LIVERPOOL TO GREAT SALT LAKE

W. O. GELLER.

G. D. Watt.

THIS PORTRAIT OF THE FIRST INDIVIDUAL IN *EUROPE* WHO RECEIVED AND OBEYED THE EVERLASTING GOSPEL OF JESUS CHRIST, AS RESTORED IN THESE LATTER DAYS, IS DEDICATED TO ALL WHO HAVE IN LIKE MANNER ENTERED INTO THE NEW COVENANT, BY THEIR AFFECTIONATE BROTHER IN THE SAME BONDS,

S. H. HAWKINS.

LIVERPOOL TO GREAT SALT LAKE

The 1851 Journal of Missionary George D. Watt

Edited by LaJean Purcell Carruth
and Ronald G. Watt

Transcription by LaJean Purcell Carruth

Introduction by Fred E. Woods

University of Nebraska Press · Lincoln

Frontispiece: *G. D. Watt*, engraving by W. O. Geller. Courtesy of Church History Library.

The University of Nebraska Press is part of a land-grant institution with campuses and programs on the past, present, and future homelands of the Pawnee, Ponca, Otoe-Missouria, Omaha, Dakota, Lakota, Kaw, Cheyenne, and Arapaho Peoples, as well as those of the relocated Ho-Chunk, Sac and Fox, and Iowa Peoples.

Library of Congress Cataloging-in-Publication Data
Names: Watt, G. D. (George Darling), 1812–1881, author. | Carruth, LaJean Purcell, editor. | Watt, Ronald G., editor. | Woods, Fred E., writer of introduction.
Title: Liverpool to Great Salt Lake: the 1851 journal of missionary George D. Watt / edited by LaJean Purcell Carruth and Ronald G. Watt; transcription by LaJean Purcell Carruth; introduction by Fred E. Woods.
Description: Lincoln: University of Nebraska Press, [2022] | Includes bibliographical references and index.
Identifiers: LCCN 2021054544
ISBN 9781496229878 (hardback)
ISBN 9781496231680 (epub)
ISBN 9781496231697 (pdf)
Subjects: LCSH: Watt, G. D. (George Darling), 1812–1881—Diaries. | Watt, G. D. (George Darling), 1812–1881—Travel. | Mormon missionaries—England—Diaries. | BISAC: HISTORY / United States / State & Local / West (AK, CA, CO, HI, ID, MT, NV, UT, WY) | RELIGION / Christianity / History | LCGFT: Diaries.
Classification: LCC BX8695.W38 A3 2022 | DDC 289.3092 [B]—dc23/eng/20220105
LC record available at https://lccn.loc.gov/2021054544

Set in Adobe Caslon by Mikala R. Kolander.

To our children:

Amy, Nathan, and Celeste

Ronda, Mathew, Andrew,

Gardner, April, and Kennan

Contents

Illustrations

ILLUSTRATIONS

MAPS

Preface

George D. Watt—Out of Obscurity and into the Light

RONALD G. WATT

George D. Watt wrote his shorthand journal during his travel from Liverpool, England, to the Salt Lake Valley, covering the period from January 28, 1851, to August 14, 1851. Unusual in its completeness, Watt's journal recorded his experiences in all three segments of the journey: his account covers the ocean voyage on board the ship *Ellen Maria*, the journey up the Mississippi and Missouri Rivers, and the land trek until they passed Chimney Rock, at which point he makes no further entries.[1] The journal also includes his record of three sermons delivered by Orson Pratt to the company of Latter-day Saint emigrants on board the *Ellen Maria* and a draft of a letter to his sister and brother-in-law, Margaret and John Brandreth, describing his experiences.

George Darling Watt is my great-grandfather. He had a very difficult childhood. After his father abandoned the family, he lived much of his life on the streets of Manchester, because his stepfather also turned him out. His mother then placed him in the poor house.[2] His grandfather Andrew Watt in Scotland rescued him from that experience and brought him to his home to live. When he became an adult, he moved back to Preston, England, but his stepfather again refused to let him stay. He then lived with some very devout people, followers of James Fielding in Preston. It was there at the Vauxhall Chapel that he heard missionaries of the Church of Jesus Christ of Latter-day Saints. He believed immediately in their doctrine and ran a footrace to be baptized first in the River Ribble by Heber C. Kimball. Watt continued at first to work in the factory and then became a policeman, but then shortly after became a missionary for the faith, serving in Scotland, where he also learned Pitman shorthand, which he used the rest of his life.[3] Watt left Britain in 1842 and traveled to Nauvoo, Illinois, then the headquarters of the Church. He returned to the British Isles in 1846, where he preached his newfound religion throughout the land.

Watt left England for Great Salt Lake City, Utah, where members of the Church had gathered, in 1851. It is at this point in his life that he began a journal, which he hoped would benefit others in their quest for that promised land. He carefully documented the ship's journey across the great Atlantic Ocean and the steamboat's trip up the Mississippi and Missouri Rivers. He began to tell his readers about the plains, oxen, buffalo, rain and storms on the plains, fording rivers, and the countless details of traveling with a wagon train, until he quit writing three days before arriving at Fort Laramie. He never carried through on his desire to publish his writings for those travelers who would come after him. He did not transcribe this private but planned-to-be-public diary. It did not help anyone else in their journey. His journal remained unread for 150 years, until LaJean Purcell Carruth found it as she was reviewing his Pitman shorthand records. She brought it to me and said, "Ron, I have found a journal by George D. Watt." Being the cynic I am at times, I did not believe that such a diary existed, until she began reading this writing that appeared to me to be hieroglyphics. Then I became a believer.

It seems to me that George Watt has followed me my entire life. He in a sense has stalked me. At first I had to write about why he left Mormonism to follow a strange, at least to me, doctrine of Spiritualism. I wrote an article on that, "Sailing the Old Ship Zion: The Life of George D. Watt."[4] I have published other articles about him, until all of these writings culminated in a book, *The Mormon Passage of George D. Watt: First British Convert, Scribe for Zion*. Every step of the way and after every publication, I would say, "I am finished with him." Then I would find that I was not. This book, *From Liverpool to Great Salt Lake: The 1851 Journal of Missionary George D. Watt*, is the culmination of my quest. At last, and together, LaJean Carruth and I have brought his writings out of obscurity and into the light.

Acknowledgments

We would like to thank the following people for their help:

Marva and Ralph Watt, Sharm Stevenson, and Suzy Sutherland for their inspiration and help in the biography of George D. Watt and their continual influence.

Fred E. Woods for writing a wonderful introduction to this book.

Silvia Ghosh for verifying transcriptions from Pitman shorthand.

Brandon Plewe for his superb maps.

Melvin L. Bashore for providing us information from local newspapers about the *Aleck Scott* and *Robert Campbell* steamboats and for the emigration numbers of Latter-day Saint pioneers.

Amy Carruth Hepworth for her help with the bibliography.

Barbara F. Watt for her patience and understanding.

The Church History Library and Intellectual Reserve for permission to publish the documents in this book and for help with photos.

Church History Library staff for their assistance in many ways, including the illustrations in this book.

John R. Sillito, Gene A. Sessions, Benjamin Whisenant, Brent Rogers, W. Paul Reeve, and John Turner for their comments and assistance.

The University of Nebraska Press, and especially our editors, W. Clark Whitehorn, Taylor Rothgeb, Elizabeth Zaleski, and Jane M. Curran, for their assistance with this book.

Also, to any others who have provided inspiration and help to us in the research and writing of this book.

Introduction

The Latter-day Saint Gathering

FRED E. WOODS

When George D. Watt won a footrace to be the first person in England to be baptized into the Church of the Latter-day Saints, little did he realize that this new religion would lead him to gather with the Latter-day Saints in Nauvoo, Illinois, and then in Salt Lake City, Utah.[1] The Latter-day Saints (often called Mormons) were a gathering people: though the church was only seven years old at the time of Watt's baptism, the Saints had already gathered to Kirtland, Ohio, as well as Missouri. When they were driven out of Missouri in 1838, they gathered again to Nauvoo, Illinois, where Watt gathered with them in 1842. In 1846 he returned as a missionary to his native England and Scotland. While he was there, the body of the church gathered to Salt Lake City, Utah, where he joined them in September 1851. This book is his journal of his second gathering, from Liverpool to Chimney Rock.

Gathering in the Early Years of the Church

The doctrine of gathering was taught soon after the organization of the church. The call for church members to gather was taught by Joseph Smith during the second conference of the Church of Christ, less than six months after its organization in 1830.[2] Obedience to this doctrine would result in dramatic life changes, and for many, it would require an arduous journey to a new homeland.

Missionary work and the gathering was limited to the boundaries within North America during the first decade of the Church's existence. In 1831 church members began gathering to Kirtland, Ohio. Missionary work was launched during the 1830s from Kirtland to various places in the United States as well as Canada. During this same decade, some Church members also gathered to western Missouri in hopes of establishing Zion in that state as well. Yet less than a decade later, Latter-day Saints were forced to flee the state of Missouri as a result of an extermination order issued by Governor Lilburn W. Boggs.

A new gathering place for these displaced Ohio and Missouri Saints was chosen in Nauvoo, Illinois. Here Saints from Canada and the eastern United States as well as foreign converts from abroad combined their faith and works to build a beautiful city out of a mosquito-infested swamp land on the eastern banks of the Mississippi River.

In 1837 Joseph Smith charged his trusted associate, Apostle Heber C. Kimball, with the assignment of opening up missionary work for the church in Great Britain. Elder Kimball was joined by Orson Hyde, also a member of the Quorum of the Twelve Apostles,[3] along with five other missionaries.[4] These men were instructed to teach the message of the restoration and were also warned by the Prophet Joseph Smith before their departure, "to remain silent consider the gathering . . . until such time as the work is firmly established, and it should be clearly made manifest by the Spirit to do otherwise."[5]

During the space of just nine months (July 1837–April 1838) these missionaries obtained over fifteen hundred converts to their new religion.[6] Their success was augmented less than two years later when more of the Twelve, including Brigham Young, embarked on another mission to Great Britain (January 1840–April 1841). By the spring of 1840, the Church was steadfastly rooted in the land. It was in this season that the Twelve decided that it was time to commence the gathering of their British converts to America.[7]

Gathering Converts from Abroad

The British Saints began their immigration to Nauvoo, Illinois, with the voyage of the *Britannia* on June 6, 1840, with English convert John Moon leading a group of forty Saints from the port of Liverpool.[8] Many experienced the difficulty of leaving their family, friends and home-

Fig. 1. *Brigham Young*, 1846 or 1847. Courtesy of Church History Library.

land. Reflecting upon her journey to America, Priscilla Staines wrote about leaving her home in late December 1843: "I left the home of my birth to gather to Nauvoo. I was alone. It was a dreary winter day on which I went to Liverpool. The company with which I was to sail was all strangers to me. When I arrived in Liverpool and saw the ocean that would soon roll between me and all I loved, my heart almost failed me. But I had laid my idols all upon the altar. There was no turning back."[9] For Staines and many other converts who followed, gathering with the Saints was a great sacrifice.

Letters Encourage Gathering of British Saints

After safely arriving in Nauvoo, Francis Moon, leader of the first group to emigrate to Nauvoo, wrote back to his British homeland to describe the temporal and spiritual advantages of immigrating: "What I might say on this subject [I hope] might have the tendency of encouraging my fellow Englishmen in the point of gathering . . . and would say if you can get to this land, you will be better off than in England, for in this place there is a prospect of receiving every good thing both of this world and that which is to come."[10]

Letters home bearing glad tidings from British proselytes paved the way for about five thousand British converts who would follow and settle in Nauvoo.[11] Such positive feedback was published in the Church periodical published in England, *The Latter-day Saints' Millennial Star*. For example, in 1841, the *Millennial Star* printed an article titled "Emigration" and commented, "The news from the emigrants who sailed from this country last season is so very encouraging that it will give a new impulse to the spirit of the gathering."[12] In addition, Church leaders also provided written instructions which encouraged immigration to Nauvoo in order for the Saints to build a temple and partake of its blessings.[13]

British converts were also influenced by the excellent organization and dependability of their Church leaders both at Liverpool and in Nauvoo. The *Millennial Star* provided useful instructions to departing emigrant Saints, and published the dates when various trans-Atlantic voyages would depart. In addition, an emigration agent was selected by Church leaders to carry out arrangements at Liverpool. As early as April 1841, an

"Epistle of the Twelve" was published in the *Millennial Star* regarding the appointment and advantages of having a Church agent.

> We have found that there are so many "pick pockets," and so many that will take every possible advantage of strangers, in Liverpool, that we have appointed Elder Amos Fielding, as agent of the church to superintend the fitting out of Saints from Liverpool to America.
>
> Whatever information the Saints may want about the preparations of the voyage, they are advised to call on Elder Fielding at Liverpool, as their first movement, when they arrive there as emigrants. There are some brethren who have felt themselves competent to do their own business in these matters, and rather despising the counsel of their friends, have been robbed and cheated out of nearly all they had.
>
> A word of caution to the wise is sufficient. It is also a great saving to go in companies, instead of going individually. First, a company can charter a vessel, so as to make the passage much cheaper than otherwise. Secondly, provisions can be purchased at wholesale for a company much cheaper than otherwise. Thirdly, this will avoid bad company on the passage. Fourthly, when a company arrives in New Orleans they can charter a steam-boat so as to reduce the passage near one-half. The measure will save some hundreds of pounds on each ship load. Fifthly, a man of experience can go as leader of each company, who will know how to avoid rogues and knaves.[14]

Later, Church agents were assigned at the ports of New Orleans as well as New York to meet the incoming Saints. Those British Saints who traveled up the Mississippi during the Nauvoo years (1840–46) were also met by supportive Saints and Church leaders, including the Prophet Joseph Smith.[15] Although there were certainly problems to be dealt with at Nauvoo, the Saints in general met most of the obstacles and labored together to build a splendid temple which adorned the city. However, by the winter of 1846 the Saints were forced to leave Nauvoo; the following year they made a new Zion in the West where Salt Lake City eventually became a modern day Mecca for the Latter-day Saints.

Emphasis on the gathering was continued after the Saints arrival in Utah, with the same amount of energy it had been given in Nauvoo. Most missionaries from this central region of the Church were sent to the British Isles during the decade of the 1840s, and by 1850 there were actually more Latter-day Saint converts in the British Isles than there were in all of North America, including Utah.[16] The following year, when Scandinavian converts began to immigrate to Utah, the Church First Presidency[17] declared to the Saints abroad, "It is time for them to gather, without delay, to Zion."[18] Some Scandinavians who endured the long Atlantic voyage aboard sailing vessels, also found many obstacles crossing the American plains. Yoking the oxen was one of the most difficult. One author noted, "Some of the Scandinavians, disliking the American way of driving oxen in yokes, hitched up the beasts of burden in regular Danish fashion. But they had forgotten one little thing—that the oxen were American . . . It was decided that it would be easier for the emigrants to learn American ways than it would be for the oxen to learn the Danish harness."[19] George D. Watt also expressed his frustration with oxen.

Many Europeans from Scandinavia and Great Britain faced more serious delays that kept them from reaching Zion in a timely fashion. Economics was the primary challenge and difficulty for many proselytes seeking to gather resources for themselves and their families. Some who voyaged up the Mississippi River before heading west on the Missouri stayed in St. Louis for months or even years to gather sufficient funds to continue their journey to Utah. There was such a cluster by the mid-nineteenth century that a St. Louis Stake was formed in 1854.[20]

The Perpetual Emigrating Fund was launched in 1849 to help provide a way for the poor to be financially assisted in their journey to Zion. It provided assistance for thousands of Saints who gathered to Utah Territory during the nineteenth century through temporary loans to immigrants, which were to be paid back to the PEF as soon as possible once the converts reached Utah, so the money could then be loaned again to other immigrants, perpetually. It continued until 1887.[21]

Additionally, resources for the gathering were partially resolved by the windfall of resources brought to the Salt Lake Valley by gold seekers and other heading West during the gold rush years. These overlanders who passed through Salt Lake City brought a certain degree of wealth to the Valley.[22] This windfall also provided additional means for missionary work to be opened up in more areas of Europe.

Modes of Transportation

Various factors influenced the number of European immigrants who came to Utah throughout the nineteenth century as well as the route they took, and their mode of transportation. For example, efforts to alleviate the demanding costs that were placed upon the poor British Saints led to an experiment with using handcarts instead of wagons. In a letter dated September 30, 1855, Brigham Young wrote to Elder Franklin D. Richards, European Mission president in charge of emigration: "I have been thinking about how we should operate another year. We cannot afford to purchase wagons and teams as in times past. I am consequently thrown back upon my own plan—to make hand-carts, and let the emigration foot it, and draw upon them the necessary supplies, having a cow or two for every ten. They can come just as quick, if not quicker and much cheaper."[23]

Leroy Hafen notes that although the Willie and Martin handcart companies left too late in the year and were caught in the early winter of 1856, overall this experiment proved successful as nearly three thousand Saints crossed the plains in ten handcart companies using 662 carts during the years 1856–60.[24]

Buying wagons and oxen at the outfitting posts for each company was very expensive; there were plentiful wagons and a surplus of oxen in Utah. In 1861 the Church began sending "out-and-back" wagon trains, which started in Utah. These trains carried provisions for the emigrants, which they cached along the way. They met emigrants at the outfitting posts. Nearly twenty thousand migrants crossed the Plains with the Church trains for the years 1861–64, 1866, and 1867. During the years 1865 and 1867, Church trains were not sent west due to the impact of Utah's Black

Hawk War, which resulted in a loss of oxen (slain by Native Americans) and also the fear of losing man power.[25]

Transportation Advancements and Rerouting

Progress in the area of transportation technology also had a tremendous impact on the gathering. For example, during the years the Saints voyaged across the Atlantic (1840–67) on sailing vessels, the average time for an oceanic trip was about five and a half weeks from Liverpool to New York. The voyage to New Orleans was more than two weeks longer. Yet with the advent of steam power, the Saints could cross the Atlantic from Liverpool to New York on an average of about eleven days.[26] What is most impressive is that not one single chartered Church vessel by sail or steam was lost crossing the Atlantic, a stark contrast to the fact that at least fifty-nine other vessels carrying immigrants sunk during the years 1847–53 alone.[27]

Steam power had the same impact on land as it had on sea. With the completion of the Transcontinental Railroad (May 10, 1869), travelers could now cross the United States from coast to coast in less than ten days. This is in glaring contrast to traveling ten to twelve weeks just from the Missouri River to the Great Basin during the wagon train years.

Throughout the years of Brigham Young's administration as Church president (1847–77), he made the final decisions regarding migration routes by sail, rail and trail, but only after wisely gathering all the information he could. For example, due to health risks, he re-routed the Saints through select eastern ports instead of New Orleans which had been the principal port the Saints had used from 1841–54. In a letter dated August 2, 1854, Young directed Elder Franklin D. Richards, stationed in Liverpool, as follows: "You are aware of the sickness liable to assail our unacclimated brethren on the Mississippi river, hence I wish you to ship no more to New Orleans, but ship to Philadelphia, Boston, and New York, giving preference in the order named."[28]

The following year, Castle Garden, an immigration depot, was erected at New York, and from that time (1855) until it burned down in 1889, nearly all European converts came through that port. And during those decades, Church emigration agents were sent to guide and counsel the incoming immigrants, commencing with agent John Taylor, a Church apostle, who arranged for lodging and employment for those European converts who could not afford to travel immediately to Utah after making the Atlantic crossing.[29]

President Young also listened attentively to his Church emigration agents at various ports and posts, who often had valuable suggestions. For example, in 1859 the railway transport route through the States for Latter-day Saint emigrants changed as a direct result of a letter New York Church emigration agent George Q. Cannon sent to Brigham Young. In this letter Cannon proposed that the Saints should be rerouted through Quincy, Illinois (instead of Iowa City), before getting onboard the Hannibal & St. Joseph Railroad, which the Saints used from 1859 to 1866.[30] In another letter Cannon wrote to Brigham Young dated January 18, 1860, Cannon suggested, "I have thought that a good many of the poor Saints might be taken through who otherwise have to remain, if they [the emigrants] could go through with part rations and be met with teams with provisions from the Valley." Thus, Cannon appears to have had the initial idea of the Church out-and-back trains, which Brigham liked and experimented upon by proving through a trial run of his nephew, Joseph W. Young, that such an idea was possible.[31]

In 1866 New York Church emigration agent Thomas Taylor chose a more economic route from New York to Chicago, which the Church supported.[32] Two decades later, New York Latter-day Saint emigration agent James H. Hart made arrangements to send the converts through Norfolk, Virginia, due to railway contract problems in New York. As a result, between 1887 and 1890 over five thousand Saints were rerouted on the Old Dominion Steam line from New York to Norfolk before taking a route heading west to Utah on various railway lines the Saints had not used before.[33]

At the close of the nineteenth century, immigration to America began to decline. During the years 1840–90 over eighty-five thousand Latter-day Saint converts crossed the Atlantic, with most coming from Great Britain, followed by about twenty-five thousand who came from Scandinavia and several thousand Swiss-German converts. In addition, there was a sprinkling of others who crossed the Pacific from various countries.[34]

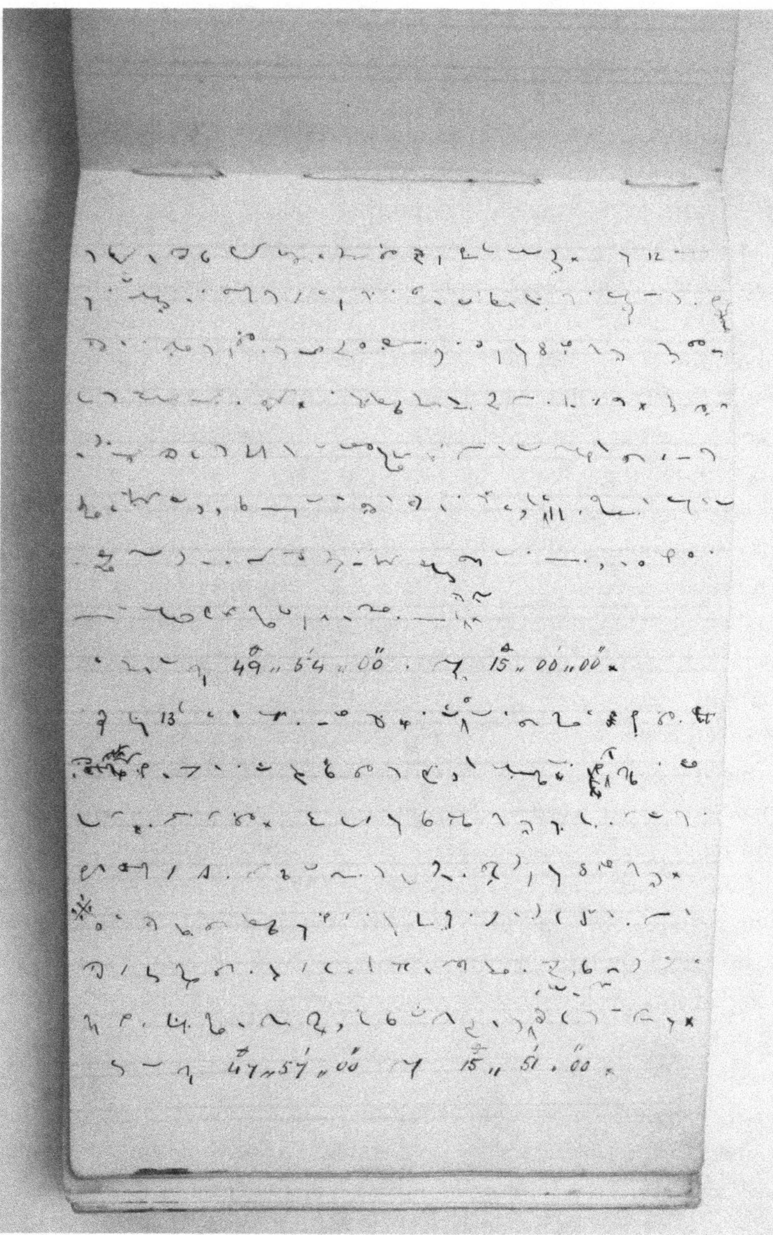

Fig. 2. Page of George D. Watt's shorthand journal.
Photograph by Ronald G. Watt.

George D. Watt's Pitman Shorthand and the Process of Transcription

LAJEAN PURCELL CARRUTH

Shorthand is compressed writing: in order to allow a reporter to write quickly, often to keep up with a speaker, much information is recorded in fewer and more readily written characters than standard orthography. Sir Isaac Pitman first published his new shorthand in 1837 in England, in a book titled *Stenographic Sound Hand*. It was the first shorthand that made it possible for a reporter to record a person's speech verbatim, as he or she spoke, and it very quickly spread throughout the English-speaking world. Pitman shorthand is written phonetically, without regard for standard orthography.[1] Consonants are represented by straight and curved lines. Lighter symbols represent unvoiced consonants, while the same symbol, though darker, represents the same sound, only voiced. For example, *b* and *p* are the same symbol, *d* and *t* are the same symbol, only *b* and *d* are darker than *p* and *t*. Vowels, prefixes, and suffixes are written with diacritics; vowels were considered optional and were often omitted. Other changes to consonants are used to add a variety of sounds. For example, a small hook at the beginning of a symbol adds *r* or *l*, a hook at the end adds *f* or *v*, and making the consonant half length adds *-ed* or *-et*.

As stated, shorthand is compressed writing. This compression of information also increases ambiguity, as a single symbol will often represent multiple words, differentiated mainly by context. The absence of vowels complicates correct transcription of words that are otherwise identical, such as *this*, *these*, *those*, and *thus*, which are all written *ths*. The absence of an initial vowel can be critical when the vowel is a negator, leaving the transcriber to differentiate, if possible, between words such as *necessary* and *unnecessary*, *relevant* and *irrelevant*, *mortal* and *immortal*. Names are particularly challenging to transcribe, as a combination of consonants, or consonants and vowels, can often represent many different names, and context is usually of little if any help. Hastily written symbols often appear different than they were intended to look.

George D. Watt was a highly skilled Pitman shorthand reporter; he used Pitman shorthand for both professional and personal writing. As noted, he wrote all the text included in this book—his journal, his letter, and three sermons delivered by Orson Pratt on board the emigrants' ship *Ellen Maria*—in Pitman shorthand. I have spent many years transcribing Watt's shorthand records and have a tremendous respect for his skill.

I found this journal in the summer of 2001, while I was transcribing Watt's shorthand records for the Church History Department, Salt Lake City, Utah. The rest of the notebook is filled with his shorthand record of sermons and other items. His draft of a letter to his sister and brother-in-law, included here, is in the same notebook. His record of the three sermons by Orson Pratt, onboard the *Ellen Maria*, are in a separate notebook.

I owe much of my career as a professional transcriber of nineteenth-century shorthand documents to George D. Watt. I have now spent many years reading his shorthand record, both shorthand that he transcribed himself and published, and shorthand that he did not transcribe, such as the materials included here.[2] His original shorthand notebooks are the best and often only source for the spoken words of Brigham Young, Heber C. Kimball, Orson Pratt, John Taylor, George A. Smith, and many, many others. These records, as well as his journal, provide us much information that we have only through his skill and labors.

LIVERPOOL TO
GREAT SALT LAKE

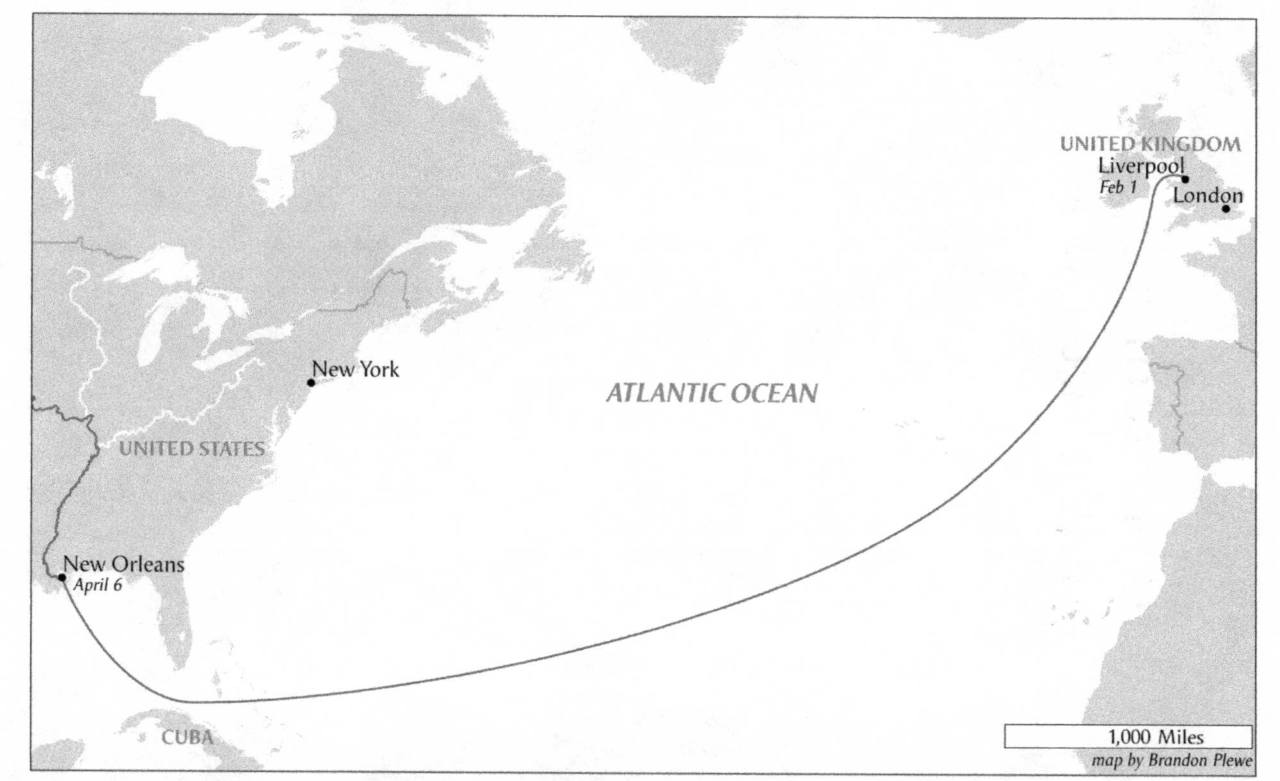

Map 1. Journey of the *Ellen Maria* from Liverpool to New Orleans. Created by Brandon Plewe.

I

The Atlantic Ocean

Our ship is scuttling along through the
deep furrows of the ocean.
—George D. Watt journal, February 21, 1851

Across the Atlantic Ocean

On April 17, 1851, from the safe climes of St. Louis, Missouri, George D. Watt, president of the Latter-day Saints on board the ship *Ellen Maria*, sat down to write to the *Millennial Star* about the voyage.[1] He told the editor that their reliable craft had one day of storm on the Irish Sea, three marriages, five births, and five deaths. He also mentioned that they held services on the ocean and that Apostle Orson Pratt preached to them.[2] Watt's letter proved to be an important contemporary record of this particular voyage—one of many undertaken by Latter-day Saint converts in this period. No one else on the ship wrote a surviving journal or life history about this calm, mundane, and even boring trip.

No one knew that Watt was writing a journal of his voyage on the *Ellen Maria*, which included his trip up the mighty Mississippi and Missouri Rivers and across the plains of the West. He faithfully recorded commentary about these events in Pitman shorthand, and he had every intention to publish it.[3] He mentioned often warning the coming pilgrims about the necessities of life aboard a ship, the problems they would face on the Mississippi, and the necessity of having enough money to purchase oxen and wagons. Why he never carried through with his publication intention cannot be discerned. Perhaps he became so involved with his new life in Utah that he simply forgot it. Today that shorthand has been transcribed by one of the editors of this book, and we know that the voyage was not as humdrum and boring as once thought. His almost poetical description of storms on the great Atlantic, being becalmed, and

Fig. 3. *Emigrant Ship Leaving from Liverpool*, wood cut. Created by Frederick Piercy. Courtesy of Church History Library.

the force of the gigantic Mississippi can hardly be duplicated. We have reproduced his words now for all the world to enjoy.

Proselyting in the British Isles by missionaries of the Church of Jesus Christ of Latter-day Saints began in 1837, when Heber C. Kimball and his party of nine landed in Liverpool and journeyed to Preston, England. The missionaries were very successful, ultimately baptizing over 1,500 new converts in eleven months, including George D. Watt. In 1838 Kimball and the other missionaries left for New York. Two years later, seven of the twelve apostles of the Church of Jesus Christ of Latter-day Saints arrived and also had great success.[4] Members of the Saints began gathering together geographically soon after the organization of the Church in 1830 in Ohio and Missouri, and at this time the Saints were gathered in and around Nauvoo, Illinois. These early missionaries began to preach the spirit of gathering in April 1840. Many of the newly converted earnestly desired to unite with their fellow religionists in America.[5] In that year forty-two Latter-day Saint emigrants left on the *Britannia* bound for New York. Church leaders arranged for emigrants to travel as groups.

The first Latter-day Saint–contracted ship to arrive in New Orleans was the *Isaac Newton*, which left Liverpool on October 15, 1840, with about fifty Latter-day Saint passengers and arrived at its desired location on the Mississippi on December 2, 1840. The route to New Orleans allowed the members to catch a Mississippi steamboat up the river to Nauvoo, creating an all-water route to the new city of the Saints. George Watt followed in 1842, the third year of the emigration, sailing on the ship *Sidney*, which was the eighteenth ship to carry Latter-day Saint emigrants across the Atlantic from 1840 with 179 other Latter-day Saints. Ships bound to New Orleans left every year from 1840 until 1855, when the Latter-day Saints switched their seagoing passengers to Boston and later New York City because trains now connected the parts of the eastern United States to the place where the Saints would start on their journey westward.

Watt returned to England and Scotland in 1846 to serve a mission in the British Isles until 1851.[6] Four ships left Liverpool carrying Latter-day Saint passengers in 1851, all bound for New Orleans. The *Ellen* left on January 8 with 466 Latter-day Saints with James Willard Cummings as their leader.[7] The *George W. Bourne* left on January 29 with 281 passengers under the leadership of William Gibson. The *Ellen Maria* under George D. Watt left February 1 with 378 Latter-day Saints on board. The *Ellen Maria* was the fifty-first Latter-day Saint ship traveling from Liverpool to New Orleans. Finally the *Olympus* left on March 4 under William Howell with 245 church passengers.

For all the Latter-day Saint passengers throughout the years of travel from Liverpool to New Orleans, the voyage was an extraordinary event and a great achievement for these land-loving souls. Most had never lived through the experiences of sailing on an immense ocean and being tossed by violent winds and waves. Perhaps they thought it would be a nice, calm journey in which the winds would propel them safely to their destination without any problems. Afterward very few wanted to try it again. Yet regular life continued on every emigrant ship. Babies were born, and the elders blessed them with names. Couples were married. Passengers old and young and sometimes in between died during the journey and were buried at sea. The Latter-day Saint passengers continued holding church services on Sunday, unless the ship was in a storm. Their leaders preached to them, thus spiritually feeding them. Usually the church members wrote about these meetings in their diaries. They recorded the names of the speakers and even subjects preached. Orson Pratt, a member of the Quorum of the Twelve Apostles who traveled with Watt's company on the *Ellen Maria*, preached four sermons to the assembled Latter-day Saints. Watt recorded three of these in Pitman shorthand.[8]

The Latter-day Saints came to their church services to lessen the boredom of the passage and to feel the spirit. Sometimes this trip could be a long, boring journey, relieved by any little thing that could gain the passengers' attention. The sighting of whales, dolphins, and flying fish were noted whenever passengers saw them.[9]

All sorts of problems might be encountered in a sea voyage, but there was no other way to travel from the British Isles to the United States. Most passengers had their berths in steerage, a dark, cold, and frankly scary place in the midst of a storm when the sailors would fasten down the hatches. Some passengers felt that they would die down there. More affluent passengers had their berths in the second cabin, which was more commodious and definitely less frightening.

Steerage passengers cooked their own food on a number of stoves on board the ship, called *galleys*, usually about three feet wide and four feet long that used coal for fuel. Provisions were handed out by the church leadership to members either once a week or once every two weeks. The captain provided their food.[10] Water was provided once a week, at least three quarts per individual. Some ships did not have enough fresh water for the voyage to New Orleans and cut rations about three-quarters of the way there. The captain depended upon storms and would instruct the sailors to catch the water in large blanket-like nets and channel it into jars and barrels. Because of the barrels that it was stored in, the water turned black, and even though it was palatable, the passengers found it difficult to drink. One of the largest complaints by passengers was the drinking water.

Storms terrified the passengers. Everybody would be hurried to their berths. The sailors sealed the hatches leading to steerage in order to prevent the flooding of the inside of the ship as water rushed across the top of the deck. The locking of the hatches caused great consternation among the passengers, who had only a few poorly lit lights, and the hold always seemed to be filled with darkness. Many, undoubtedly, could feel the walls closing in on them. The ship would be tossed around in the sea, and it would pitch one way and yaw the other; sometimes it was put on its beam ends, almost tipping over. Passengers screamed and felt helpless, and almost all vomited. The sailors instructed passengers to tie down all their baggage. Most did not understand why, and many either left them unattached or tied them very loosely. In a storm they learned a great lesson. All items not tied firmly would bounce around like they were dancing. Many felt that the ship would sink. The next day or whenever they could, the passengers cleaned up after their messes of the night before. Even though boats were small and storms large, yet no Latter-day Saint–contracted ship sank during the Atlantic Ocean crossing.[11]

Most of the squalls were minor ones, but others were almost catastrophic. The *Kennebec* in 1852 lost the top part of its foremast, the front mast on the ship. The near disaster of all the Latter-day Saint–contracted ships was the *Olympus*, which left on March 4, 1851, about a month after the *Ellen Maria*. For three weeks shortly after they left Liverpool a storm raged along its path. After one day of sailing without a storm, another one hit the ship. The foremast broke and went into the sea. At midnight after the ship took in great amounts of water, the captain, fearing that it would sink, sent a messenger to Elder William Howell, the president of the Latter-day Saints, informing him that "if the God of the Mormons can do anything to save the ship and the people, they had better be calling on him to do so." In his message he also told Howell that the ship was taking in more water than the pumps could throw out. Elder Howell called some of the brethren to him, and they prayed, each taking his turn, and while the prayers were proceeding the storm abated and ceased. The captain said that only God's hand had saved the ship. Before their journey was completed, forty-one people, composed of crew and nonmember passengers, were baptized.[12]

Passengers in steerage had additional difficulties. They were cramped into bunks two high and probably eighteen to twenty inches wide that had to accommodate more than one person, sometimes a whole family. Privacy was nonexistent. The ship provided pots for toilets. Bodily smells were strong in these closed conditions. British people bathed little, and the long journey simply increased these odors. Add to that the odors of human wastes during a storm, and the aroma could be overwhelming. Seasickness began almost from the point of embarkation until people became acquainted with the motion of the ship, and even then when a squall happened, many people became sick again. This process repeated again and again.

The ships were small and rolled with the waves; walking on the deck was sometimes impossible until the passenger became accustomed to the roll of the ship. Jane Rio Griffiths Baker, who sailed on the ship *George W. Bourne* in 1851 about a month before the *Ellen Maria*, commented at the end of February, after being on the ship about five weeks, that she finally had her "sea legs." "I can now walk about the ship when she is rolling or pitching, with tolerable ease."[13]

The most dangerous problem could be a shipwreck. Fortunately no Latter-day Saint ship had a disastrous encounter. In 1851 the *Ellen* had a wreck but a very minor one. Shortly after leaving Liverpool, the boat, as John Woodhouse described it, "received a violent shock." When he went on board the next morning, he found it anchored in Cardigan Bay, North Wales.[14] A schooner had hit the *Ellen*, and all on board the schooner drowned. The *Ellen* found a replacement for a damaged part and two weeks later continued on its journey.

Another fear for all was an epidemic such as measles, small pox, or cholera. In 1850 two Latter-day Saint emigrants died from small pox on the *Josiah Bradlee*. Thomas Day mentioned in his journal that he called "the elders together and we earnestly prayed that the disease might be stayed which was done and the small pox disappeared."[15] The worst case for a ship between Liverpool to New Orleans was the *Clara Wheeler* in 1854. It had twenty-two deaths caused primarily by measles.[16] A normal crossing usually only had three to five deaths.

There were six types of vessels that were used by the Latter-day Saint emigrants in the nineteenth century: ship, barkentine, brigantine, brig, schooner, and bark. A ship, such as the *Ellen Maria*, was the vessel usually used, so we will only discuss that type. A ship had three or even five masts mounted with square sails. All ships had jib sails, which were triangular sails between the masts. These helped the ship keep a steady course. Most of the shipbuilding by 1850 was done in the United States. The construction of a ship took at least a year, but more likely three to four years to complete.[17] The full-rigged ships with square sails dominated the ocean trade. The *Ellen Maria* weighed 768 tons with dimensions 151 × 33 × 17 feet. It was built by Harrison Springer at Richmond, Maine, in 1849.[18] It was only two years old when George D. Watt and Orson Pratt boarded it with 376 other Latter-day Saints. Some nonchurch members were also aboard, but it is not known how many.

Crew of a Ship

A full-rigged ship required a large crew. At the head was the captain, who had supreme power on the ship and whose orders had to be obeyed by all the crew members. The captain was the dictator on board, especially toward the crew and even the passengers. Watt described George Whitmore, the captain and part-owner of the *Ellen Maria*, as a "practical philanthropist, seeking continually to smooth the path of his fellow creatures from this mortal struggle. The saints hitherto have been blessed by his kindness."[19] Watt later changed his mind a little concerning the captain. He thought he was a kind man to the passengers, as long as money or provisions were not involved.[20]

The first mate, sometime called the prime minister or chief mate but more often just the mate, was the sailing master and quartermaster. The captain told him what he wanted done and allowed him the responsibility of seeing that it was and done well. The mate kept the logbook, for which he was responsible to the owners and insurers, and had charge of cargo and its delivery.

The second mate was neither officer nor sailor but had to furnish the men with all supplies needed to help with their work. He was expected to work with the crew. He ate and slept in the cabin but ate at the second table, not with the captain and mate. On board the *Ellen Maria* the second mate talked freely with Watt about the harshness of the captain to the crew. He also wrote Watt a letter about being baptized after the voyage. It is not known whether he was.[21]

The steward was the captain's servant and was in control of the pantry. The mate and steward were most often at odds with each other because the mate wanted to have authority over all the others on the ship. For example, on one occasion aboard the *Ellen Maria* the steward wished to give a family some soup from the pantry, but the captain prevented him from doing this act of kindness.[22]

Finally, the cook looked after both the crew and the second cabin. From time to time, if there was extra food available, he would give some food to crew members, especially when the crew members had the night watch or perhaps in return for favors that they had done for him.[23]

We cannot be sure how many sailors were on board the *Ellen Maria*. A full-rigged sailing ship needed at least thirty sailors to operate it efficiently.[24] They divided the time with being on duty and off duty, usually on deck every four hours. A sailor was always busy when he was on duty. There were no idle hands, and it was the officers' responsibility to keep them busy. The sailors were the lowest class on the ship. They had sometimes been impressed into sea service against their will. It was the seamen or sailors whom Watt feared the most. When the Latter-day Saints went to the sailors to find a sister who might have been led there, Watt said that going there raised the ire of the sailors, "but this is nothing compared with the sorrow that must follow in the case of a poor female being robbed of her virtue by reckless seamen."[25]

The high point of Watt's account concerns his description of the storms that the vessel encountered. Therein he calmly writes his shorthand in very descriptive terms while the ship is being tossed by the waves and driven by the winds. His ability to express himself is superb. For example, in one storm he writes, "Outside the wind is heard raging on like the voices of a thousand malignant spirits screaming the requiem of some distant wreck."[26]

Journal from Liverpool to New Orleans, January 28, 1851–April 6, 1851

[Image 394][27]

Sarah Preece <born 8th of August 1850 ~~aged 6 months~~> died on board of the *Ellen Maria* on the 11 February, the daughter of Richard and Susan Preece, natives of Herefordshire, England.[28] [*Illeg-*

ible] admitted to the calling for 20 crates instead of ten. March 2nd.[29] Sunday February 9th 1851.

The saints[30] on board of the Ellen Maria met on the poop deck[31] to celebrate the ordinance of the Lord's Supper[32] for the first time since sailing from Liverpool[33] and as the weather hitherto would not permit of the privilege. Nearly all the saints aboard washed and cleaned and had recovered <from> their sickness in a great degree. The captain of the vessel tried to make us comfortable and did all things he could to effect it. The morning is fine and calm though in the distance misty.

Elder Watt opened the meeting with singing <the first hymn.> President Pratt[34] prayed to the Lord for the blessings we needed in the circumstances in which we were placed. Sung again "Glorious Things of Thee are Spoken etc." Elder Pratt spoke to the people. The following is a summary of his remarks. He brought forth an example of a man who was rich and trusted with the things of this life; he would not know how to appreciate the blessings his Heavenly Father had given to him, for he [had] not previously been afflicted with the miseries of this mortality. So the saints are tried by their Heavenly Father even unto death. Christ was tried, descended below all things and was afterwards raised above all things. [He] referred to the troubles of those who have to be placed in the steerage. He had three times passed the ocean in the steerage and could pity those who had to pass through the same. Jesus was tempted and tried and had to learn things by afflictions and therefore know how to succor others placed in similar circumstances. Just so it is in my own heart: when I see the brethren in need, [to] know to help them, I reflect back and think how I have been in the same circumstances. I never want to be in the same circumstances again, and look forward to the time when those who have these afflictions to dwell in will have splendid palaces to dwell in, and mansions in the upper world.

[He] made a few remarks for the benefit of those who have never travelled much. You will find it important to put up with all the little inconveniences we have and roiled feelings. If you see any brother and sister you have to find fault with, let us try to think there may be a mote in our [*illegible*][35] eye; take the mote out of our own eye. After that we will do our brethren a good turn for all his evil deeds and win him with love and kindness. Also beware not to let our passions have power over us. If we cannot control our passions, [we] cannot control our household. The first thing a man has to learn in power and authority is to rule himself. This takes time. A man has to smother his feelings often. When a man feels his passions rising, stop short and reflect. I make these remarks because of the trifling circumstance [that] took place on the [Mersey] river; you know what it was.[36] Every man must think and try to repent of any wrong we may have done in this manner and forgive those who have contraried. I make these remarks because we are about to take of the sacrament, that we may offer our sacraments up before the Lord in righteousness, that he be not angry with us. If any have done wrong, repent in their hearts and confess your sins one to the other. Any not in the Church of Jesus Christ of Latter-day Saints, you are surrounded with a people like yourselves; judge not according to appearances, according to appearing. It is the privilege of all those who have been baptized to take of the Lord's Supper. Have not the convenience here as in other circumstances. Yet he says it matters not what we [Image 395][37] eat or what we drink,[38] but are to do these things to show we are willing to be subject to him and obedient to him in all things.

We want a favorable wind [*illegible*]. How [do we] obtain [it]? Do right, and if [the wind is] favorable or not, we shall be happy, the Lord will be satisfied in it, and he may listen to our prayers and cause the wind to blow from a more favorable part of the heavens. He has done such things. Let us exercise faith in this matter. Do not let us boast of our faith; let us lay aside all boasting. What are we? We are nothing of ourselves. What are we? We profess to be the disciples of Jesus and profess to love him and we will seek to set an example of righteousness before all men and all women. It is impossible ~~for us~~ for us to love him if we do not love one another. What say more? The Lord bless you and cheer your hearts and deliver you entirely from sickness and let love prevail in your midst until we arrive to the end of our journey. The sacrament was attended to.

Brother Toone[39] spoke a little to the meeting upon the subject of dealing with each other as brethren that when anything is borrowed it be returned again etc.

James Stratton[40] and Francis Clark[41] was presented before the meeting to be married. Any objection that might be made to this marriage was called for. No objections. Both from the Cambridge. Elder Orson Pratt celebrated the ordinance of marriage. Elder Watt then made a few remarks on the the[42] manner a company of people in such confined circumstances all ought to act towards each other. After singing the meeting was dismissed by a blessing[43] from Elder Watt.

The weather ~~remained~~ remained fair and calm throughout the whole service.[44] [Image 396]

[Beginning of Chronological Journal]

I hereby give a faithful account of my second voyage across the great Atlantic Ocean for New Orleans,[45] in which I shall intersperse remarks that may occur to my mind touching any situations and circumstances that shall take place in the course of this voyage worthy of notice. In writing this account I shall try to keep in view the edification of my friends and brethren whom I have left behind, that they may be better prepared to endure the many inconveniences that must be met with in crossing the great waters if they should at any time feel to do so. Without further ceremony I will at once proceed to my account.

Myself and family went on board the "Ellen Maria" on the 28th of January 1851. She was then lying in the factory docks. The registered burden of this ship in America is between 7 and 8 thousand ton[s] but according to the English measurement between nine hundred and one thousand ton.[46] She is an American built ship of great symmetrical dimensions and very commodious for passengers.[47] Captain [George] Whitmore, who commands this vessel and who also owns a considerable portion of her, is an American by birth. He seems to be a practical philanthropist, seeking continually to smooth the path of his fellow creatures from this mortal struggle. The saints hitherto have been blessed by his kindness. On Thursday the 30th we left the docks and cast anchor in the river where we lay until Saturday about twelve o'clock.

The thanks of this company is due to Elder <William> Dunbar[48] for ~~duties~~ services done to them while ~~they~~ the ship lay moored in the docks. In the allotment of berths to passengers he acquitted himself to the satisfaction of the whole company. We have not heard a murmur. His energetic strong and commanding ~~manner~~ aspect towards the many thieves that rushed on board to rob the emigrants <of their money and clothing> under night's dark mantle saved the unsuspecting saints much sorrow, while the thieves inched their path by him; not one penny or garment was lost (which was not the case with the other two ships that went out in January) thanks to the Lord and the vigilance of Elder Dunbar. It would be well for the saints who may emigrate hereafter to place a strict watch upon their things while they lie in the Liverpool docks, as there is a company of men who make it their business to rob the boxes of the emigrants after night [Image 397] taking advantage of the law that forbids any light to be used on the ships while in the docks. We suffered no one to enter the ship after dark without knowing their business. If a thief gets down among the luggage he can cut the cords of the boxes, pick the locks and help ~~themselves~~ himself to money, clothing or any other article of value and may at the same time be rubbing hard against the owner of these articles; "a hint to the wise is enough".

On Friday the 31st we doled out provisions for the first time, out of which arose a situation that I consider is not unworthy of notice as others may be profited and warned by it. A man by the name of William Davies[49] from Wales (a member of the church) with his wife and three children determined to take his departure from the ship and return to his native Welsh mountains; he therefore sold his bed, his tins and other utensils to the passengers at what they would fetch and by that means raised enough of money to pay one of the river boatman to ferry him to shore; his wife wept, his poor children screamed, the passengers ~~prevailed upon~~ plead with him, Elder [Orson] Pratt ~~plead with him~~ and tried to show him the folly of his course, but he gave ~~him~~ Elder Pratt impudent language and was inexorable to all the persuasions of his brethren and the tears of his wife. He left the ship. The reason why he took this foolish ~~step~~ step was because he could not get his provisions just at the time he called for them, a great many more having to be served before him. His wife and children were hungry, it is true, and the poor man was no doubt much tried by that circumstance, but [he] had not learned enough to be patient in such trials, for others were hungry too. However, when he found himself in Liverpool without money and friends, he repented and returned to the ship, feeling ashamed for his rash course, while his wife rejoiced and the saints pitied <him for> his folly. By this example of petulance and impatience let others take warning, remembering Lot's wife.[50]

*[51]On Saturday the first of February the wind was fair, and about noon the tug came along side and took us out to sea unto the seventh. We experienced a scene of sickness more or less;[52] on the fifth <in the afternoon began to> it blow very hard. Increased until the morning of the sixth when it abated a little. It would be ~~hard~~ <difficult> for me to describe the inside of [Image 398] a passenger ship in a gale of wind. On the night referred to we had the wind in our teeth,[53] as a sailor would say, so that we had to beat against the wind and waters, which gave the ship an ugly <prevailing> side motion <accompanied by all sorts of motions that could be produced by a nor'easterly>. My wife took up her quarters upon a box near the center of the vessel where she could have the privilege of holding on to some luggage lashings, for she was afraid of being thrown out of the berth, it being a top one;[54] I repaired to our berth and passed the night not only watching and praying but holding on with my fingernails, lest I should suddenly be landed on the floor

Fig. 4. Cover of George D. Watt's shorthand journal.
Photograph by Ronald G. Watt.

among pots and pans and boxes that were dancing a dance peculiar to this one loose on the deck of a ship in a gale of wind.

The peculiarity of the sounds around [us] in such a circumstance adds no little interest to the scene, though perhaps of a kind not very pleasurable to the human ear. Outside the <wind> is heard raging on in its relentless course ~~screaming through the shrouds like a thousand~~ <like the voices of a thousand ancient> malignant spirits screaming the requiem of some distant wreck. Inside is heard the ~~scream~~ plaintive cries of an infant mingled with the terrified ~~cries~~ <screams> of the <children> more advanced in years,[55] the ~~immense~~ disagreeable sound caused <by the efforts of> a hundred females to discharge from their discomforted stomachs the provisions they refused to digest, <with> the deep groans of the <otherwise> athletic men who, in these circumstances, stripped of their strength, not by losing their locks as did Samson in the lap of Delilah,[56] but by losing their equilibrium on the bosom of the great deep;[57] and as a ~~choir~~ chorus to this other music, accompanied to the raging of waters a thousand ~~tins~~ <cans>, kettles, pans and bottles thundered forth their tinny voice accompanied by the banging of boxes broken loose from their moorings. This is the kind of vocal and instrumental music old Neptune[58] seems much to delight in;[59] however dreadful this may appear to some yet the tale is not half told.

When the morning sixth of February broke in upon us the scene was very truly at once pitiable and amusing,[60] there was none able to be up except a few of the old people, who seemed to weather it much better than the young and middle aged. On the deck was to be seen all sorts of mixtures ~~which you will excuse~~ <from the> mention of which I beg leave to be excused;[61] here I will notice one little incident that took place this morning for the amusement of my readers. [Image 399] A certain man who used to live not a hundred miles from [*illegible*] near Preston is the hero of these circumstances. It seems that he had in a can about four pints of treacle.[62] It is true he had a lid upon it but he had neglected to lash it to something permanent, however. In one of the heavy lurches of the vessel, away went the can of treacle and all this made quite a sloppy mess in front of the berth. Our hero <being somewhat of a [Norway seaman?]> was diligent to gather up such of it as he well could, <but he felt very fearful lest he himself should be ~~landed~~ cast away upon this sea of sweet,> but the main part of it had passed through under the luggage to the other side of the ship.

The most amusing part of the circumstance ~~took~~ was, after the treacle was <partly> gathered up; a bull dog by the name of "Major"[63] would of course be near his master's berth but when <he trod> ~~came~~ upon the place where the treacle had been spilt. he found it necessary to hold on with his toenails, which by and by was of no use to him and down he slipped, on all fours, until he came in contact with the first luggage that stopped him in his slippery passage;[64] after he had fulfilled one journey in this way, he would take a circuitous course to regain his master's berth, but as soon as he again touched the slipslops, there was nothing more certain than a speedy passage <on all fours> and a safe landing against the post luggage. Poor Major looked the picture of pain and despair and seemed as much puzzled <to know the reason of all this> as a drunken man did who tried <in vain> to light his pipe at the spout of a pump.

Another circumstance among the many I <will be> tempted to introduce here because of its kindred affinity to the one I have just ~~introduced~~ mentioned. A young man from Preston they call Isaac[65] thought he would go upon the poop deck to take the fresh air after such a night's rocking,[66] the ship gave a lurch to one side, Isaac lost his footing and found himself perhaps not very comfortably situated upon the wet deck,[67] this would not have been so bad could he have had the privilege of arising to his feet again but when he had to take a ~~opposite~~ <journey> [~~end/not~~?] from one side of the deck to the other, not on all fours, but in a seated position, wiping the deck in his passage and leaving a wake behind him of some considerable breadth. We rejoice to say that neither he nor Major sustained any material injury. ~~This~~ I notice these little incidents because I consider them to be necessary points in a faithful picture of a voyage across the Atlantic. And they perhaps might be able to give new understanding to my friends.

**February seventh.*

This is a very fine morning, the sea ~~calm~~ <a little rough but the vessel moving steadily through it> and the sun shining beautifully from the heavens. Today we cleaned beneath decks [Image 400] which is done by ~~sweeping~~ scraping, sweeping, and mopping. Our first duty was to get upon deck all the sick men and families, some of whom had not been out of bed for some days, we had some difficulty in accomplishing this as a many seemed to have no [*illegible*] for this; however we got them up except two. The fresh air much revived the sick and they felt thankful that they had mustered courage to venture upon deck, joy beamed upon every ~~countenance~~ countenance,[68] this however was changed to a wonderful scene of confusion. The vessel shipped a ~~sea of~~ <shower of spray> which gave the ill <~~sick~~> ~~passengers~~ [*illegible*] of them a thorough good washing. Here was <men>, women, and children sitting not very comfortably, I should think, in the midst of salt water, drenched to the skin,[69] this did them no harm at all but good;[70] with a great deal of caution and vigilance on the part of some of the brethren they were all safely deposited below in their clean berths without any being hurt though a many are wet and frightened.

Saturday February 8th

The passengers are much recruited from their seasickness,[71] the weather fine and the sea approaching a calm. We got a many of the sick upon deck today but the recent washing was not forgot which deterred many from availing themselves of the fresh air. <~~Evening we~~> In the afternoon I succeeded in getting a congregation on the poop deck. To them we read the ship rules and made such suitable remarks as the Spirit of the Lord and the circumstances of the people suggested to us,[72] Elder Pratt addressed the people much to their comfort <at this meeting Elder Watt was presented ~~to~~ before the people for their vote of confidence as the president of the company. Brothers [Wilber?], Toone, Baker,[73] and Jones[74] from Wales as his counselors>. In the evening may be seen on all hands the preparations going on necessary for the celebration of the Sabbath, which consisted chiefly in the cleaning and polishing of boots and shoes.

**Sunday 9th February*

The morning calm and beautiful. The ship not making much head way. The passengers were to be seen busying themselves in preparing for the meeting which was to be held on the poop deck. The chief part of the company assembled together about half past ten and set themselves upon such things as they had. A great portion of them were seated upon the deck which was dry. Elder Watt opened the meeting by giving out the first hymn "The Morning Breaks" etc. which was sung with spirit and devotion. Elder Pratt made an appropriate prayer and delivered a proper address for the circumstances we were then in.[75] The sacrament was duly administered after which several spoke touching the duties of emigrants ~~one~~ to each other on board of ship. The meeting dismissed with singing and a blessing from Elder Watt. Elders Pratt and Watt <then> visited the sick, [Image 401] prayed with and comforted them. The day closed without any more change in the weather, and all hearts rejoiced, retiring to rest with songs ~~God~~ of praise to the God of Joseph. This is our first public meeting to celebrate the worship of God.

<*>*Monday February 10th.*

This morning we found ourselves in a calm but the sea betokens of that ~~reminding~~ recently there has been a gale of wind. The <sea> comes rolling in majestic swells from the north west while the surface of these <watery> mountains and valleys are as smooth as oil. God is seen in his majesty in this world <of> briny waters. The saints are all around their galley[s] anxious to cook breakfast; until this morning we have not hitherto seen much disposition manifested for cooking and eating. But <now> food is quite in demand ~~this morning~~ for the sickness has well-nigh subsided, such as red herring, pickled cabbage and onions or pickles of any kind, preserves of the sour class;[76] salt fish etc. <are the things desired and sought for> lemons, oranges and apples are much in demand.

Late in the afternoon we spoke a ship[77] named "H W [Buron?][78] from Liverpool bound for Philadelphia. In the evening it was reported to ~~me by one~~ to us that a female, one of the sisters, was in the forecastle among the sailors. Now this is contrary to the rules ~~of all~~ which govern all emigrant ships, and against which the captain of this ship had particularly warned us;[79] we applied to the mate that he might turn her out but he gave us liberty so to do,[80] accordingly we went to the forecastle and inquired if there were any females there, but discovered we had been misinformed,[81] this aroused the ire of the sailors against us because we kept a strict look out after our sisters and would not let them be led astray. The sailors came to us in a body and offered some insult,[82] however <the vexation of this> this is nothing compared with the sorrow that <must> follow in the case of a poor female being robbed of her ~~virtue~~ virtue by reckless seamen. Scores of innocent females <who were not acquainted with the deep wickedness of this class of men> have thus been blighted and plunged into irretrievable woe. Let all presidents over companies of saints pay marked attention to this part of their duty, fearing not the frowns of men or the disapprobation of women.

We will commence our recording of the ship's course from today. We are in latitude 49° 30′00″ and longitude 10° 35′00″ which places us over a hundred miles southwest of Cape Clear[83] by which it may be seen we have plenty of sea room being in the great Atlantic.[84] [Image 402]

Tuesday February eleventh.

The night has been somewhat squally but the morning is fine with a wind south by west enabling us to steer a westwardly course with the sails tight hold to the wind. A northwest wind would be more favorable for us. Throughout we have had to thank God for his mercies to us so far, enabling us to clear the Irish Channel, in which dangerous place ships are often detained between 20 and 30 days.

Sarah Preece <aged six months> the daughter of Richard and Susanna Preece <natives of Herefordshire> died today a little after noon.[85] The child was sick before it came on board the ship and was expected to die in Liverpool. This circumstance caused some curiosity among the passengers who had not seen any person buried in the sea. It may not be uninteresting my friends to ~~know~~ <read> an account of the process of burying the dead on the sea. The corpse is washed as ~~usual~~ usual and given into the hands of the sailors who sew it up tight in canvas long enough of length at the feet of the corpse to receive about 50 pounds or a hundred weight of coals or rock or any other weighty substance to sink it to the bottom of the ocean. This is also sewed in with the dead person. After it was dark, Elder Pratt and myself and the captain assembled at the berth of the bereaved parents to administer comfort to them and tend to interment of their infant child;[86] in the mean time, while Elder Pratt was making an appropriate prayer, the body of the child was placed upon a board by the sailors and born to the lee side[87] of the ship waiting for orders to plunge it into the fathomless waters. After prayer was over, the command was given and the infant's remains sank down, down, down to the depths beneath. I will not weary you with my reflections caused by this heart rending scene. It sufficeth me to say that the sea will give up its dead on the resurrection morn where the grief stricken parents ~~of this poor child expect~~ expect again to meet their infant child. Spoke a ship today but did not ascertain her name. We are in latitude 49° 36′ 0″ and longitude 12° 46′ 00″.

Wednesday February 12th

<We have had a quiet night.> In the forenoon we spoke a ship named the *Tuscarora* of Philadelphia. This morning is a little squally <fair sailing> under closed reef top sails and main sails also under single reef.[88] The first mate who ~~seems to have~~ <has the> charge of the sailing department seems rather timid about carrying sail when the ship would carry a great deal more. [Image 403] However, it is better to be cautious than foolishly adventuresome where so many souls ~~are~~ <would be> at stake if anything was [to] happen. About 12 o'clock today the wind shifted around to the

quarter for which we had prayed the Lord to send. It is now blowing from the northwest giving us a southwestwardly course. All the reefs are out <sails> and our gallant ship is sneaking through the waters at about 8 knots per hour. Our heart seems glad for every kindness, caress and smile.

The appetites of the passengers are now becoming sharp like a two edged sword. It would amuse you to see the curious messes that are dished up not in consequence of the badness of the food but the lack of knowledge manifested by some who come from districts where oatmeal is not used,[89] it is cooked in all sorts of ways but the right way,[90] if <we> had had a sprinkling of north of England and Scottishness among us to a greater extent so much good oatmeal would not have been murdered in cooking,[91] but as necessity is the mother of invention they will perhaps find out how to mix and cook it <ere long>. We are now in latitude 49° 54' 00" and longitude 15° 00' 00".

Thursday February 13th

We all enjoyed a good night's rest. The wind <is> in the same direction with ~~sudden~~ steadying sails and a <main [*illegible*]> quarter set to catch all the wind possible. These sails are chiefly used by navigators in the ~~southern~~ <low> latitudes, the winds being light and requiring light sails. We have averaged about 6 knots per hour today having a light wind from the starboard quarter which [*illegible*] a little towards night making our pass through a smooth sea at about 8 knots per hour.

*As we were passing some passengers today sitting on the poop deck we had the pleasure of seeing them dine on a leg of mutton which had been previously salted and boiled which they were eating cold to mustard pickles and ketchup,[92] this made us wish we [had] prepared ourselves a dainty previous to leaving Liverpool,[93] if this hint will be useful to our <who intend to emigrate> friends[94] they are quite welcome to it. We are in latitude 47° 57' 00" longitude 15° 51' 00". [Image 404]

Friday February 14

Favorable <light> winds and <~~fair~~> making no progress in ~~sailing~~ sailing. We are in latitude ~~46° 54′ 00″~~ 46° 20′ 00″ longitude 15° 16′ 00″.

Saturday February 15th

Favorable winds until the afternoon when the wind sprung up from southwest giving us a westerly course at about 5 knots per hour. We are in latitude 45° 51′ 30″ longitude 16° 30′ 00″.

**Sunday February 16th*

Elder Toone from Leamington had a child die this morning about 6 o'clock aged 11 weeks.[95] It also was sick before it came on board and its parents expected to bury it in Liverpool. It had never been nourished from its mother's breast in consequence of its not being able to suck.

The [wind] is still from the southwest direction blowing a steady breeze. Our meeting opened at the usual time that is at <half past> ten o'clock by the ship time which would be about 12 o'clock by the English time. After singing and prayer by Elder Toone, Elder Pratt addressed the meeting upon the principles of obedience to the laws of God which have <certain> bounds and penalties attached thereto. Treated upon the various sins of which man can and cannot be forgiven in this life. We obtained a verbatim report of this speech but to give it here would swell this letter to an unwarrantable length.[96] <Elder Watt addressed the passengers as to their duties in keeping the laws of the ship *Ellen Maria* which Elder Pratt had referred to>. Sacrament was administered, a child blessed and some sick prayed for. So concluded the services of the day with a blessing from Elder Watt. After meeting Elder Toone's infant was plunged into the bowels of this fathomless abyss of waters. We are in latitude 45° 44′ 00″ longitude 18° 25′ 00″.

Monday 17 February

We are in latitude 45° 45′ 26″ longitude 20° 53′ 15″. The winds are variable and the ship is not making much progress.

Tuesday February 18th

Variable winds, generally unfavorable. We are in latitude longitude

Wednesday 19th February

Stormy with a wind from the northwest we are in latitude [Image 405] longitude .

Thursday 20th February

Fair winds until evening when it lowered and changed to a head wind and to the southeast about 2 o'clock in the morning of Friday. We are in latitude longitude .

Friday 21 February.

LATITUDE 41° 26′00″ LONGITUDE 20° 42′00″.

The wind increased all day and in the evening blew a hurricane, getting up the sea into a vast succession of hills and valleys. The most of our sails are furled and the rest under double reef waiting for the approach of the distant monster which we expect suddenly to pounce upon us without mercy. The <west and> southwest sky near the horizon at sun set displayed some of the most beautiful tints, which peep through the angry blackness which ~~was~~ is fast approaching us. The sun has gone down ~~from us~~ to brighten and cheer the animated beings of other climes,[97] blackness now covers the heavens. The gale has struck our ship roaring like a thousand thunders through the rigging. Our noble vessel gently leans to itself as if conscious <of the> superior force against which she <has> ~~had~~ to contend. The gale increased in intensity and force the captain and first mate ~~are~~ display on their countenances all the anxiety ~~of those who were called upon to exercise their wisdom~~ of men having the charge of <many> souls and much property committed to them. The gale still increases,[98] now the voice of the first mate is heard ~~like that of a child's midst the thunder~~ giving orders to furl the ~~main~~ fore top sail the ropes and stays are immediately slackened and the sail is free,[99] all hands are now seeking their way up the rigging <when it would be next to impossible for a landsman to keep his feet on deck>. We have lost sight of them in the darkness above. We have now three sails up, namely the main top, which is under double reef, the spencer, and one of the jib sails.[100] The dark waters beneath us are made angry by the ~~merciless~~ merciless winds,[101] they are foaming, roaring, and and[102] swelling powers in awful majesty as though they had waged war with the furious element above them.[103] While our ship is scuttling along through the deep furrows of the ocean like a thief surrounded by the administrators of justice as if truly aware [Image 406] of her dangerous position. The blackness of the heavens is gone but the gale is still raging in its fury. The starry firmament above give[s] us some little light upon the scene which is ~~truly~~ <awful> green and I ~~I~~ must say [*illegible*] description. It may be thought that the passengers were all frightened half to death but such is not the case for some are singing and some are ~~praying preparing for bed~~ <offering up their evening devotions previous to retiring to rest> and some are reading and others conversing and some playing music. While the wind continues in its fierceness the vessel is much more still than when there is but little wind and a heavy sea. After midnight the wind ~~had~~ became <not so fierce> and left a heavy sea which continued to rage with unabated force,[104] the ship now begins to roll from side to side as she is sailing in a parallel direction to the waves. It is now everybody's business to hold on to their berths or they would be landed on the floor <of the deck>,[105] I had to get a rope and lash myself and family in our berth for often the vessel was thrown on her beam ends almost.[106]

Such a scene as this is not quite without interest even to a sick person, for the boxes began to break from their places and like as many trains would make passages from point to point as the ship ~~moved~~ <rolled>. The men might be seen in their undressed condition chasing their boxes pans kettles bundles and barrels to secure them again.[107] But, as though the spirits of the deep rejoice to see poor lost lands-men in such a predicament, when a person thinks he has got his box in his power and at its place, no sooner has he mounted this restless piece of furniture than the ship gives a lurch, off goes the box like a passenger train carrying the owner with it to another part of the ship. This would be not be so bad if he could stop there but he must <unwillingly enough> come back again and <be> carried as far ~~as~~ on the other side of the ship <and thus make 4 or 5 such passages> before he can [*illegible*] carriage and see <a fleet[ing]> opportunity of freeing himself from his unfavorable situation. This is only one case among many such like.

A curious little scene took place right front of our berth;[108] ~~Amos Fielding[109] and myself had neglected to tie our water bottles the night before~~ and two water bottles that had not been tied the night before took a notion to dance a reel. A little brown one [Image 407] leaped from its place and danced over the deck. Its large brown neighbor, seeing this, concluded to join in the dance was [*illegible*] rolling and tumbling over the deck, then a provision box that stood by introduced its four corners into the reel. This would be called in Scotland a threesome reel,[110] these danced away, proving fatal to the little brown bottle for on coming suddenly in contact with the larger bottle, it fell in pieces scattering its watery contents over the deck;[111] a glass pickle bottle full of onions, that was ~~situated~~ situated on the top of a pile of boxes, through these accidents concluded to fill up the breach, so down it came to join the dance and fortunately enough escaped being broke. "Amos your pickle bottle is on the floor" cried out some one.[112] This aroused a man from his berth who broke up the dance of the bottles and the box. The pickle bottle was ~~placed~~ put back to its place but not long afterwards it bounced upon the floor and was smashed if not into a thousand pieces, into twenty at least. The onions finding themselves freed from their prison had a fine time at playing at roly-poly. Here we had onions, vinegar, and water and a broken pots [*sic*] with a mixture of tin cans, pieces of salt pork, a box containing flour, meal, rice, and biscuits spilled on the floor <in confusion>. Our ~~my~~ friends may learn from all this that it is necessary for themselves on the ocean to tie every thing firmly with good strong cord, a supply

Fig. 5. Ship *International* in storm, etching.
Courtesy of Church History Library.

of which it would be wise for every emigrant to bring with them. The wind came from the southwest.

Saturday February 22nd

The wind unfavorable and somewhat violent, the sea was heavy and passengers generally sick through the heavy rolling of the ship. The wind is from southwest. This morning a Welshman was put in irons for exposing a naked light in the steerage. This was not the first offense but [he] had been reproved for it twice before. He was seated on the deck so as to be exposed to all the passengers and a pair of handcuffs put on his wrists. The man made no resistance whatever. And many of the passengers brought candles with them and lanterns. Now this is wrong and exposes the ship to burning dangers. We would advise all passengers to make up their minds to do without candles and be contented to ship lights that are provided.[113]

Sunday February 23d

The wind still stormy and the sea heaved. Had no meeting today upon deck as it would be impossible for the passengers to keep their feet [Image 408] in consequence of the violent rolling of the ship last night and many are sick and unable to be out of bed. In the afternoon a marriage was solemnized by **D Jones**[114] between **Edward Williams**[115] <elder> from **Llunelli**[116] Branch.

Camrarthenshire[117] [*sic*] **aged** 30 and **Ann Morgans**[118]

Cwmbach Branch (near **Aberdare**) **Glamorganshire**[119] **Aged** 24 in the presence of

John Prue Elder
John Harris[120] **Do**
Wm Williams[121] **Do**
Thos Phillip[s][122] **Preist** [*sic*]

Elder Watt preached to <the portion of> the passengers in steerage about one hour. A good spirit prevailed and a disposition to do the will of God and those who he has appointed to look over the welfare of the company.

Monday February 24

The sea is still rolling heavily and the wind high, blowing from the same quarter, retarding our progress to the west and threatening to prolong our voyage. The company is generally well except a few aged people and <a few> young children.

Tuesday February 25th

LATITUDE 36° 26′00″ [LONGITUDE] 18° 36′30″

The wind is blowing from the south sometimes inclining to the east. The vessel has made a due west course all day running about 2 ½ miles per hour. The air feels light and salubrious and the motion of the ship is but slight giving the passengers a chance to gather upon deck to take fresh air and the sick to recover a little from their seasickness. Nothing of importance occurred to day all things go on in peace among the passengers. [Image 409]

Wednesday February 26th

LATITUDE 36° 13′00″ LONGITUDE 20° 56′00″

The wind continued in the same course as yesterday until the evening when it lulled into a calm. The passengers generally well. No complaints today.

Thursday February 27th

LATITUDE 56° 12′20″ LONGITUDE 18° 46′30″

This morning we have a calm. All sail is unfurled and flapping against the masts caused by the motion of the ship <moved> by the swell of the sea. We found it very hot in the second cabin in the night;[123] the sun rose beautifully from below the eastern waters which soon shone with that brightness common to our native isle in ~~England~~ the midst of summer. The passengers after <breakfast> and prayers began to gather upon the deck to bask in the gentle sun light;[124] their sickness seemed to be gone forgotten while they are busied some with knitting, some sewing, some [*illegible*] music, some washing, some cooking, and some ~~basking~~ <rolling and basking> themselves in the sun, not doing anything but that. Some complaints were made this morning relative to the closeness of the steerage, inconsequence of the great amount of luggage therein stowed, for none of the passengers' luggage has been stored below, and there being a great deal of it leaves the passengers but little room. However we are a deal better off in the *Ellen Maria* <in this respect> than those in the *Ellen*[125] and the *G W Bourne*.[126]

Friday February 28th

LATITUDE LONGITUDE .[127]

The company enjoyed a good night's rest it being very calm weather. This morning we have scarcely a breath of wind. The company is all in good health with but a few exceptions.

Saturday 1st March

LATITUDE LONGITUDE .

The weather still calm and the wind, what there is of it, favorable. Spoke an [amphritite?] frigate this afternoon [Image 410] from Bermuda bound for Madeira[128] had been out to sea 23 days. She [*illegible*] named the "[Lowell?]".

There are some fears today that the cabin passengers and sailors will fall short of provisions in consequence of the delay experienced in the voyage. There being no more than one month's vittles aboard and we have not traversed more than a fourth of our journey. The captain is a kind man in his manners and external deportment to the passengers but very hard in his dealings with his fellow men,[129] he has therein not supplied enough of food for the passage,[130] such is the statement of the first mate,[131] and talked of rather publicly by the second mate,[132] how far this may be true the future alone will reveal.

Sunday March 2nd

LATITUDE LONGITUDE .

We are still becalmed,[133] what wind we have is breathing from the northwest. All ~~is~~ are busy preparing for the the[134] meeting on deck. The meeting of the saints was convened at the usual time. We had a general assembly. Elder Toone opened the meeting with singing "Ye Sons of Men a Feeble Race etc." Elder Watt prayed. After which which[135] Elder Pratt addressed the [saints] eloquently and powerfully upon the dealings of God with mankind formerly and what he will do in the future, quoting prophesyings from the Bible and Book of Doctrine and Covenants. For a full report of this speech refer to the book of ~~his~~ the speeches of the beloved apostles.[136] The sacrament was delivered as usual and the saints dismissed with a blessing from Elder Watt. A good feeling prevailed through the whole meeting. Elder Pratt's infant child[137] is much afflicted with bowel complaint and canker. She was ill when she came on board with a sore eye. It has healed and she has worsened in other ways.

Monday March 3rd

LATITUDE LONGITUDE .

The sky is cloudy and threatens a wind. The moon changed early this morning[138] and about 3 in the afternoon a wind sprung up from the southeast to the joy of the whole company, for we are all anticipating a long passage having had [Image 411] many head winds and <a few days'> calms. In [the] evening and through the night there was a little <small> rain and fog through the day.

Tuesday March 4th <Pan cake Tuesday>

LATITUDE LONGITUDE .

~~About~~ The wind still being from the southeast and our ship is ~~steering~~ <lying on> her course with her yards braced up close to the wind. We are making somewhere about between 5 and six knots per hour. About 11 o'clock this evening we spoke a vessel a schooner from [*illegible*] in Brussels. She reported our longitude to be 23° 6′ 00″. She had been out at sea 23 days. Did not ascertain where she was bound for. Elder Pratt's child is worse this morning.

Wednesday March 5th

LATITUDE LONGITUDE .

All is well this morning as usual. Brother Pratt's child no better. The wind favorable and blowing a steady breeze.

Thursday March 6th

LATITUDE LONGITUDE .

No change in the wind or in the circumstances of the people. All is peace and contentment so far as our condition will admit of. Elder Pratt's child neither better nor worse.

Friday March 7

LATITUDE LONGITUDE .

No change in the wind or in the circumstances of the people in general. There is today a little difficulty caused by a sister of the name of Hill from Liverpool telling that she saw a sailor kiss a Miss Phoebe Bromley[139] which through her [Image 412] circumstances and the statement of her friends seems to be false;[140] this Sister Hill has had the misfortune to tattle to several leaders which has caused the friends of the girl who ~~is~~ are very respected to feel much grief. Elder Pratt has been some concerned with the affair. Elder Pratt's baby is much better this morning.

~~*Saturday*~~

Saturday March 8th

LATITUDE LONGITUDE .

This morning about the break of day George Spicer, aged 2 years and eight months, died of dysentery and was interred in the usual manner. The son of Sarah and George Spicer[141] of **Grantum,**[142] Lincolnshire, England. The mother and three children are on their way to America and had left their husband and father in Grantham. Elder Pratt's child much better this morning. The wind is still favorable and our vessel is pressing her way at the rate upon an average of 8 knots per hour.

Sunday March 9th

LATITUDE LONGITUDE .

There is no change whatever in the weather. The morning is somewhat cloudy and there is a change.
At twenty minutes past five this morning Frederick Joseph Robbins was born. The child and the mother is doing well. Also Sister Sarah Spicer was delivered of a son between seven and eight o'clock. She buried a son yesterday and was safely delivered of another today. We had a good meeting today on deck Elder Pratt spoke for fore part of the discourse was reported.[143] Brother Toone and Watt administered the sacrament after which Elder Watt made remarks upon the act of training children and the duties of husbands and wives, though he confessed his limited knowledge on the subject. About 3 o'clock [Image 413] in the afternoon the sky threatened a squall a

head of us. The officers of the ship immediately made such preparations as they considered necessary for the occasion. The evening until about twelve o'clock presented a scene of the most frightful thunder and lightning with heavy torrents of rain, not much wind. The sailors were busied in catching fresh water both for culinary and laundry purposes.

Monday March 10th

LATITUDE LONGITUDE .

The morning is clear and cool for this climate but the wind had deviated somewhat against us and which is also of a light character. We lost by the last squall about 16 hours sailing. We are not moving more than 4 to 5 knots per hour. Elder Pratt's child is better today. Hear no complaints of any kind among the passengers.

Tuesday March 11th

LATITUDE LONGITUDE .

Fair wind this morning. All sail set but it is light. We have moved the luggage out of the second cabin which has given us a great deal more comfort than before. This has caused us quite a busy day. Elder Pratt not so well today being troubled with a boil complaint. The child not so well so that they entertain not much hopes of her recovery. The wind has strengthened much towards evening and is pressing our ship from eight to nine knots per hour through the water.

Wednesday March 12th

LATITUDE LONGITUDE .

We have a fine wind this morning and an odd sun. Sometime about four o'clock **A.M.** poor pug was thrown overboard by some person who thought he had lived long enough on this terrestrial ball. He had been a dog in his mistress's house [Image 414] for 17 years. In the course of that time [he] had the misfortune of ~~breaking~~ <getting> his leg broke, which cost his mistress five shillings to ~~get~~

<have> it set <by a [*illegible*] bone setter>, but the bandage being too tight gave poor pug a great deal of pain and at the same time ~~not long~~ <did not heal> his shattered limb,[144] his mistress saw,[145] and felt for his pain and undertook to bandage it fresh which gave the wounded animal much ease and ended in a good cure. From that time pug imbibed a truly heart felt affection for his mistress and would not leave her side by night or by day. In this case it was a true saying that love begets love for his mistress might be seen carrying <her> favorite in her arms up the ladders and down the ladders and over the <slippery> decks in all weathers. In the morning she might be seen washing the ~~much beloved animal's~~ face and combing the <hair of the> much loved pug,[146] before he could be permitted to go a visiting with his mistress.

He was of the lap dog bred with a neat head <and ears with a considered amount of sense too> but a bit too large for a lady's lap dog. His color was light brown mingled with a little white in sundry places. He had [*illegible*] hair about the neck and shoulders and appeared very decrepit with age. <He was apt to fits and would run to his mistress to hold him when he felt them coming on.> His voice sounded like an old man's and was rendered quite harmless in the mouth, for where once on a time might be <seen> a row of beautiful ivories is to be seen the toothless gums with here and there an ill-colored pug tooth. Poor pug as if [*illegible*] of his ~~his~~ [*illegible*] <feet> would not leave his gentle mistress a yard, and if she had occasion to leave him in charge with any person he would cry almost like a child until her return, and looking as well as he could (for he was almost blind) in the direction he had supposed his mistress to have gone. His mistress feels it sore at heart. They [ought to have?] had many a weary tug.

But few there is to to [*sic*] heal the smart for all seemed tired of poor old pug. [Image 415]

Thursday March 13th

LATITUDE LONGITUDE .

The wind is still favorable but of a light character. The weather is very hot and the second cabin for want of ventilation is almost past living in.

Friday March 14th

LATITUDE LONGITUDE .

The prospects and weather about the same. A spirit of satisfaction is general among the passengers as well as health of body.

Saturday March 15

LATITUDE LONGITUDE .

The weather and other circumstances the same. Some dissatisfaction manifested by the ~~some of the~~ passengers and some of the sailors in consequence of Amos Fielding['s] dog being permitted to go abroad unchained. He has bitten some and threatened to bite others.

The captain asked me to let him have some butter belonging to the passengers which in consequence of the little amount made difficult to dole out to them for which he promised to give us flour and beef which dole out better to the passengers. There was about 45 pounds of butter <with a keg>. Began today to give the passengers 3 quarts of water instead of two which we gave for about 5 weeks. Changed my bed from the berth to the boxes.[147]

Sunday March 16th

LATITUDE LONGITUDE .

A beautiful morning and a fair wind as we have had now for many days. The passengers are amused with the sight [Image 416] of a young whale following our vessel for two hours sometimes diving beneath it and sometimes swimming alongside of it and sometimes sporting in the front of it. The fish seemed about 25 feet long.[148]

The saints assembled for meeting at half past ten by the ship time under an awning, which was spread over the poop deck to protect us from the sun. Elder Toone opened the meeting. and Elder Pratt prayed, and Elder Watt spoke those things that came into his heart, after which Elder Pratt made remarks commending the teachings of the spirit through Elder [Watt] and recommended them [to] the saints for their observance. The sacrament was administered as usual. Frederick Joseph Robbins was blessed before the congregation. A spirit of peace and rejoicing was made manifest on the countenances of the saints Elder Toone dismissed the meeting with a blessing.

The following is a copy of a letter received from the second mate today

to George Watt

Sir

Not being much of a hand to convey my ideas upon any subject verbally, I will try what I can do with my pen upon a subject that has occupied the first place in my mind for a length of time, more especially since we left Liverpool this passage, but you must not startle when I tell you that the subject is Mormonism.

A few months ago you asked me to let you baptize me,[149] now I will tell you plainly how I have felt, and how I now feel concerning the same.

About twelve months ago or more I was in London,[150] and one Sabbath I was at a friend's house, where I accidentally met with a Latter-day Saint when we had a great deal of talk and argument but somehow or other he always got to be winner of me a long way out. When leaving he told me he should like to see me again, but we never met. [Image 417] A [*Millennial*] *Star*[151] he had left at this house fell into my hands but I could make nothing of it so I gave Mormonism up for a bad job thinking it <nothing but a delusion> a regular cheat the public.

My next attack at Mormonism was at Liverpool but here I had a better tutor <tutor> or rather <~~tutors~~> tutors <tutors>. This was a young lady of very respectable family <~~connections~~> connections who had embraced the gospel contrary to her parents' wishes and unknown to them. From her I had the Mormon principles explained to me. I believe it to be true but still a cloud hung over me on it, a sort of a doubt on my mind.

[Prior to] this voyage I called at her father's house and to my surprise the old gentleman told me she had gone crazy with religion and left him. I determined to find her out and did so to reason with her upon the rash step she had taken for an unprotected female to leave home and parents but she very coolly remarked what she had done she was sure was right and that she valued her soul's salvation above all other things;[152] it was then that the first rays of light began to break through the cloud that hung over me.

And when I heard the testimonies of yourself and Brother Pratt the wall seemed to vanish before good sound reason and secure proof. Now Mr. Watt (I cannot call you brother yet) it is my desire to become a member of the Latter-day Church as soon as a convenient opportunity offers and I hope that every professing Mormon has as good a heart for the cause

As you[r] humble servant
John [Curtis?][153]

> P.S. It is my intention if possible to go right through to the valley. Clear off from all the crafts and temptations of this evil world but we can talk that over and make arrangements again.
> J. [Curtis?]

[Image 418] The following is my answer to the above letter

Ship *Ellen Maria*
March 16th 1851

Dear Curtis

Your account (which I have just received) of how you was first made acquainted with the principles of the gospel of peace gave me much joy. I do assure you [blank space] to your [action?] to join this people, I say amen to with all my heart, for after you have done that sir you at once enter into plenty of sea room where you may sail through life with unreefed topsails and royals set, and sometimes with setting sails. You may here have to encounter both white squalls and black ones but if you remain true to Mormonism you will find in it power enough <to make> to live in the worst gale that ever blew.

With best wishes for you
I am your servant for Christ's sake
G. D. Watt.[154]

Brother Pratt's health is poor having been troubled with a boil complaint. His child is not much better.

Monday March 17th

LATITUDE LONGITUDE .

No change in the weather or circumstances of the people. Elder Pratt still poorly. The child no better.

Tuesday March 18th [Image 419]

LATITUDE LONGITUDE .

No change in the circumstances of the people or weather. Elder Pratt still very weak and the child no better. Captain Whitmore seems not to have laid in proper provisions for the cabin. We cannot attribute this to anything but to the wretched onerousness which seems to be walk of men.[155] Sister Pratt[156] is much afflicted in her mind because of her sick family and not having it in her power to get for them those necessary things their condition of body requires. She did not provide any kind of fruits expecting that all needful would be provided by the captain. Although the captain is so ornery so as not to allow the steward to give a poor family that had been laying in a sup of soup. Yet he is very well and mild with the passengers and willing to make them comfortable in any way that will not cost him anything.

The wind sprang up from the larboard side of the ship rendering the <lower> sitting sails of little use. We are doing well with this wind.

Wednesday March 19th

LATITUDE LONGITUDE .

We have had a fine wind and have had a good run last night making upon an average 8 knots per hour. The company is generally in good health with the exceptions of a few children.

Thursday March 20th

LATITUDE LONGITUDE .

The weather very hot and the wind has gone from us almost it is now very light. Great expectation of seeing land tomorrow but the wind having become light it is feared we shall be disappointed. Brother Pratt's child worse. She is not expected to live to see [New] Orleans. Happiness prevails in the company and general good health. [Image 420]

Friday March 21st

LATITUDE LONGITUDE .

The wind is still of a very light character which is detaining us much in our journey

This evening was married by Elder O Pratt James Turnbull[157] of **Torpichen**[158] Parish Linlithgow County but born in Glasgow,[159] to Mary [Nickel?][160] a widow who was born in Port Glasgow James had never been married.

witnesses
G D Watt
John McPherson[161]
Hugh **Moloe**[162]

After prayers this evening I went upon the poop deck to take the fresh air after having been largely hot through the day for I never go upon the poop in the day time in consequence of the strength of the light which much affects my head. This evening I was very weak, not having been able to eat much food through the day;[163] while there Sister Martha, a young woman in Brother Pratt's family, came to me and wished me to go with her and look at the bed the captain had kindly offered her on deck, it being most uncomfortable to sleep in the cabin. This bed was composed of a large sail upon which the sailors had been working through the day. I sat upon it and then lay down upon it. Sister Martha, making herself well with me, and we having been acquainted in Liverpool sat down beside me. I still kept my lying position. Afterwards Sister Hill and Marian Ross[164] came and also sat down beside the sail upon which I was laying. Afterwards Sister Maddison[165] a second cabin passenger and her daughter came and sat down too. Then Emily[166] another sister from Liverpool ~~who was~~ is also in Brother Pratt's family there not being room for her to sit down beside me. She lay down on the sail [Image 421] on the sail[167] beside me.

Now all this took place in a very few minutes. Sister Ross left us and immediately after Brother Pratt came up from the cabin and walked up to us for this sail bed was beside the man who was managing the wheel. Elder Pratt walked about a little after making some passing remarks and then addressed me in words something like the following: Brother Watt you must allow me to tell you that ~~that~~ you are showing the passengers a very bad example and you as the president of the company ought to know better. I immediately answered by saying that I was not aware that I was doing anything wrong. He said he <u>knew</u>[168] I was.

I immediately left the company and repaired to my berth. This Martha and Emily had lived at Brother Pratt's house in Liverpool. It seems he had agreed with them to bring them both out to America also Sister Marian Ross and give them a cabin fare. Sister Martha had been very sick all the voyage so as to not be able to do anything for herself or any other person. It seems that Sister Pratt took umbrage at this and treated her very hardly indeed not allowing Emily or Marian Ross to do anything for her, as well as speaking disrespectfully of her to some of the passengers.

Now I felt for the poor sister and sympathized with her in her condition. I walked her over the deck now and then and fulfilled the office of a brother and a man to the sick girl in the face and eyes of those who neglected her in her hardest sickness. This caused her to manifest the love of a sister towards me and would be with me when she could see an opportunity. I am afraid this has given Elder Pratt and his lady offense. Emily is a strong girl of a very good natured temperament and sometimes would take a romp among the passengers but we all yet believe a good virtuous girl. Her manner has by some means or other obtained for her the disrespect of Elder Pratt and his lady. These <girls> not having hurt me in the least degree of course. I have not manifested a shyness to them any more than to the passengers. Now I am led [Image 422] to think that Elder Pratt has supposed me too well with these girls which is not the case. Elder Pratt's rebuke which was given in the presence of all and also before the men at the wheel grieved me much so that I have determined not to be on the poop deck more neither mingle with the passengers. Had Elder Pratt taken me to one side and told me his feelings I should have thanked him and kept a strict watch upon my position whether lying or sitting in the future. Retired to rest much grieved in spirit. Elder Pratt's child is no better.

Saturday March 22nd

LATITUDE LONGITUDE .

The wind has almost died away. Finished the reporting of my late violation which I have been occupied for three or four days. Its tone is much improved as well as its appearance. Saw the mountains of Santo Domingo[169] about ten o'clock. In the evening the wind sprang up to quite a breeze so that we make about 8½ knots per hour. The island of Santo Domingo lies east and where our course is due west and has therefore been in sight all day.

Sunday March 23d

LATITUDE LONGITUDE .

In consequence of the variableness of the wind and the frequent changes necessary to be made in the sails of the ship, our meeting did not take place until four or near five in the afternoon. We had a full meeting. Brother Toone opened with singing. Elder Watt joined in prayer after which Elder Toone spoke a short time preaching on the awful condition of those who apostatize from the church of God. These remarks were called forth through his having heard of some that were so inclined. His words were appropriate and good. [Image 423] Elder Watt then addressed the meeting to some length encouraging the poor to put their trust first in God and then in the strength of their own arms. He pointed out to them what the poor of the English nation had accomplished and what they do still accomplish. Proving thereby that they had the power in a new and fertile <or fertile> country to produce the same blessing for themselves as they have produced for their former kings and rulers. The congregation seemed much encouraged and blessed by our administrations. Elder Pratt did not choose to speak as his health was so poor in consequence of watching with his sick child. The meeting was dismissed by a blessing from Brother Pratt. We are running about eight knots per hour before a fine breeze of wind which has its influence in cheering the hearts of the passengers.

Monday March 24th

LATITUDE LONGITUDE .

This morning at three o'clock Marinda Pratt departed this life after a lingering sickness. The child was not well when she came on board. She is to be preserved in spirits and molasses until she arrive[s] at New Orleans. The wind this morning is not so [brisk?] as it was in the night. We see <to the south> the small island that lies between Santo Domingo and Cuba.[170]

Tuesday March 25

LATITUDE LONGITUDE .

Today we saw the island of Cuba which presents a very bold shore with lofty mountains. The winds are light from the land. The company enjoyed itself [*illegible*] health and peace. We are all in hopes of soon seeing the haven of our expectations. [Image 424]

Wednesday March 26

LATITUDE LONGITUDE .

We have had a fine breeze from the land towards evening. We are very near to the shore; the mountains of Cuba appeared to be no more than a couple of miles from the ship. About two in the morning the wind ceased and the ship drifted to within five miles of the rocks but fortunately a breeze sprung[171] up from land and saved us.

Thursday March 28<7>[172]

LATITUDE LONGITUDE .

The wind is light this morning we passed the Cape de Cruz[173] about dinner time a good breeze sprang up in the evening and towards nine o'clock carried away one of her <lower> [*illegible*] booms and sprang the other. The ship is making about nine knots per hour. William Davies was cut off from the church at a meeting of the [*illegible*].[174]

Friday March 27<8>th

LATITUDE LONGITUDE .

This morning Sister Wilde the wife of Brother Henry **Wild**[175] <from South Hampton> was delivered of a very fine daughter who is to be called Ellen Mariah <Martha>. A fine ship passed us this morning we did not speak [to] her but a show of colors was exchanged between the two ships.

Saturday March 29th

LATITUDE LONGITUDE .

Brother Pratt settled with me giving me <£> 8 .. 10 .. <£> 4 10 s .. 0 .. for the company which was made into the poors fund. <£> 2 <s> 0 .. 0 due to myself and <£> 2 .. <s> 0 .. 0[176] for [Image 425] treacle which the company had to embalm his infant child. Went around among the company today seeking out the poor and destitute and made as good a disposition of the means of the poor fund as possible so that all if possible might go up the river. The ship is lying on her course with light but steady wind.

Sunday March ~~28~~<30>th

LATITUDE LONGITUDE .

We have a fine morning and a good wind. About meeting time we saw the land to the north of us. We had a full meeting and we expect it to be the last we shall have on board of ship. The meeting was opened by Elder Toone. Prayer by Elder Pratt after which he spoke to the saints, giving them some general instructions how they should act on their arrival at New Orleans. Elder Watt was appointed to charter a steam boat for the company and to take a deposit of ten shillings from each passenger. After lengthy remarks upon the future glory of Zion and the saints and the destructions that shall come upon the wicked, Elder Watt laid before the company the state of the provisions and it was agreed that half of the surplus provisions be given to those who have served the company and the other half be given to the poor according to the wisdom of the president allowing all those who wish their share of the half to obtain them. ~~2~~ Pounds two and sixpence which was due to the company for treacle which Elder Pratt had used to embalm his child was agreed to be given to the poor. We blessed two children namely [Alma Lora?] Spicer and Ellen Maria Martha Wilde and cut two off from the church namely two were cut off from the church namely [blank space] William Davies of the Abercrombie Branch Monmouthshire Conference and Evan Howells[177] [*illegible*] Branch in the same conference. William Davies was the man that left the ship while she lay in the river. [Image 426]

Monday March ~~30~~<31>th

LATITUDE LONGITUDE .

We have a fair wind pressing us on through the Gulf of Mexico. All is expectation among the passengers that soon there will be a termination of their tedious journey. The passengers all well. Elder Pratt informed me that Martha and Emily would pass up the river on board the steamer in the steerage and gave me instructions to procure for them a berth in some family to cross the mountains stating that Martha was not healthy and could not do Mistress Pratt's work and Emily was slow, and under the anticipation of hot weather he feared she would be slower still. And that Sister Pratt would have American girls to do her work.

Tuesday ~~March 30th~~<April 1st>

LATITUDE LONGITUDE .

We commenced to finish up the doling out of the provisions to the company. Nothing of importance occurred to day.

Wednesday April 2~~st~~<nd>

LATITUDE LONGITUDE .

*Finished the doling out of provisions to the company. I bought 14 barrels of meal with a hope of making something by it in New Orleans. We have a head wind today which is hindering us very much and will tend to abride our hopes of seeing land tomorrow morning. About 8 o'clock this evening Sarah Lane the wife of the wife of [*sic*] John Lane[178] was safely delivered of a daughter.

Thursday April 3 [Image 427]

LATITUDE LONGITUDE .

We saw one of the [*illegible*] lights about seven in the evening. This made all hearts rejoice with exceedingly great joy and every mouth except those who were insensible of the mercies of God to give forth praise to him. We were too late for a steam boat so we lay to all night.

Friday April ~~3~~<4>th

About 10 o'clock this morning the steam boat <[*illegible*]>[179] took us in tow and about 12 at noon we safely crossed the bar without sticking and we cast anchor in the river until afternoon about

4 o'clock when we were taken in tow again and proceeded on our way up the river.[180] In the afternoon myself with Elder Pratt and a many others went on shore to get some provisions but we were much disappointed and found none worth naming.

Saturday April 5th

We are on our way up the river and the passengers are much delighted with the scenery of the Mississippi.

Sunday April 6th

Arrived safe in New Orleans without losing any of our passengers though early on Sunday morning before day break a young man by the name of John Richards[181] fell over board off the steam deck into the river. The current took [him] under the paddles of the steam boat. He being a good [Image 428] swimmer found his way to the top of the water and gave the alarm. A life buoy was thrown from the ship *Ellen Maria* and fortunately he caught hold of it or he must have sacrificed his life to his want of caution while on the <unguarded> decks of those ~~unguarded~~ Mississippi River steam boats. The engines are not working ~~in consequence of~~ <for the vessels are> lying to for the night. A boat was manned which soon returned again with the half drowned man on board. By these circumstances let all take warning.

Immediately after the boat was moored, Elder Pratt and myself went ashore and chartered the large steam boat *Aleck Scott* securing berths[182] for 292 <adult> passengers at $2 per head and a hundred weight of luggage allowed to each passenger. The rest to be paid for at the rate of 25 cents per hundred weight. Cabin passage $15 per head to go on board on Tuesday after noon with the expectation to set sail for St. Louis the same evening.

2

The Rivers

The *Aleck Scott* cleared the wharf . . . and bent her course against the mighty currents of the great Mississippi.
—George D. Watt journal, April 9, 1851

Up the Mississippi and the Missouri Rivers

The first successful commercial steamboat began with Robert Fulton. Fulton was born in Pennsylvania in 1765 of Irish parents.[1] He went to England as an aspiring artist but instead became interested in applying the steam engine to a river boat. He met Robert Livingston, an American and a signer of the Declaration of Independence, in Paris. Livingston convinced him to return to the United States and develop a steamboat for American waters. He built the first commercial steamboat in New York, the *Clermont*, which plied the waters of the Hudson River between Albany and New York City. In 1811 he constructed the *New Orleans* in Pittsburgh, and thus began the steamboat era in the Mississippi River basin, which lasted more than fifty years.

Though the earlier use of flatboats and keelboats had helped in the development of those western rivers, these boats did not lead to much actual growth. The steamboat, however, triggered great growth throughout the region. It helped increase the population throughout the entire Mississippi River basin. For example, Cincinnati grew from a population of 9,600 in 1820 to 115,000 in 1850, and St. Louis increased from 4,900 to 77,000 during the same time.[2] Traveling at least five to eight miles an hour, a steamboat could go down the Ohio and Mississippi faster than ever, and it could come back up the river with speed that the keelboats never had. The steamboat quickly took over the Mississippi River and its tributaries. Keelboats could not compete with these lumbering giants. The steamboat became the mode of transportation for all agricultural products, from the edible products of the northern states to cotton in the south. No longer did farmers need to subsist on their farm products: they could now ship crops thousands of miles, which allowed them to put more land into production.[3]

The Mississippi River was navigable by steamboat from its mouth in the Gulf of Mexico to St. Paul, Minnesota. New Orleans became the chief port of this gigantic river basin. The lower part of the river became the trunk line for goods and passengers traveling up the river. In 1820, 15 steamboats were built to begin this era. The number of boats per year increased every year thereafter.[4] In 1850, 109 steamboats were built in order to handle the demand of moving products from the north of this new nation to the southern tip and return. The tributaries of the Mississippi spread its tentacles from eastern Montana with the Missouri River to Pennsylvania with the Ohio River, and the southern part of the country to the White, Red, and Arkansas Rivers. It seemed that any place could be reached with this river system and these boats.[5] The steamboats carried both products and people. Later steamboats resembled palaces on the waters, catering only to the rich.[6]

After the introduction of the steamboat into these western waters, the design of the boat changed in order to accommodate the rivers. From the mid-1830s to mid-1840s the hull became flat and light. This was made possible by what the builders called a "hog chain," which was not a chain at all but a small metal rod that ran the length of the boat. It gave the boat strength and prevented sagging. The builders dropped the screw propeller and put in a paddle wheel, with either two wheels, one on each side, or one in the stern. The paddle wheel was easier to repair than the screw propeller and had less tendency to have problems with snags. The small hold below the decks now was limited to cargo. The engine changed from a low-pressure to a high-pressure engine, which avoided awkward gearing and inefficient transmission of power. It was mounted on the main deck. The steam pushed large gears, which turned the paddlewheel.[7]

The high-pressure engine was well adapted to the conditions, but it was more wasteful. Steamboats now needed more fuel. The engine used a great abundance of wood, which was plentiful. Farmers clearing their farm land of virgin forests sold their poorest grade wood to the steamboats. Often they left it on a raft tied to a dock in the river or in an established wood yard where the crew could access it quickly. The boat would make a stop and crew and even passengers would assist in throwing it on board, taking about an hour each time.

The steamboats of this period had three decks: main, boiler, and hurricane. The main deck housed the engine including the boilers, some of the cargo, a blacksmith's shop, bunks for deck passengers, and hatches for the hold. Deck passengers were usually limited to the main deck. The boiler deck, situated just above the boilers, had cabins for passengers. It also contained a bar, a saloon, which was a restaurant, men and women's washrooms, and a baggage room. The hurricane deck, located just above the boiler deck, had a series of cabins in the middle of the deck for the crew, called a Texas, with a pilot house on top of it, ringed with windows on three sides which gave the pilot a great view of his surroundings.[8]

Initially, the steamboat was used to transport primarily agricultural products throughout the Mississippi River basin. The owners quickly realized that they could also convey people who were coming to New Orleans from European countries. They built cabins for the higher-paying first-class passengers and took poor immigrants as deck passengers for less money. Deck passengers found accommodations in the midst of the cargo. They could purchase food from the saloon, but most brought their own on board or purchased it in the port cities.[9]

A steamboat could have a crew of between thirty and forty men, which included a captain, two pilots, a chief clerk, two engineers, two mates, a carpenter, a barkeeper, a watchman, and a number of young apprentices, often considered officers-in-training. The cabin crew consisted of the first steward, cooks, waiters, cabin boys, and chambermaids. The cabin boys and chambermaids received their position only for the season. The deck crew consisted of firemen and deckhands, often called roustabouts, who manned the pumps, handled the cargo, and supplied the wood. Engineers supervised the firemen, and the deckhands did much of the manual labor. The pilot received no regular salary but worked on a contract, which made him the highest paid individual on board. He needed to have an extraordinary knowledge of the river.[10]

In her diary Jane Rio Griffiths Baker, an emigrant of 1851, wrote a wonderful description of her steamboat, the *Concordia*, which took her from New Orleans to St. Louis: "The engines are on the deck, the stoke-hole quite open on each side and the firemen have an uninterrupted view of the country." She explained that another staircase led to an upper deck that she called the "Hurricane Deck," which had cabins on each side and a cabin in the middle for the better-paying passengers. There was also a saloon where the passengers could dine. "The ladies cabin is placed astern . . . and is splendidly furnished with sofas, rocking chairs, wood tables and a piano. . . . There is also a smoking room for the gentlemen, opening out of the saloon in which are card-tables, etc." She further commented that another set of stairs led to the last deck that had cabins on each side and a cabin in the middle. "The one forward encloses the steering wheel. Here stands the pilot secured from wind and weather." She added more information explaining there were two ten-foot-tall funnels from the boiler that in a headwind left the upper deck covered with hot cinders.[11]

The largest problem for steamboats came with what was called *snags*. People continually threw trees and limbs into the water, and oftentimes the erosion of the river's sides caused trees to fall into the water and be swept away. When the trees continued down the river, they became waterlogged and soon dropped to the bottom of the river. When others collected in the same spot, the pileup could cause great damage to the hull of a boat. To improve navigation of the rivers, a snag boat patrolled the waters and removed them, but enough snags remained so that the situation remained dangerous.[12] Snag boats did their job, but this gigantic river system could have used many more. Snags and rocks sank many boats. One source indicated 289 steamboats were sunk in the Missouri River between 1819 and 1897.[13]

The second problem for steamboats was the tendency of the boilers to explode, which was caused by not enough water or too much pressure in the boiler. Boilers had to be constantly maintained or else pressure could build up. The worst case scenario for a great number of Latter-day Saints was the explosion of the steamboat *Saluda*. The *Saluda* arrived at Lexington, Missouri, on March 31, 1852, with approximately 175 passengers and waited several days for the river to become calmer so as to make it around the bend. The day before the explosion the William Dunbar family, another Latter-day Saint family bound for Kanesville, boarded the ship. Dunbar had been the security guard on board the *Ellen Maria* before it left Liverpool. The next day, April 9, the *Saluda* left its safe harbor, and minutes later it exploded. Dunbar survived, but his wife and his two daughters died. The explosion is thought to have killed seventy-five people.[14]

Watt's trip up the Mississippi and Missouri Rivers was not this dramatic. He had been on a steamboat before when he came up the Mississippi in 1842–43. In 1851 he voiced a fear of the river. He told his readers about a boy who fell into the river as the *Ellen Maria* was approaching New Orleans. Again he emphasized his concerns for future travelers when Elizabeth Shelley fell overboard somewhere below St. Louis and drowned.

Watt got off the boat in St. Louis in order to purchase a wagon, which he stored on the next boat going up the Missouri River. It seems that he was now ready for his trip.

Journal from New Orleans to Kanesville, April 6, 1851–May 21, 1851

Monday[15] April ~~6~~<7>th

This day is a scene of happy bustle; the excise man or custom house officer is among us. All are busy getting their luggage on deck to have it examined which work was accomplished today. In the evening we had a ~~tug~~ job boat to take our luggage to the steam packet for $35 to be at our ship early in the morning.

April Tuesday ~~9~~<8>th

Got our luggage all removed and without any accidents to the passengers we were all safely put [Image 429] on board the *Aleck Scott*. Our conditions for the steerage passengers are as comfortable as could be expected for such a large company. All expect to have had berths to sleep in and [*illegible*] made their beds upon boxes.

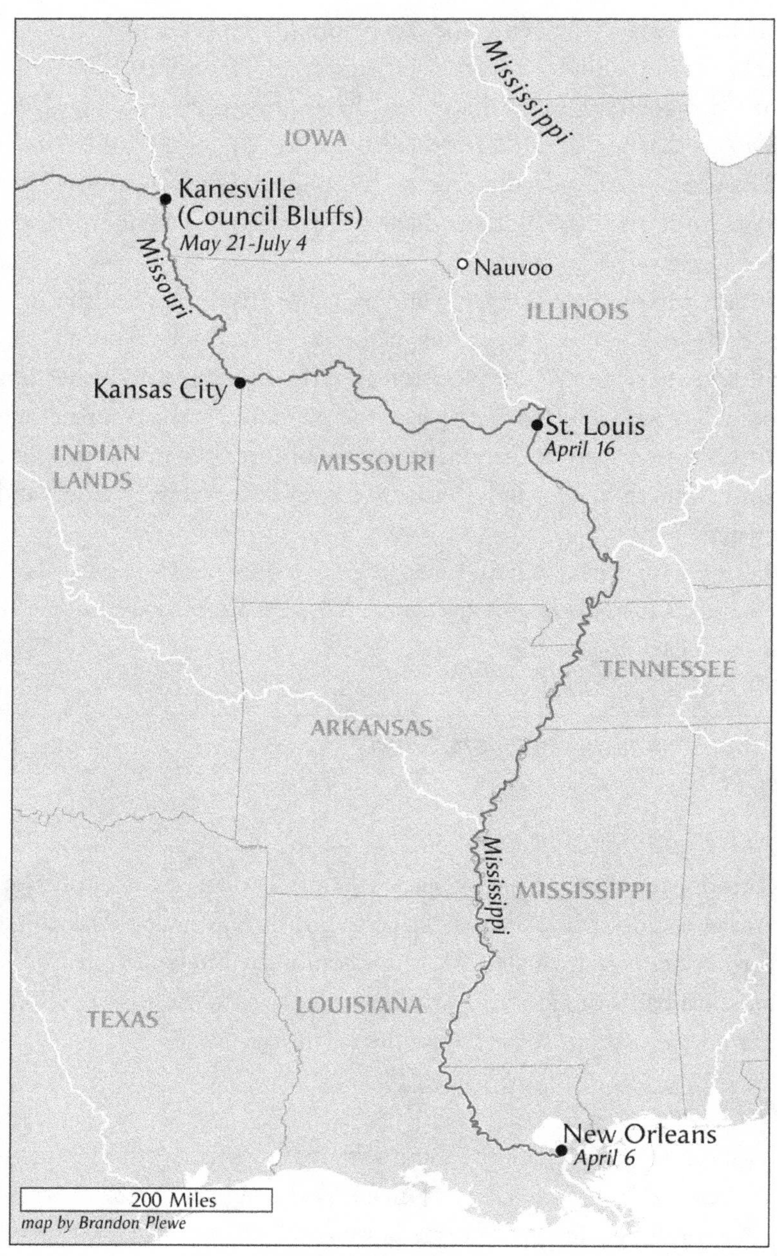

Map 2. River journey from New Orleans to Kanesville, Iowa. Created by Brandon Plewe.

Wednesday April ~~8~~<9>~~th~~

Early this morning Ann **Entwistle** the wife of Samuel Entwistle <from the town of Bury Lancashire>[16] was safely delivered of a son and they are ~~mother~~ <both> doing well. The child is to be named Alex Scott Entwistle.[17] The *Aleck Scott* cleared the wharf this evening about 7 o'clock and bent her course against the mighty current of the great Mississippi.

Thursday April ~~9~~<10>th[18]

We espied a wood in the forenoon and many of the passengers flocked on shore some left their children unprotected to satisfy their own curiosity. The wood was well nigh. All got in and the boat was about to proceed on the course when the alarm was given that some one was overboard. Our attention was drawn to the place and we saw William Lewis Hawkins a boy of about 10 years of age the son of James [Hawkins?] struggling in the water. Every bosom seemed ~~filled~~ filled with consternation and dismay expecting the child would surely drown. One James Freeman, a young sailor from the *Ellen Maria*, boldly leaped into the water and rescued the child from ~~death~~ watery grave. I am sorry to say that and many of the parents (not all) that sailed on board the [Image 430] the[19] *Ellen Maria* having manifested the greatest looseness in their attention to the welfare and safety of their children. Let this be a warning to all parents who may hereafter travel upon this dangerous water.

Nothing worthy of record occurred at all.[20]

Sunday April 13th

Elder Pratt was requested to address the ladies and gentlemen in the cabins of the *Aleck Scott*. This request was almost universal. About half past ten he read a chapter and Elder Watt prayed after which he gave a brief but somewhat minute summary of the doctrines and principles believed by the Latter-day Saints dwelling more particularly upon the Book of Mormon and the covenants and blessings of the church of God. Elder Watt concluded with a blessing. Almost all

Fig. 6. *New Orleans*, steel engraving. Created by Frederick Piercy. Courtesy of Church History Library.

wanted to purchase the Book of Mormon and a general inquiry was got up so that ladies and gentlemen [flocked?] to Brother Pratt, making inquiries about this strange people.[21] There are tens of thousands of respectable people of this land whose minds have been biased from the pulpit and the press. Were they better informed as to this people, [they] would be our friends if not join our cause. Thus are our present impressions <from the circumstances surrounding us>.

Monday April 14th

Thereto we have had a prosperous passage and have lost none by accident;[22] alas I have a woeful tale to record under this date. Oh that I had been spared the task but who can understand the heights and depths of divine wisdom. This mournful affair may be for a warning to saints who may in future traverse these waters. [Image 431] <About nine o'clock **P.M.**> Elizabeth Shelley[23] aged 55 years the wife of James Shelley from the Worcestershire conference left her family at their berth to renew her washing which she had been engaged in on the former part of the day. <Before commencing her work> she took the bucket to draw some water when she was suddenly plucked into the current. She was seen floating for a minute or so in the distance when she sank to rise no more. The engine was stopped as soon as the alarm was given and a boat manned but all too late. A sudden [visitation?] this, and a bereavement that is felt sorely by all the family but [*illegible*] so by the old man. Sister Shelley had enjoyed the best of health the whole of the passage but aught a moment's warning was plunged into death <She was drowned in [*illegible*] 16 that is in [*two words illegible*][24] River run the 16 island and the mainland on the end between side of the island>.[25] Blessed are the dead that die in the Lord. She rests from her labor.

In the *Millennium* [*Millennial*] *Star* I am unable to say <in> what volume is recorded a letter written from St. Louis warning the emigrants not to suffer their old women and old men and children to draw water from the rapid stream of the Mississippi for it is <almost> more than a strong man can do. Another warning is here given. Let it not be forgot lest the messenger of death shall visit the dull of hearing and slothful to hearken to these awful ~~testimonies~~ <counsels> in their own family circles and pierce their heart's core with thorny sorrows. He that heareth these words and doeth them I will liken him to a wise man.[26]

Tuesday April 15th

This morning <a strong man> one of the *Ellen Maria* passengers (not in the church) was drawing water when the bucket came in contact with the current. His strength was not equal to the sudden jerk the bucket gave him. He lost [Image 432] balance and fought hard and was about to be precipitated into death when fortunately two of the brethren caught him by the feet and saved him.

Wednesday April 16th

Landed in St. Louis about 4 p.m.[27] While in this place I busied myself in preparing for my journey across the plains. Twenty pounds was all the money I possessed with which I had to purchase a wagon and provisions and oxen for the journey besides defraying my expenses up the river of the Missouri to the Council Bluffs. This money of course did not begin to be enough to answer all these ends. My trust was in the Lord and my heart continually breathed out prayers to him to raise me up a friend. This he did in the person of of[28] Brother John Hardy from the Clitheroe conference,[29] he loaned me 30 pounds[30] and promised me more if I wanted it. I immediately purchased a wagon and provisions for the journey, with a tent and many other necessary things for our comfort on the way, which consumed what money I had. Brother Hardy will also let me have money to purchase my oxen as well as.[31] I feel myself unworthy of this kindness from the hands of God but how good he is to those who have served him in the work of his ministry. He knows what things they need to enable them to fulfill his pleasure he will reward them in this world. He will soften the hearts of those who have means to bestow it upon his servants. He clothes the lilies of the field.[32] He feeds the wild beasts of the forest and will not suffer his saints to want in good things. When I became this fortunate my heart magnified the name of God who became my friend in a strange land.

We chartered the steam packet *Robert Campbell*,[33] the captain of which boat engaged to put us off at Council Bluffs[34] [Image 433] at four dollars and a half per passenger and one dollar per hundred for luggage. And many of our company that came over the sea with us stopped in St. Louis but we and another company who came from Cleveland in America, we made up a company of about 200 passengers.

Sunday April 20th

Met with the saints in the hall where the St. Louis Branch met for worship. Elder Pratt spoke in the fore part of the day and in the evening. I spoke in the afternoon to a crowded audience.

Wednesday April 23d

The *Robert Campbell* left the wharf at St. Louis and bent her way up the Mississippi and struck the mouth of the Missouri about noon.

Fig. 7. *St. Louis*, steel engraving. Created by Frederick Piercy. Courtesy of Church History Library.

We came to Rounds Bend in the evening, [where we] lay to for the night on the left bank, and in the morning began to throw out freight for it was found impossible to pilot the bar at Rounds Bend as there was only 3 feet of water and the boat drew more than four.

Thursday April 24th

The captain requested us to allow him to put off passengers' freight promising to take up the passengers as far as the town of Kansas and return for their freight and not go again to St. Louis until he had accomplished the trip to give the passengers seven barrels of flour and board four of [Image 434] of[35] our men as watchmen to stay with the luggage on these terms. We consented to his request and the men began immediately to put off our heavy boxes, our provisions for the plains, our wagons and all we possessed except our provision chests and a many left their clean linen. After remaining on the bar ~~for~~ between two and three days we got off and pressed on our way. ~~And was landed at~~

Thursday May 1st

We were put on shore in the town of Kansas situated in Jackson County, Missouri. About 12 or 14 miles from this place is situated the grounds that was designated by revelation as the spot on which the city New Jerusalem should stand. This place is filled with the bitterest enemies to the saints and a many of these inhabitants was at Nauvoo when the saints was driven and at the killing of the Prophet Joseph.[36] These crowds make no secret of the affair but boast of the wonders they performed in this disgraceful affair. The man who murdered the little boy at Haun's Mill[37] lives in this place. I am informed he goes at large boasting of this diabolical murder. Oh <ye men of Missouri> ye inhabitants of Jackson and Clay Counties, especially who entered into hellish agreement with your sister state <Illinois> to murder the just and true sons of God, why were ye not satisfied with the Haun's Mill tragedy? Wo unto you, for there is a troubled day for you to meet and awful retribution for you to endure. It shall come upon you without mitigation. Every grain of it shall be rewarded to you there shall be none to ~~plead~~ plead for you. There shall be none to pity you. You shall be soaked in your own blood. Rottenness shall consume the marrow of your bones and in the belly of hell shall you wail ~~in the~~ <under> your just damnation ye cursed of earth. [Image 435] The saints are all over this place some living in one house and some in another but the chief of them live in a large log and frame building belonging to one Mr. Brewster who is favorable to the Mormon people his house is situated on the bank of the river on the west side of Union Hotel.

Friday May ~~8~~<9>th

Today Sister Jane Wilde[38] from Hampshire aged 81 died about 9 o'clock p.m. This old sister had stood the journey first rate to about 3 weeks before her death. She had been much afflicted with dysentery, which ultimately ended her life. She died without a groan or complaint, for we did not know that she was dead for half an hour after she was gone.

Saturday May ~~9~~<10>th

Sister Jane Wilde <and Brother Pratt’s baby> was buried in the Kansas[39] grave yard in a nice dry clean grave situated in the heart’s core of Zion about 14 miles from the site of the New Jerusalem that is to be built in the last days. And this grave yard lies on the east side of the city. It is a gentle rising hill. The grave is on the south east side of the hill. Her work is done and she rests.

Saw David Candland and three others from the Bluffs on the steamboat all busy on their way to the ~~eastern~~ state of New York <Elder Candland and Brown was for Nova Scotia.>

Sunday May ~~10~~<11>th

Sometime in the night a dreadful thunder storm passed over this town but no damage was done to the property [Image 436] or inhabitants.

Monday May 12th

The river which has been exceedingly low, commenced to rise to the joy and satisfaction of the saints who are waiting here for the return of the *Robert Campbell.*

Tuesday May ~~12~~<13>

The river is rising very rapidly. The *Robert Campbell* expected up to day or tomorrow.

Friday ~~Tuesday Wednesday~~ May ~~14~~ 16th

The steam boat *Statesman* came to the river from St. Louis, bearing Elder Robbins[40] and company from that port bound to the Bluffs.[41] Reported the *Robert Campbell* [was] over the bar a[t] Rounds Bend and waiting for the rise. About fifty of our passengers went on board of this boat, which was contrary to my counsel and directions to the company. They were enticed on this wise.[42] It seems that Brother Robbins had agreed with the captain of the *Statesman* to supply him with so many passengers, if he would lay them down at the Council Bluffs. He however could not raise the complement at St. Louis and therefore tried to do so in Kansas from our company. Elder Pratt referred him to me for my mind upon the subject of their going with this boat. I opposed the idea stating what did, in reality, come to pass: that those who remained would be exposed to difficulty thereby,[43] as well as themselves. Elder Pratt in the mean time said he would go up with that boat if the captain would ensure him of being laid down at the Bluffs. This the captain would not do without being ensured [Image 437] that he should have fifty passengers to remunerate him for going so far. Contrary to my wishes and the interests of the company, Elder Robbins took a book and commenced taking the names of those who would go up with them and Brother Pratt, and the complement and more was soon made up, for all knew that Elder Pratt was going on board of her if so many passengers could be raised. They started and left the balance of us in Kansas.

Saturday May ~~15 16~~<17>th

About four o'clock in the afternoon the *Robert Campbell* was seen coming up the river to the joy of all the hearts of the saints who were left. No time was lost in getting her luggage and families. The captain was much dissatisfied on hearing that so many of the passengers had left him, for he had given them six bushels of flour and had not taken pay for any of their luggage up to Kansas, which they had taken away on the other boat. Some difficulty is anticipated through this affair. We paid fairly to Kansas and bent our course up the river in full expectation of catching the other boat and passing by her. The captain had not taken on any passengers in hopes of reshipping his former company.

Wednesday May 21st[44]

Early in the morning we landed at the Kanesville[45] landing.[46] The *Statesmen* had left there the evening before last, sometime after sundown. The captain is weighing every ounce of our freight <allowing none to passengers> and charging for infants half price, which was contrary to the bargain I had made with him. He [is] tight on us in consequence of those passengers leaving [Image 438] him to go with

Fig. 8. *View of the Missouri River and Council Bluffs from an Elevation*, steel engraving. Created by Frederick Piercy. Courtesy of Church History Library.

another boat. He has charged Elder Pratt with the passages of those who left him, setting that as the example influenced them to do so. He is also charging him more for his freight. The day is wet and very uncomfortable. No luggage can be put [off] today. The roads are disrupted, muddy with thunder and lightning in [northwest?].

The aspect is quite dreary which makes some of the weak saints wish they had stayed at home. My money is all done. I have nothing to pay my portage up the river but the Lord will raise me up a friend I have no doubt.

Kanesville Interlude

Use it well, your garden's sure to grow.
—G.D.W., "Answer to Our Rebus in Our Last"

George D. Watt did not write in his journal for a little over a month, from May 22 to July 4, 1851. Sometime after arriving in Kanesville, he quarreled with his wife, Mary. Smarting from her temper and his own,

Fig. 9. *Entrance to Kanesville*. Created by Frederick Piercy. Courtesy of Church History Library.

Watt angrily left the camp on foot. In the midst of sparsely populated Iowa, he accidentally happened on the house of Robert Williams, one of his missionary companions in Manchester, England.

Williams wrote in his autobiography eight years later that "George came tramping by my house. I was very sick and boy [his son] as well." When Watt walked into his sparsely furnished house, he found Williams lying sickly on his cot. Williams wrote: "Says I George, you are welcome to my humble fair." After a short discussion, "George told me of his words with his wife and he remained with me 2 weeks hid up, to try to make his wife better in her feelings for she was a rip with a tongue but a good wife to him and a kind hearted woman." Watt convinced his old friend to immigrate to Zion and promised to transport him and his nine-year-old son, Alfred, in his wagon.[47] Probably while at Williams's house, he read the June 11 edition of the *Frontier Guardian*, the local newspaper published in Kanesville by Orson Hyde. On the last page, he came across a riddle in poem form entitled "Rebus by Amicus." A rebus is a riddle made up of symbols whose names resemble intended words or syllables. He must have read it carefully.

Rebus by Amicus

Eight letters does my whole contain,
And three my first will spell,
A boundless, wide, sublime do-main;
The veriest child may tell.
It boasts the grandest works of art,
The mightiest earthly power;
To man it wealth, and woe imparts
Each anxious passing hour.
My second is a living thing,
A creature useful, strong;
And sometimes wealth and honor brings,
To whom it doth belong.
My whole's a monster that is rarely seen,
My 6 5 7 2, the choicest flower amid the green;
My 1 5 6 8, is painful, tiresome, filthy, mean,
My 3 1 7, an ill-famed bride, indeed, I ween
My 7 2 8 6, as good a man as e'er has been;
My 4 5 1 8, a garment made without a seam
My 4 5 2, a tool oft used at morn's first gleam,
My 7 4 5 6 2, a place of wind, of wet and steam
My 2 3 6, a member useful, truthful, lean.
An Answer requested[48]

Watt decided he would solve the rebus. To people in our century it would have been difficult to solve. However, people in the nineteenth century viewed it as a crossword puzzle. He studied it diligently and wrote down his answer. He then carefully composed his own poem answering the riddle.

Answer to Rebus in Our Last

by G.D.W.
Your first, the boundless ocean wide
Your second, a horse, the Indian's pride;

Your whole a SEA-HORSE.
Your 4, 5, 1, 8, a scotchman's hose,
Your 6, 5, 7, 2, an English rose,
Your 7, 2, 8, 6, will name a seer;
Your 2, 3, 6, the human ear;
Your 4, 5, 2, a gardener's hoe,
Use it well, your garden's sure to grow,
Your 7, 4, 5, 6, 2, the sea-shore,
Your 1, 5, 6, 8, a painful sore;
Your 3, 1, 7, a slave to his glass,
A poor, silly, simple, drunken ass.

Watt must have felt quite proud of his answer. He dropped it off at the newspaper's office and Hyde published it.[49] It is doubtful that George saw the item in the newspaper. By this time he was off with his two wagons to the rendezvous place with the John Brown Company.

After working through the rebus, Watt returned to his family. He reconciled with Mary, and she must have felt some remorse when she saw him once again.

In 1867, when he returned to this spot, he told an addition to his story that he had not included in his journal. He explained that he was no more than two hours from the main camp when his oxen balked and would not move unless he yelled at them, and then they would move only a little. After two days the oxen got stuck in a mud hole. "I sat down on the bank a little while, to rest and take a calm survey of my situation, when an officer of the company came riding up on the charitable mission of hunting up stragglers. 'Why Brother Watt, what are you doing here?' 'I am trying to go to Zion but I cannot get these stupid creatures to take the wagon out of that mud.' He took my whip, and out came my wagon apparently with very little effort."[50]

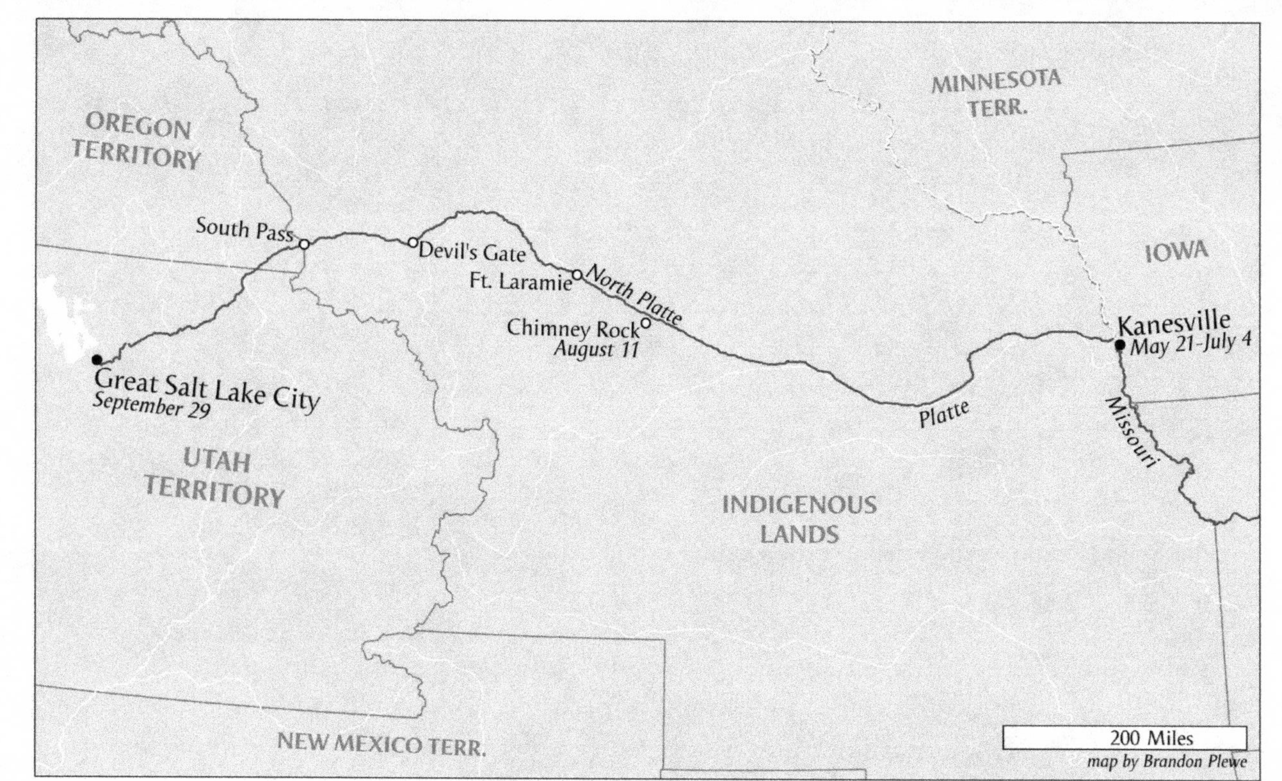

Map 3. Trail from Kanesville to Great Salt Lake City. Created by Brandon Plewe.

3

The Trail

People do not know what kind of a temper they got until they try have to drive and manage a team of stupid oxen!
—Letter, George D. Watt to John M. and Margaret Brandreth

On the Trail to Chimney Rock

The western trail was first blazed by fur trappers and explorers in the early part of the nineteenth century. Finally in 1835 pioneers began to make a wagon road that would go all the way from Missouri to Oregon and California. From 1843 through 1845 John C. Fremont and party traveled extensively through the West, describing it in detail to the world. The latter year Lansford W. Hastings published an account that suggested wagons could travel through the Great Salt Lake area to California. The Donner-Reed party, traveling to California, tried that route the following year with disastrous results. In 1847 Brigham Young and the Latter-day Saints fleeing from religious persecution followed the same trail to the Salt Lake Valley.

The organization point for the Latter-day Saints was about two miles west of the old Winter Quarters site. The trail then connected to the Platte River. The Platte had a wagon road on both the north and south side. Most of the church emigrant trains kept to the north side of the Platte River. The Oregon and California trains usually stayed on the south side, but both varied at times. The barrier between them was not much. The Platte River was wide but shallow, probably not more than two or at the most three feet deep. When the Platte split into the North Platte and the South Platte Rivers at the present day North Platte, Nebraska, the emigrants followed the North Platte into western Wyoming, visiting Fort Laramie. Then the trail turned southwest with the North Platte and then followed the Sweetwater River. The wagons had to cross the

Sweetwater nine times. To reach the Continental Divide the wagons had only a gentle incline. Thereafter the pioneers had only creeks, the Big Sandy being the first, for water until they reached the Green River. By 1851 when Watt traveled it, many thousands of Latter-day Saints had used that road and would continue to use it until the coming of the railroad in 1869.

For Watt this would be the most difficult part of his journey: he had a wagon and oxen that he would have to drive overland to Utah almost a thousand miles, a journey that would be difficult for a one-time factory worker. He and his family had traveled by ocean ship and river boat. Now they had another conveyance, a covered wagon, to transport them across plains, hills, and mountains. His trip before had been easy. Essentially, he could sit back and let someone else handle the vessel, but now he was the crew. He had two wagons and a teamster, Samuel Patterson, to help him. He had oxen to drive, which troubled him, since he had no experience in doing that.

The wagon was a simple vehicle, unlike the ships and boats of his more recent past. These covered wagons, or "prairie schooners," had a wagon box, usually four feet wide by twelve feet long; big wooden hoops called bows, which supported the waterproof canvas, with drawstrings for the front and back; four wheels, the front two being smaller than the back; iron tires, four hubs on the wheels, a tongue with a doubletree and a singletree attaching it to the wagon to equalize the load on the oxen, a neck yoke attached to the tongue for the oxen, two axles, which the pioneers called axletrees, a brake lever, and one brake block attached to the rear axle. Inside the wagons the wooden hoops had hooks, to which the pioneers would attach pots and pans, guns, jackets, dolls, and anything else that would hang. The movement of the wagon caused a chorus to sound out from all these attachments. Inside the wagon would be food for their three month's journey, clothes, farm implements, and some luxury items. If the wagon was too heavy, the latter would be the first to go, and the trail could be littered with these articles. The wagon could hold about two thousand pounds. In the case of the British Saints, they would not have that much in their wagons since they had already slimmed down for the voyage from England. Because these English Saints did not have farm implements, they slept in their wagons. The wagon also needed at least four oxen, or as Watt described it, two yoke of oxen with harnesses. Watt used three yoke of oxen, six oxen.

This was not an inexpensive journey. Watt had tried to borrow money from the Perpetual Emigrating Fund Company, a fund that loaned money to poor emigrants, but Orson Hyde told him that was not possible. So Watt borrowed enough money from four individuals to make the journey, altogether 125 English pounds, or about $610 in 1851; that would be about $23,000 in today's currency.[1]

The John Brown Company was organized on July 4, 1851, the last company to proceed on this overland journey that year. As Watt wrote, "Brother Brown was appointed to pick up the fragments of emigration and organize them into a company and bring them out. I shall join this company as I am indeed a fragment."[2]

The company was subdivided into several groups, each called a ten, which usually was composed of ten wagons, although there could be more or even fewer. The company had a captain who made sure the company made good time on the trail. He decided when and where they would stop at midday and for the night. He was also responsible for when the company started the next morning. Each of the tens also had a captain who was responsible for the well-being of their group. A different ten led off each morning, so everybody had a chance to have the best air. A wagon train made a considerable amount of dust in their journey.

Preston Thomas,[3] who was selected as the clerk and also the official journalist for the company, became the captain of the first ten; Joseph Chatterley, the second; George D. Watt, the third; and Alexander Robbins,[4] who arrived later that day, the captain of the fourth ten. John Brown, an experienced trailsman and westerner, was selected as the captain over the entire company. Brown, only thirty years old, had made this journey three times before and had been a member of the Brigham Young vanguard company in 1847. He knew the trail well. The next day six more wagons arrived from St. Louis, and Edward Rushton, who was a member of that group, was appointed to be the captain of the fifth ten. Jane Rio Griffiths Baker, another of the journalists in the Brown Company, traveled with his group. On June 6 an Oregon-bound group asked to join them. Brown divided their people up among all the groups. Watt's ten received two more wagons with an additional eight people.

When Robbins arrived, Brown organized a small committee, including Watt, to evaluate Robbins's wagons on weight and see if one or more could be left behind. To satisfy the committee, Robbins stored some of his freight materials and left one wagon, taking six wagons with him. This same committee inspected Edwin Rushton's eight wagons and approved them all.

On July 10 eight more wagons joined the company, including those of Elias Smith and Emily Smith Hoyt, the last two journalists of the company's trip who were assigned to Preston Thomas's ten. Watt's ten, according to the "John Brown Emigrating Company Journal," included altogether thirteen wagons and 51 people, the most people that any ten had. Robbins had the smallest number of people, but his twenty-three wagons were loaded with freight. Now the Brown company had 235 people.[5] Altogether thirteen wagon trains left that year and thirteen freight trains, totaling 1,974 people.

At the end of the day the pioneers pulled their wagons into a circle at night, unhitched the oxen, and usually let them graze inside the circle if the grass was sufficient. After about a month, they let the animals graze out of the circle to find enough feed. Those with tents staked them down every night and dug ditches around them in case it rained. Sometime after dinner they chained the oxen to the wagons. If the immigrants slept in their wagons, which the Watt family did, the movement of the oxen during the night jiggled the wagons, interrupting their slumber. Each morning a bugle sounded at daybreak, or else the watchman came round and woke up the teamsters by rapping on the wagons. The teamsters began hollering and calling their animals, usually to wake up the cooks.[6] After breakfast the oxen were yoked and hitched to the wagons, and the company started off.

It had been a wet spring and early summer. On the night of the organization of the John Brown company there was a storm accompanied by thunder and lightning; three days later, while the company was on the trail, there was more rain, followed by more the next day. They had no rain for a little more than a week, when a giant storm hit them. Watt said it "blew down all the tents in the camp, exposing the inmates to the violence of the storm." He commented that the "wind was so violent as to run back several wagons about twenty feet." Robert Williams, who was in the Watt party, also described this storm as violent. Watt cried out to Robert Williams to save his canvas wagon covering, which Williams did.[7] Five days later another storm hit and "drenched" Watt "to the skin."[8]

Maintenance on wagons made the company stop for repairs often. Any movable conveyance has a tendency to break down. Even though there were few parts to a wagon, a distance of over nine hundred miles over rough terrain caused great strain on the wagons, and they broke down. Watt had two wagon tongues break. Both he and Alexander Robbins broke wagon tongues the day after the company organized.[9] A little over two weeks later Watt's other wagon tongue broke.[10] They obtained wood from trees near the trail to replace each one. On July 7 Robbins broke an axletree, and about two weeks later he broke a wagon wheel. On July 27 and 28, the wagon train stopped and first tightened the tires and then set them on again, so they could continue their travel.[11] It happened to many of the wagons along the trail. The pioneers had started their journey in rain, and the iron tires had been put on the wagons when the wood was full of moisture. In their journeying the wheels had shrunk, but, of course, the tires had not. On Sunday the company stopped for the purpose of mending wagons, and the blacksmiths busied themselves shortening the tires. The next morning they set fourteen of them before moving on.[12] Wagon wheels seem to be the easiest thing to break. The day after the entire train had to wait before leaving because a wagon wheel had been broken by a teamster or, as Thomas wrote, "was broken down carelessly yesterday evening by a raw teamster."[13] The primary day for fixing small problems on the wagons was Sunday, but in emergencies they stopped any day of the week.

The wagon trains faced certain obstacles as they crossed Nebraska, mostly rivers and creeks. The first large one was the Elkhorn River, which ran into the north side of the Platte River several miles from the Missouri River. The spring had been very wet, forcing the companies that started earlier to go north in order to cross the Elkhorn River at a narrower place, adding several days to their journey. By the time the Brown

Company left, the Elkhorn River had receded enough to allow them to cross the river at the usual place, which meant they could catch up with and even travel ahead of the earlier companies. By July 30 Baker said that there were three companies ahead of them: the Morris Phelps Company, the Garden Grove or Harry Walton Company, and the John G. Smith Company, which the journalists called the Shurtliff Company.[14] The four companies continued a game of leap frog for several days. On July 30 Watt saw two companies about two miles ahead of them and mentioned that the next day several of the other emigrants had joined their company. The next day Brown camped near the Smith Company. The following morning the Smith and Garden Grove companies passed Brown's company. On August 3, Sunday, the Brown Company stopped to worship while the Smith Company continued. The animals of these three companies traveling in close proximity to each other competed for grass along the trail.

The pioneers of this period repeatedly saw buffalo along the trail. Watt's experience did not vary from this pattern. On July 27 he wrote that somebody from the company, "not of the church," went out and killed some buffalo in eastern Nebraska. He did not see the buffalo that day, though. The next day every journalist commented on the animals. There were thousands of them. Watt commented that they "traveled through large herds of buffalo. I suppose tens of thousands of them." The following day he wrote, "Surrounded with buffalo all day. We had to stop to let them ahead [of] our train and horse men were appointed to turn them in their course after large herds issued from the River Platte, galloping at full speed, [and] threatening destruction of our cattle and wagons."[15] He complained that some animals had been killed and left to rot. He thought this was a terrible sin and felt that they should consume all that they killed. He helped cut up a young bull and found the meat to be finer than the common ox.[16] After July 30 no journalists mentioned large herds of buffalo. Jane Rio Griffiths Baker said that someone from her group killed buffalo on August 2 but left them on the prairie for the night. By the next morning the wolves had devoured the carcasses.[17] The animals must have remained nearby in much smaller herds. On August 26 Elias Smith was in a hunting expedition that killed four or five head; this was the last time any of the journalists mentioned buffalo.[18]

Journal from Kanesville to Chimney Rock, May 21, 1851–August 14, 1851

Wednesday May 21st[19]

Early in the morning we landed at the Kanesville[20] landing. The *Statesmen* had left there the evening before last, sometime after sundown.[21] The captain is weighing every ounce of our freight <allowing none to passengers> and charging for infants half price which was contrary to the bargain I had made with him. He [is] tight on us in consequence of those passengers leaving [Image 438] him to go with another boat. He has charged Elder Pratt with the passages of those who left him, setting that as the example influenced them to do so. He is also charging him more for his freight. The day is wet and very uncomfortable. No luggage can be put [off] today. The roads are disrupted, muddy with thunder and lightning in [northwest?].

The aspect is quite dreary which makes some of the weak saints wish they had stayed at home. My money is all done. I have nothing to pay my portage up the river but the Lord will raise me up a friend I have no doubt.

Thursday May 22

Brother Hardy loaned me nine pound[s] with which I paid my [portage?] up the river. I praise the Lord for raising me up such kind friends. May he reward them with a thousand fold. About this time my troubles and anxieties became increased. I found myself in a strange country and among a people who were all poor like myself and trying to make their out fits to the church in the valley. I was without money and had a large amount of luggage to convey to the valley, namely the luggage of two families. One wagon I found to be [too] little to answer my purpose. I must have another wagon or leave part of my folks behind, namely my mother[22] and sister.[23] Brother Wilson from Cleveland had a wagon to sell that would just answer my purpose; I went to Brother Shelley who kindly loaned me sixteen pounds with which I bought this wagon, for which I paid sixty five dollars.

A few days previous to these circumstances, I went to Brother Hyde[24] and acquainted him with my situation and told him my wants,[25] he said he could not help me except[26] I could raise him a loan of two thousand dollars for which he would give a check on the perpetual fund[27] in [Image 439] in[28] the valley. Now this was an impossibility for me to perform. I had hopes previous to this that I might obtain some help from the Perpetual Emigration Fund but now my hopes were all blighted;[29] a few days afterward I got Elder Pratt to remind Elder Hyde that I was sent for by the First Presidency. This however did not benefit me one iota but I received the same answer as before. I saw that there was nothing for me now but to help myself,[30] Brother Hyde encouraged me so to do by remarking "that God helps them that helps themselves;[31]

I turned my face towards my friends that had thereto helped me out of some tight places. I now [need] four yoke of oxen to draw my two wagons which would be burdened with about fifteen hundred pounds on each,[32] I had no money to get these oxen. What must I do,[33] oxen at this time is from sixty five to eighty dollars per yoke. I made application [to/too?] again to Brother John Hardy and his brother George who kindly loaned to me fifty pounds more which was not enough to purchase such cattle **or** cattle[34] as was necessary to carry over the mountains my burden;[35] I therefore made application to Brother Shelley who loaned to me fifty pounds more and Samuel Patterson, my teamster, added to this sixteen dollars. I bought my cattle and as I considered had got every thing rightly fixed for my journey. My heart was glad and thankful to the Lord for all his tender mercies to me, but my sorrows was not yet over.[36]

We left Kanesville about the twenty sixth of June, and on our way to the ferry, a distance of about six miles from that place, one of my best cattle fell down a steep bluff and dislocated his hip bone. This entirely disabled me and made me unfit for the journey,[37] here was one yoke of my cattle broke up.[38] I was now unable to prosecute my journey; by the assistance of some brethren I was safely landed in Ferryville on the banks of the Missouri River. While crossing a bottom of some four miles of mud and water sometimes the water would be up to the body of the wagons.[39] In this bottom two yoke of my [Image 440] of my[40] oxen left me and returned back the way they had come. These I lost for several days. All the companies had gone on except a few who like myself was delayed by misfortunes. One of my yokes of cattle was found and the other remained lost for near one week. They was found however at last which immediately gave me no small degree of joy.[41] I was was[42] still a yoke of cattle short and how to raise that odd ox I could not tell, but the one that was hurt I sold to the flesher[43] for ten dollars. A good ox would cost thirty;[44] while I was in this situation Brother Carrington[45] loaned me ten dollars. I had now twenty dollars to buy an ox with and pay my ferriage which came to two dollars and sixty cents;[46] I was about thirteen dollars short of raising an ox to work with my odd one.

I got some brethren to draw me up from the river to <Pratt's> camp a distance of about a mile and a half. The large camp was about six miles out. I now found myself on the wide prairies with a crippled team and unable to proceed without some assistance from some quarter or other. I waited to see what the Lord would do for me and never once gave up the thoughts of proceeding forward on my journey. I was organized in the first fifty as captain of the fifth ~~of~~ ten under the presidency of Elder Cummings,[47] who was captain of the hundred,[48] I could not get up to my company and none of them came out to help me up,[49] finally Elder Pratt moved off and left me lonely <helpless> on the prairies.

The [Lord] however did not forget me but so ordered circumstances so as to open my way before me in the following manner. Elder Littlefield[50] had received three yoke of fine cattle which, for want of broke cattle to work with them, he found it impossible for him to proceed on the journey,[51] he gave up and Brother Brown, a poor fund agent from the valley, gave me the use of the cattle and a cow with the broke team that I had I could work this team temporarily. My way was now opened hitherto. I had been short of team. I have now [a] team. Then I need buy no ox. [Image 441] The mysterious workings of thy providence oh Lord is wonderful to we mortals. I give God all the glory for these manifestations of his kindness to me when it would seem that I was deserted by all. Brother Brown[52] was appointed to pick up the fragments of emigration and organize them into a company and bring them out. ~~I have~~ I shall join this company as I am indeed a fragment and was picked up by them.

July fourth eighteen fifty[-one].[53]

The last company was organized.[54] The morning was wet and cloudy and cold. Elder Thomas[55] was proposed by G. D. Watt to be the president of the first ten. Carried. Elder.[56] Chatterley[57] from England was next proposed to be the president of the second ten ~~company~~ <carried> and Elder Watt was proposed as the president of the third ~~company~~ <ten>,[58] carried. Brother Brown was sustained as the president of the whole camp. Elder Robbins and his wagons has not yet arrived. We are waiting for him.

Today Elder Roberts [A.?] [Sander?] left for Pratt's camp, which is about twenty miles off. He went in obedience to an express which Elder Pratt sent for him yesterday. At three o'clock p.m. the camp was called together to consider the situation of the wagons and teams and the loading, also the state of the provisions of the emigrants. Elder[s] Brown, Thomas, Chatterley, Terry, Norton[59] and Watt were appointed as a committee to examine the wagons loading the state of provisions and the strength of teams. Elder Robbins got all his wagons up to this place this afternoon about two o'clock. We are now camped about four miles from Ferryville.[60]

We have examined the wagons and loading and provisions and found that all are good and capable for such a journey as lies before us. After examining the teams we found that all could go on their journey comfortably, except Brother Robbins. He had eleven wagons, which averaged nineteen hundred weight in each [Image 442] and had two yoke of small cattle and one yoke of cows to each wagon. These cattle [were] wild and unruly, unaccustomed to the yoke, with the exceptions of three or four yokes. The committee decided he could not go with that team and advised him to leave [behind] until next year about fifty hundred weight, which it is expected he will do. This freight he was engaged to take through to the Salt Lake for a Mr. [Blakely?], who paid the freightage of some [*illegible*],[61] which places poor Robbins in a bad fix. Brother Robbins has not yet decided what he will do in this matter but expect he will to night. It is now nine p.m. Elder Robbins has decided to send back to Ferryville fifty hundred of his freight.

Saturday July fifth eighteen fifty[-one]

After a night of thunder and rain the morning broke unclear with a little wind. The camp is waiting for Elder Robbins who is now busy preparing to send back some of his goods. About seven o'clock p.m. two men arrived in the camp who had been on their way to Oregon but in consequence of the cattle taking a stampede and losing thereby fifty head their company could not proceed;[62] a few wagons wished to accompany us to Salt Lake. They reported that the [Elk] Horn Stream[63] was down sufficiently to admit of crossing with safety as they had returned that way with their [imperfect?] teams with little difficulty. Captain Brown seems inclined to take that course instead of doing the Horn Stream. There is three reasons for so doing. First it is the old route, second it is the straightest route, and third we are counselled to go that way. I feel much inclined for that route.

About twelve o'clock noon with our wagons and teams started for the Six Miles Grove, which we made after breaking <three> tongues and one axletree,[64] we reached this camping ground about one hour [Image 443] before sun down <formed a corral with the wagons in which the cattle was herded at night.[65]> About twelve o'clock midnight Brother Rushton[66] captain of a company from St. Louis by land arrived in camp with his company;[67] some who left with [Bennets?] came through, among whom is Brother Hawkins and family. Elder Robbins has a little more than he can do, notwithstanding he has put out fifty hundred weight.

Sunday July sixth eighteen fifty[-one]

Morning beautiful, sky clear, little wind, and sultry hot. About ~~8~~ eight a.m. a returning Oregon company stopped at our camp;[68] [they] reported the Stream [Elk]Horn [was] passable. Four or five wagons wish to join our company upon which an expression of the company will be taken.

About nine o'clock the bugle sounded and a meeting was convened to <more> fully organize the company. Elder Robbins was proposed captain of the fourth ten <carried>. It was moved [and] seconded that Edwin Rushton be the captain of the fifth ten carried. Moved and carried that we go the old route the First Presidency recommended; carried. Moved and carried that a few returning wagons that came in this morning be received into our company. It was then reproposed that Elder Brown be the captain of the company carried. Elder Thomas was again proposed as general clerk of the camp. Carried. General instructions from the president to the company. The committee of inspectors then inspected the wagons that came in last night and this morning. The wagons, provisions and teams were passed by the committee as fit for the journey. Brother Rushton's wagons was inspected at the same time and passed. We made the Six Mile Grove today travelled about four miles.

Monday July seventh eighteen fifty[-one]. [Image 444]

Today we made the Elkhorn a distance of about nine miles. The day was cool and cloudy some thunder at a distance. Our cattle did well today and all got safe over the Pappea Creek[69] without any accident; this refers only to four of the ten. Captain Robbins and his ten were detained in consequence of a break down in one of the axletrees of ones of his wagons. Brother Hall[70] is making coke[71] and several of the company are gone to the ferry boat to prepare for crossing tomorrow. Previous to our coming here the ferry was forsaken of the ferry men, but hearing that a company was passing this way we found them there to receive the ferry fee, which is to be two bits ~~for~~ <per> wagon and ferry ourselves over.

The afternoon and evening clear with a hot sun. Elkhorn quiet within its banks. A yoke of cattle and a cow was found today supposed to belong to some companies that have passed up the Horn Stream. <Six 6 p.m.> Captain Brown received from the camp the sum of two bits per wagon for the use of the boat and gave it to the <ferry> man who however was[72] [*illegible*] after the Indians to <recover some> stolen horses <which had been stole> from a Frenchman who was with him. Elder Hall made two coke pots;[73] the night is somewhat hazy, [with] thunder and lightning at a distance to the north;[74] some little rain through the night.

Tuesday July eighth eighteen fifty[-one].

The morning cloudy and blustery with a black gathering of clouds in the south and a little rain. Elder Robbins has not yet come up to the camp. We pass the Horn today in tens. Elder Rushton's company to pass over first. The companies all got over this stream in safety and without accident. We swam all our cattle with the exceptions of a few that were forded over for the purpose of drawing out the wagons on the other side. [Image 445] In swimming our cattle, the cattle of the [*sic*] our ten, one of my best oxen got down below the landing and seemed in imminent danger. There was few men on the other side to render him any assistance,[75] on seeing this, Benjamin Votaw,[76] a man not in the church but teamster to Brother Margetts,[77] boldly plunged into the water and swam [stemming?] the current to help to relieve my drowning ox. When he approached the animal it plunged and threw water upon the man, which well-nigh choked him, but both he and the ox was rescued from the stream.

About one mile and a half distant from the Horn is another creek, unfordable, but not more than six yards wide. This we also crossed in safety and swam our cattle. A wagon belonging to the captain Rushton laden with dry goods, in consequence of unsuccessful management, sank the boat and the wagon wetting dry goods very much, so as to give some loss. With this exception all the rest of those was got over these waters safe. Captain Robbins and his train came into the bottom in middle of the day and remained there until next day. The day was fine.

Wednesday July ninth eighteen fifty[-one]

The morning wet with thunder showers, the heavens dark and gloomy. Before sun rise the Camp of Israel engaged in preparing for the day's march. Before seven o'clock the trains were on their way to the shores of the Platte River. We travelled about ten miles over a soft and marshy bottom. On the way we passed a place where Elder Babbitt[78] had thrown a great quantity of letterpress paper, which had got wet, while he was on the small island down the Horn and the creek. This paper, instead of being scattered over the earth and on the perils of the great bearing glad tiding of great joy or proclaiming and exposing the wickedness of vile man,[79] its virgin sheet was scattered wide [Image 446] over the wild and uncultivated plain to be trodden under foot by man and beast.

After great exertion we reached the Platte with worn down teams and worn out bodies. All the camp was in corral before sun down. Travelled ten miles. The Platte rose over a body of sand; [it] is a shallow stream and muddy. Its banks <here> on the west side are high but on the east side they are low. Brother Hall from England had a wagon break down also Brother Robbins. The day cleared up and the sun sank beautifully in the west portraying steady weather. Reported by Captain Brown that Robbins was safe over the Horn and the small creek and would be in camp tomorrow;[80] Captain Brown and three others had been assisting him over this water all day. It was my watch.[81] A whole town watches [itself/at once?].

Thursday ~~Friday~~ July tenth eighteen fifty[-one].

The weather beautiful and seems to be delightful for the season. We waited here today for Captain Robbins' company and to make some repairs wanted by the company. Captain Chatterley is burning coke for that purpose.[82] This morning one man we took in with us on the way got dissatisfied and would turn back. He is an Irishman with a sanguine temperament. His wife and two or three daughters refused to go with him,[83] he put out their things and yoked up his cattle to the wagon in the midst of our remonstrations and reasonings and persuasions of his friends but he would not harken to reason. So they let him alone to cool down all himself, which he finally did. His provisions and loading is now lying on the ground. Adam Meek[84] is the man's name, and one of the party that we found returning from the Oregon expedition.

This after noon eight more wagons joined our camp. In this company was Elias Smith, cousin to Joseph Smith, [Image 447] the prophet. He owns three wagons. Captain Robbins' company all came in late in the afternoon. The remainder of the day was spent in mending broken wheels and wagon tongues,[85] <also> ~~in~~ getting spare ones from the forest. The <weather> has kept clear and fine with a hot sun making the roads good.

Friday~~<Saturday>~~ July eleventh eighteen fifty-one~~<stayed on the Platte>.~~

Beautiful morning with a cool breeze. Calculate to start out today. Left the Platte and travelled over a heavy bottom. Made our camping ground again on the banks of the Platte.

Saturday ~~Sunday~~ July twelfth eighteen fifty-one

Travelled a few miles nothing of any importance transpired. Crossed Shell Creek.[86] <Camped upon the Platte in the wood.>

Sunday July thirteenth eighteen fifty[-one].

Travelled about six miles over a heavy road to a place where we could have some wood. <Camped upon the Platte>[87]

Monday July fourteenth eighteen fifty-one

Travelled through some bad places, Elder Holt[88] broke a wheel. The road generally soft. Camped on the Platte. Made about nineteen miles.

Tuesday July fifteenth eighteen fifty-one. [Image 448]

Made about ~~nineteen~~ <fifteen> miles and camped upon Plum Creek.[89] Crossed Beaver [River] today.[90]

Wednesday July sixteenth eighteen fifty-one

Beautiful morning,[91] last night a heavy dew. Crossed Plum Creek all right after repairing the bridge. Made the [poyners/pioneers?] ford about noon and rested our cattle for two hours. Crossed Cedar Creek in the afternoon and camped a few miles from it.[92]

Thursday July seventeenth eighteen fifty-one

Passed a road of bottom land and high land with deep ravines. Rested our cattle upon the ledge of a piece of tableland previous to entering the bottom land country, a way we need come, about quarter mile from the bluff. One wagon was upset in the water belonging to Mr. Judkins,[93] a traveler with us. It was soon righted and not much damage done. Four of the companies got over this creek and camped on some high land on the other side. Captain Thomas's company was left on the other side of the creek.

About sunset the heavens looked black and angry and about half past ten a tremendous thundershower came on with vivid and continued lightning. It blew down all the tents in the camp, exposing the inmates to the violence of the storm. The rain was mingled with hail stones and fire, [but] no damage was done with the lightning. The wind was so violent as to run back several wagons about twenty feet; in some of them was a ton burden. This rain raised the creek so as to make it impassable. [Image 449]

Friday July eighteenth eighteen fifty-one.

A bridge was built across that [*illegible*] (which has no name in the guide)[94] and in the evening about two hours before sundown the whole camp proceeded to the upper ford of the Loup Fork. Arrived there about sundown. I left by the camp while hunting.

Fig. 10. *Camp at Wood River*. Created by Frederick Piercy. Courtesy of Church History Library.

Saturday July nineteenth eighteen fifty-one

The ford not passable, the waters having [*illegible*] themselves in a deep stream.[95] The officers held a council and concluded to observe the Sabbath and banish all worldly care and pray to the Lord and humble ourselves before him.

Sunday July twentieth eighteen fifty-one

On the banks of the upper ford of Loup Fork. Rested from all our labors and held meeting at two o'clock p.m. in the midst of the corral. The spirit was present with us somewhat [*illegible*] and a few bore testimony. About two o'clock Esther Kempton[96] from London departed this life. She was unmarried and seemed to be about fifty years of age. She travelled with Elder Margetts, formerly president of the London Conference. She was buried in a small mound on the right hand side of the road as you pass down from the tableland to the ford of the Loup Fork and was interred about sunset. She lies in a clean, dry, but lonely grave. Little George[97] fell and hurt his face. [Image 450]

Monday July twenty-first eighteen fifty-one

Early in the morning the ford[98] was again examined and the road across it staked out. It was reckoned to be the best place to pass this stream. The [word missing] was put in the water and they passed over and returned. This settled the quicksand and seemed to raise the road some few inches. The wagons were next put across and were all safely over by one o'clock. The tongue of one of my wagons was broken on the opposite bank which was the only accident that befell the whole camp in crossing that quicksand bottomed stream. There was some chairs, grease cans and other little articles lost down the stream. The water came up to the wagon bodies but not into them. The ford ran half a mile down stream. We made our camp on the bluffs about six miles from the ford. No wood and bad water for culinary purposes.

Tuesday July twenty-second eighteen fifty-one

After travelling a heavy road, partly through bottomland and partly very sandy bluffs, we camped on the other side of Prairie Creek.[99] At noon Brother Allan[100] our blacksmith suffered a yoke of his cattle to stray away with the departing trains which detained our train about two hours behind the rest of the company. Was caught in a thunder storm and drenched to the skin. Travelled to day I suppose about eighteen miles.

Wednesday July twenty-third eighteen fifty-one [Image 451]

The morning is misty and damp. The day cleared up and became excessively hot. In consequence of and many of the cattle not having been watered and a long drive without water some of them gave out one died and one was left which I suppose is dead. This was the ox I loaned to Elder Robbins. He was strained to pieces with too hard pulling and my large ox Lam gave out. We had to unyoke him before we got to the camping ground. We discovered that he had the hollow horn[101] which we are curing. He is much better. We camped upon the banks of the Platte and I suppose we have travelled fourteen miles.[102]

Thursday July 24th eighteen fifty-one

Offered Lam a line to rest and drew my heavy wagon with two yoke of oxen and my other wagon we used three yoke of wild ones. Did not travel far sparing our cattle.

Friday ~~Thursday~~ July twenty-fifth eighteen fifty-one

Made Fort Kearny.[103] Captain Brown went there with leaders. Monroe[104] about ~~8~~ eighty miles ahead of us. Heard nothing of the trains that went the north route.

Saturday July twenty-fifth eighteen fifty[-one]

Traveled about twenty miles and camped upon Elm Creek. The cattle performed this journey without [*illegible*]. The road was good and steady. [Image 452]

Sunday July ~~26~~<27> /~~50~~<51>

We let the cattle rest. Had no preaching or meeting today. The day was spent in mending wagons, preparing for setting tire, etc. A very hot day and a thunder storm at night but not very severe. Some of the company, not of the church, went out and killed five buffalo and left them on the prairie to rot, not having the means of bearing them away.

Monday July 28 /51

The morning fine and cool somewhat cloudy. Setting tire, etc. The trains began to move about ten o'clock in the day,[105] we unyoked at Buffalo Creek and discovered large herds of buffalo on the plains.[106] Several hunters went forth to kill meat for the camp and several was shot and a many of them left to rot on the prairie. Elder Robbins shot four and could not use them or carry them away. This is a sin and a shame. I helped to cut up a bull about four years old. The buffalo is larger than our common ox considerably and the meat is much finer. My stove fell off the wagon and was broke very bad indeed. It was after sunset before the companies was in corral. The

Fig. 11. *Scott's Bluff.* Created by Frederick Piercy.
Courtesy of Church History Library.

cattle had no time to eat. We travelled about fourteen miles and camped upon the banks of a dirty slough where there was no wood but plenty of buffalo chips. Robbins had a wheel broke to pieces on entering into the corral.

Tuesday July 29th /51 [Image 453]

Set Robbin's tire and was on the road in good time. Travelled through large herds of buffalo, I suppose tens of thousands of them, and camped upon the Platte. We made about fourteen miles. Met a company of two wagons returning from Salt Lake, [who] brought an unfavorable report. In this company was Mr. Thomas Bateman[107] on his way to England to set right the churches according to his account. He is not in good fellowship with the church according to a letter from his son in law to Elder Margetts of this camp. About half past eleven a dreadful thunder storm passed over our camp unroofing wagons and terrifying women and children but no material damage was done.

Wednesday July 30 /51.

Surrounded with buffalo all day. We had to stop to let them ahead [of] our train, and horse men were appointed to turn them in their course after large herds would issue from the River Platte, galloping at full speed, [and] threatening destruction of our cattle and wagons. However no accident occurred. The day was hot and sultry but the cattle was not [*illegible*]. We camped upon the banks of the Platte. About two miles ahead is camped another company that came around the divide and late in the evening another was seen making to the river. Mr. Wilkin's[108] ten has separated from his fifty and has also camped close by. Nothing has been heard of Pratt, Cummings,[109] etc. Elder Hyde[110] was robbed by the Indians of almost all he possessed. The companies on that route have had several stampedes. Lost a great many cattle and killed one man of the Garden Grove[111] company.[112] [Image 454]

Thursday July 31/51

This is a nice cool morning, rather cloudy. Several emigrants from the neighboring company joined this company. We travelled over a sandy road today which was heavy for the cattle. The day was hot and the night wet and stormy with thunder and lightning.[113]

Friday August first /51.

Travelled about 17 miles and camped close to Shurtliff's[114] company. This company and another passed on ahead of us in the morning. Travelled about 12 miles in a hot sun <over> a heavy sandy road which was hard upon our cattle. I stopped my ten before the general camp stopped in consequence of the melted condition of many of our cattle. Came to a cold spring that threw out a great volume of water. This was very refreshing to man and beast.[115]

Saturday August second /51

Passed the two companies in the morning and while we nooned, they both passed us. Shurtliff's company went on and the other

Fig. 12. *Camping on the Platte with Chimney Rock in Sight.* Created by Frederick Piercy. Courtesy of Church History Library.

company stayed at the last timber. We passed them again in the afternoon and camped about two miles this side of Shurtliff's camp. Made about 18 miles today which was walking a good road.[116] [Image 455]

Sunday August third /51

Shurtliff's company gone this morning we stayed here to worship God and rest ourselves and cattle. Meeting at two o'clock. We had a good meeting. The spirit of the Lord was with us in very truth. A stranger whose name I have not yet ascertained spoke to the meeting and felt much in favor of the Mormon principles.[117] He came into our company from Felt's fifty and travelled with Mr. Judkins as they were acquaintances. And many spoke spoke[118] upon different subjects and all went to their wagons much cheered and comforted. The day was fine.

Fig. 13. *Fort Laramie*. Created by Frederick Piercy.
Courtesy of Church History Library.

Monday August 4th /51

The train started in good time and passed over two very hard sand hills making about 15 miles.[119]

~~Monday~~ Tuesday August 5th /51

The day cloudy and warm inclined to thunder. Past over a very hard road of sand and sand hills.[120] Made about 17 miles and camped upon the banks of the Platte. Our cattle was tired with this day's work. Learned on the road from writing on a bone that the 4th and 5th tens of Shurtliff's company had camped here on Sunday third instant.[121] All well. Signed David Wilkins. I ~~am not~~ <am> unwell today and not fit to do much in the way of teaming etc. Mother unwell.

Wednesday August 6th /51 [Image 456]

The morning cloudy with a rain bow at sun rise. It is cooling and bids fair for a good day for the oxen.[122] We met several Mormons returning from the gold mines and some from Salt Lake in the same company. They rode upon mules and horses. Reported that all was going on well in Salt Lake: good crops, good health, money scarce and flour 4 dollars per bushel. Travelled 19 miles. Field's[123] camp about 2 miles back.

Thursday August 7th /51

Crossed a bad sand hill about ¾ of a mile over and nooned beside the lone tree. This lone tree is about 30 feet high and grows close on the banks of the Platte. It is most destitute of leaves and seems scrubby and unhealthy but it is a tree and the only one for a great many miles on the south side of the Platte.[124] In the afternoon Monroe came to our camp. He started about ten days before we did and he reported that his camp was about 15 miles ahead. We made about 19 miles.

Friday August 7<8>th /51

Travelled until noon on a fine level road and nooned opposite to <a returning> camp <of merchants from the Salt Lake>. The companies behind us nooned about half a mile below. Made a little over 20 miles and camped on the banks of a of a[125] beautiful flowing stream.[126] [Image 457]

Saturday August 9th /51

Crossed a high bluff. The ascent was good and hard. The descent was sandy. We nooned on the bottom. While we nooned Phillips camp passed us. We passed them again and camped upon the banks of the Platte having made about 15 miles. Phillips camp stopped about 2 miles below.[127]

Sunday August tenth /51

Captain Chatterley and Robbins repairing wagon wheels and setting tire all day. No meeting in consequence thereof. In the fore part of the day the ten belonging to Shurtleff's company that had been left behind through losing their cattle passed this camp. Also the

~~Garden~~ Garden Grove Company[128] who had lost 21 head of cattle. The day was very windy and myself and wife were unwell all day. A slight storm of wind and rain in the evening which cooled the atmosphere considerably.

Monday August 11 /51

Travelled over a good road and made I suppose about 15 miles. All weary. Camped opposite Chimney Rock.[129]

Tuesday August 12 /51

The day was cool,[130] and good for cattle. We made about 17 miles. Beautiful ancient bluff ruins on the south side of the river. These ruins are some ancient fortification of tremendous magnitude and strength. [Image 458]

Wednesday August 13th /51

The day somewhat warm and the road good generally with a few hard places of sand. We travelled about 19 miles and camped by the side of a small creek on the south side of the road in which the guide reports to be trout but we found none.[131] Good feed for cattle in wood but not many buffalo chips.[132]

Thursday August 14th /51.[133]

[No entry for this date.]
[The last page of the notebook contains Watt's brief shorthand notes of the House of Representatives' meeting on January 5, 1852, including his appointment as reporter.]

Letter from George D. Watt to Mr. and Mrs. Brandreth, Describing His Journey to Salt Lake City

[Transcription of shorthand draft of letter written by George D. Watt. He stated in this letter that they had traveled five hundred miles over the plains; he likely wrote and mailed this letter at Fort Laramie, which is about five hundred miles from Ferryville, Nebraska.]
[Image 276]

Mister and Mistress Brandreth Dear Brother and Sister

We take up our pen to write you a short communication from this place; hitherto we have not written directly to you, but have written to others in Preston, and requested them to allow you a perusal of the letter. This seeming neglect does not arise from a want of that respect which your kindness to us on ~~parting~~ parting, as much as kindred itself certainly demands, but for <want of time> and opportunity to pen and compose such a letter as would be at once interesting, <instructive>, and amusing to you. We[134] designed to drop you <all therefore>[135] a note from the midst of the wilderness, if a chance presented itself. ~~I am pleased that I can send you this letter~~ And also to write you a long communication from the valley, when our minds were free and rested from the toils anxieties and vexations of a journey like this.

We have now traversed 5 thousand miles of the sea, [and] near 2 thousand have we travelled on the Rivers Mississippi and Missouri and 5 hundred across these plains.[136] The journey across the sea and up the rivers are fraught with many dangers. Our lives are in the hands of ~~incomprehensible~~ wicked and reckless sailors the chief part of it, so that it requires much cunning and wisdom to get along on this part of the journey without losing your lives and property. We have been preserved through all these dangers, for which we render thanks to our Great Father who art in heaven. We all enjoy this day our [*illegible*] health, strength, and spirits. In crossing the sea there is a continual sameness. In passing up the rivers, we were treated to a continual change of scenery of the most beautiful and enchanting character, such as calls to our minds the imagined scenes we have read in ~~fairy~~ fairy tales or seen painted [Image 277] upon the scenery of a theater.[137] We cross these plains in wagons drawn by oxen. We have two large wagons and 13 head of cattle. We have three yoke of oxen to each wagon and one cow. Mother and Jane occupies one wagon and myself and family the other.

The Americans have been trained to use oxen to plow, to travel with, [and] for every purpose our English horses are used, except to ride them. An American feels quite at home with a whip in his hand, and two or three yoke of oxen by his side. But if ever an Englishman felt himself far from home, it is in when he has to commence, whip in hand, to drive and manage oxen. This is a lesson of no small magnitude, I do assure you, a lesson that a many never can learn. The folks in England talk about the patience of Job, and possessing their souls in patience, and to be of an unchanged temper; but people do not know what kind of a temper they got until they ~~try~~ have to drive and manage a team of stupid oxen. It has become an acknowledged fact in this country, that no man can drive oxen properly without swearing but we have proved that to be an untruth,[138] although we have not been without ~~our~~ great temptations to commit this evil.

We sleep in our wagons, and eat our vittles from the broad prairie table, covered with its natural grassy carpet. We travel from 15 to 20 miles per day, six days in a week, and rest our cattle and our men on the seventh. This company numbers about 60 wagons. We have a captain over the whole, and captains are appointed over each ten. It is the duty [of] the first captain to see that all the trains are yoked up and started properly on the way every morning. and to seek out a proper camping ground at night where our cattle can have good grass and water. It is the duty of the captain of ten to commit the orders of the first captain to his ten and see them obeyed. [Image 278] Thus we travel in order and peace. When we camp at night, we form a corral of our wagons in this shape. [Circle drawn with small opening on left side.] We can drive our cattle in there, and protect them from Indians, if there is any danger, and also protect ourselves.

There is much on this journey across the wilderness to please, and amuse, and astonish the lover of nature: the endless plains covered with grass and flowers of every grade and hue from the rose to the common unassuming daisy. These wide spread prairies are covered generally with what is called buffalo grass. It is short and tufted, but very fine in the blade, and excellent to fat up cattle. It is the richest and nicest kind of feed, but when we come upon the banks of the streams, there we find thousands of acres of the best kind of rye grass that you have seen grow in the select parks of England. Our cattle wade into up to their bellies. While we travel daily, our cattle keep fat, and some old cattle that were thin on the commencement of the journey are now near fat enough for the knife.

For 50 miles we were partly surrounded with buffalo, so that they endangered our camp, [if/for?] they frighten our domestic cattle and cause them to stampede. We were under the necessity of sending men forward on horseback to divide the herds, that we might pass through. The plains were black over with this monstrous creature, as far as our eyes could see. Hundreds of nations of Indians have been fed with their flesh, and clothed with their skins, for hundreds of ages, and yet they swarm on these plains like our cattle on the English market grounds. They answer the description given to them in books of natural history. Were you to have a buffalo beef steak placed before you on your own table at home, and you kept ignorant of it, you would say you never eat[139] a more delicious piece of beef in all your life. Hundreds of pounds of this meat is left [Image 279] to rot on the plains, or be devoured by the wolves, which are very plentiful. Here is venison in abundance, hundreds and thousands of deer, antelope, hares, and elk, beside the fish that gambol in the merry but lonely waters that moisten these plains.

4

The End of the Trail

> The endless plains [are] covered with grass and flowers of every grade and hue from the rose to the common unassuming daisy.
> —Letter, George D. Watt to John M. and Margaret Brandreth

From Chimney Rock to Great Salt Lake City

George D. Watt did not state why he stopped writing his journal. He had already recorded the trip across the Atlantic, the steamboat trip up the Mississippi and Missouri Rivers, and part of the overland trip. There are some possible hints. On August 5 he wrote that he and his mother were sick. Maybe every day thereafter when he thought about it, he was so tired he could not pick up his pen to write. Perhaps it was the oxen. He certainly did not like to drive oxen, at which he had no experience before this journey. He thought they were stupid animals. Even with this dislike, he would have needed to spend more time in helping the others of his group, which left him little time at the end of the day. He may have felt that he could not write to those fellow Britishers about his difficulty with the oxen. He could write his sister, but if he put this into his journals, he would discourage others who were expecting to leave. He could not do that. He would be complaining and thus would drive those others away from coming to Zion. He may have simply given up. He thought about that experience in 1867, when he arrived near Council Bluffs, Iowa, and he wrote a letter back to the *Deseret News*, telling the newspaper and its readers about his experience with oxen.

There are four other accounts of the John Brown Company in 1851: Preston F. Thomas kept the official company journal, while Jane Rio Griffiths Baker, Elias Smith, and Emily Smith Hoyt[1] each kept personal journals.[2] Each record has its strengths and limitations; together they give an excellent picture of conditions of the trail, the mileage, and other events of their lives on this long and arduous journey. These four records are used together in order to tell the story of their overland travel to the Salt Lake Valley after Watt ended his record on August 13, 1851.

The company encountered no American Indians during the part of their journey covered by Watt's journal. On August 14 the company saw an Indian for the first time. For the next few days Indians came into their camp. Baker mentioned that the Sioux were with them for the entire day, and their women had dresses neatly covered with beads.[3] Two days later, they passed Fort Laramie where they saw many Indians, camped all over the countryside. The company did not stop at the fort, although somebody delivered letters there, but continued several miles beyond. On August 19 the company again encountered more Indians, who were going toward Laramie. Six days later two government Indian agents informed them that all the tribes were going to a great council. Their leaders would represent them in this council with the federal government. Three days later on August 28 the members of the company saw a little army of Shoshone Indians going to Laramie, the last group they encountered. Brown informed the men to load their rifles, which they did. The Indians passed by without incident.[4]

The season turned hot and dry after the very wet spring and early summer. They had problems finding sufficient grass for their cattle in western Nebraska and Wyoming, an area normally dry with little grass, except by the streams and rivers. They needed to find enough feed for their cattle to regain their strength every night. In many cases they could not do it. The other companies on the trail exacerbated the problem. The Brown Company was now together with the Morris Phelps Company, the John G. Smith Company, which the journalists called the Shurtliff company, and the Harry Walton/Garden Grove Company. In the last few weeks of their trip, Brown slowed his company down in order to save their oxen. The animals of these three companies traveling in close proximity competed for the grass along the trail. Indians' ponies had also consumed the feed in the area of Fort Laramie. The journals are filled with the words "poor grass," "little grass," or "tolerable good grass" throughout.

The trip was hard on both man and beast, but especially hard on the animals. Captain Brown had enough knowledge of the trail and the hardships to know when to stop. He seemed to have a goal of moving approximately a hundred miles in a week, but he did not hold to this when he knew the animals needed nourishment and rest. Later Brown allowed the cattle outside the corral barrier at night. On the second night the cattle grazed several miles away. When the men of the company did not find the cattle immediately, they thought that Indians had taken the animals, but they discovered the cattle and started late that morning. Besides letting the cattle graze outside the corral, Brown often moved the wagon train a few more miles past their intended stop to find better grass. He also began resting the company in the middle of the week, especially when they found grass long enough to allow the animals to graze. At the Bear River, he moved the entire group off the trail and traveled several miles down the river to find a good grazing spot. Several times Brown stopped the whole company to mend wagons and rest the cattle. By the first of September the oxen were giving out, and several died. Baker lost six oxen on the journey for various reasons, including exhaustion.[5]

Brown was also concerned with the wagons breaking down. Most of the men became very proficient in fixing their own wagons, but again the train had to stop while this process took place. Robbins, the captain of the third ten, had the greatest difficulty. His wagons were loaded primarily with goods and so were heavier than the others.

Another of Brown's goals was to keep the wagon train together and to make sure he did not leave anyone behind. He never allowed the groups to get separated from the main company. At least once Robbins had wagons break down, and his group stayed back and did not corral with the others. Brown sent Preston Thomas back to find Robbins and bring his ten up to the wagon train.

The latter part of the trip, Brown was much better at stopping on Sunday and allowing meetings. He preached at one, Preston Thomas at another, and George D. Watt at another. The meetings revitalized the entire group and gave them the courage to press on.

Each subgroup had the opportunity to lead the wagon train on certain days. This allowed that group fresh air, not filled with dust. Watt's ten had a problem of not being ready to lead when they had the opportunity to do so. Baker and Smith mentioned that in the early part of the trip. The other journalists seem to blame Watt for being slow. Perhaps the answer for his slowness and even for not writing in a journal also lies with the members of his group of ten. He had fifty-one people and thirteen wagons that he presided over. He had a driver, Samuel Patterson, for his other wagon. He had two wagons so both he and Patterson were needed. Thomas Margetts, another Englishman, was with him. Joseph Allan, who was also British, had three wagons with a wife and two small children. He also had John Yardley, another Britisher, who had two wagons. Perhaps his wife Zillah Allan drove the other one. Joel Terry, an American from New York, had a large family but no other driver, unless he turned to his wife and perhaps his sister, Amandah. The last two wagons were owned by Mary Child, who had John Lynden with her, who could drive one of the wagons. Watt also had two wagons in his group of ten with eight people traveling to Oregon. Any of these could have been responsible for the slowness of his ten.[6]

On August 16 the John Brown Company was at Fort Laramie. They continued up the Platte River and then crossed over to the Sweetwater. They passed Independence Rock on September 1, almost halfway through Wyoming, and the next day reached Devil's Gate. Many walked through this narrow pass. They crossed the Continental Divide on September 9. Thereafter water and grass became very scarce. On September 19 they passed Fort Bridger and camped past the fort. Some entered the fort and bartered for necessary goods. Four days later they arrived at Cache Cave, where Watt and others chiseled their names on the wall inside the cave. Nine days later they camped on the foothills overlooking Salt Lake where they saw the lights in the valley. The next day, September 29, 1851, they all entered the city. Brown had done an amazing job. He had kept them all together for the entire journey. There had been no large or small rebellions like those that had split other emigrant trains.

Many of the company would be disbursed throughout many of the towns of the territory, but Watt remained in Salt Lake City. He was a highly skilled Pitman shorthand reporter and began to use his skill immediately. In October 1851 he reported the trial of Howard Egan for the murder of James Monroe in the First Judicial Court. He was hired as the official reporter for the 1852 Utah Legislative Assembly. He used the same shorthand notebook for the legislature that he had used for recording his journal and reporting sermons by Brigham Young, Heber C. Kimball, Orson Pratt, and others. There is no evidence that he ever transcribed his journal or made any effort to publish it as help and instructions for the British Latter-day Saint emigrants who would follow.

George D. Watt's Life after the Journal

George D. Watt has no other known journals. However, he continued to use his pen in many ways. He reported the speeches of the authorities of the church and others in Pitman shorthand. He wrote letters to various individuals including his wives, Brigham Young, Willard Richards, and many others. He wrote articles for newspapers and even some fictional articles about a vagabond boy in England, which he titled "The Little George Stories." In this life sketch after his journal, we intend to give the reader a view of this extraordinary man through some of his writings, which describe his interests and his personality. From 1851, when he first arrived in Utah, until 1868, when he left Brigham Young's office, he was involved with all of the prominent events that happened in the territory. Even after he left Young's office he wrote letters and newspaper articles.

On September 29, 1851, George D. Watt and family arrived in Salt Lake City. He busied himself with recording different events in shorthand in the new community: court and legislative proceedings, baby blessings, missionary and other setting-apart blessings, talks, and sermons at church meetings. Since his skill was so good, he was able to record a speaker's words almost verbatim, though he occasionally missed reporting a word or phrase. Brigham Young already knew about his talents as a shorthand reporter before his arrival, from Watt's work in Nauvoo and by the report he made at the trial of the accused murderers of Joseph Smith in Carthage, Illinois. Willard Richards, Young's counselor in the First Presidency of the Church of Jesus Christ of Latter-day Saints, also knew him. Richards had hired Watt in Nauvoo to work in the Church Historian's Office. Perhaps through their help, he gained employment with the Utah Territorial Legislature. When the territorial legislature convened, Watt was the recorder, and he faithfully took a verbatim account of much of the proceedings.

Willard Richards was now the editor of Great Salt Lake's newspaper, the *Deseret News*. He asked Watt to report the speeches of President Young and others for the newspaper. In January 1852 Watt began his work. Every Sunday Young and other church authorities preached. Watt's responsibility was to be there with his pen and paper and record those speeches. In their discussions Watt and Richards never discussed his wage. Watt probably presumed it would depend on how much of what he did was put into print or else it would be by a separate publication that Richards would authorize. He continued through most of September 1852 without any pay; then he finally wrote Richards a letter, complaining that he had never been paid for his services. Thus began what became a heated exchange of correspondence between the two men.[7] Watt used the saying on the newspaper's masthead, "God Helps them Who Helps Themselves," to introduce his problem. Watt then explained what that meant to him. "I understand that the saying to mean, 'that every man shall reap the reward due to his labor, whether it be much or little.'" He said he had a family to support; "this I wish to do, and this I will do by the blessing of the Almighty." He could not do that without an income. At the end of the letter Watt wanted Richards to know that his feelings toward him were the same, but he needed support for what he did. "I have no enmity in my heart, I love you but I cannot tamely submit to have the fruits of my labor taken from me altogether, when it is right by every just law that I should enjoy them."[8]

Richards felt that Watt could have taken some of his reports and sold them for his own benefit. He was incensed that Watt would write him and send it through a public area, the post office, and that in finding fault with his course, Watt was finding fault with his God: "you find fault with my God: and that ground is very slippery, and if you don't get off it quickly, you will find it hard to stand." Watt replied that he needed to be rewarded for his labor. "I want to know what is mine as clearly as I know what is yours,—when I work, I want to know how I am to be rewarded temporaly [temporally], for it is I must confess very little satisfaction to me to work upon the principle of being rewarded in the resurrection, though that may be well enough, if everybody else worked so." He ended his letter with the entreaty, "You can lead me but you cannot intimidate me: while a kind word from your lips vibrates through my soul like the sweetest sounds of harmony." The rift between Richards and Watt continued for many months. Watt continued to be present at the meetings, faithfully taking shorthand reports, but they were not printed in the *Deseret News*. He was the official reporter for the semi-annual General Conference of the Church of Jesus Christ of Latter-day Saints and sent the transcriptions of the General Conference to be published in the newspaper. In May 1853 Watt suggested that he be allowed to publish a booklet of speeches that he had recorded. He would be responsible for the publication and receive the profits from his venture. The three members of the First Presidency of the church, including Willard Richards, approved his request. Thereafter Watt began to publish the *Journal of Discourses*. He helped heal the rift between him and Richards by sending copies of his reports to Richards, who published them in the *Deseret News*. Richards died in March 1854. Watt wrote the report for the funeral proceedings, which was published in the *Deseret News*. He ended by saying that the mourners retired from the cemetery, leaving "the remains of one of the best and greatest men that ever trod the earth, to sleep in peace, until he shall awake to immortality and eternal life."[9]

Watt served in the Utah militia, or Nauvoo Legion, as it was called, to defend Utah from U.S. troops sent by President James Buchanan in 1857 to put down a rumored but nonexistent rebellion. He wrote his wife Alice three letters during that period. He was convinced that they would be able to defend themselves in Echo Canyon. He said, "They have grade rock defenses with port holes on every point commanding a good rifle range of the road for a distance of over a mile." Even though he sent letters home, he received no letters from his wives. He again wrote, "I had just come in from a long and tedious days journey, was hungry—weary—and worn—and dirty, and on top of that no letter for me." His unit was recalled to Salt Lake City a few days later.[10]

After his appointment to the Board of Regents of the University of Deseret in 1852, Watt was appointed to a committee to develop a new phonetic alphabet for the English language. He was very influential in the development of the Deseret Alphabet, including the design of the characters.[11] The Deseret Alphabet was an attempt by Brigham Young to perfect the English orthography, having one letter for each sound.

At that time some members of the Church of Jesus Christ of Latter-day Saints practiced plural marriage. Watt would eventually have six wives. He married his first wife, Mary Gregson, on June 13, 1835, in Preston, England. He married his half-sister Jane Brown on January 5, 1852, in the Endowment House in Salt Lake City, shortly after his arrival in the valley. Then he began seeing Alice Longstroth Whittaker. She had previously been married to Moses Whittaker, who died in January 1852. One night he walked her home, but she did not invite him in. Feeling disheartened, he wrote late at night, "When you informed me I could not go into the house to spend an hour with you and bade me good night and that too in such a careless tone . . . a gloom of grief passed over me." He continued, "You have touched the tenderest courts of my nature, you have become mingled up with my very existence." He thought that she did not reciprocate his love. "Why friend you cannot imagine the distress of mind, the bitterness of the pain it gives to me if this pure unsophisticated love that knaws [at] my heart, if you speak or act towards me as though my feelings are not real or if you consider they are to treat it as foolishness or esteem it as wickedness." The next morning, feeling better, he continued his letter, "I hail the break of merry morning. My body and mind is invigorated with balmy sleep, and . . . gratitude to God for his daily mercy." It is possible that this letter convinced Alice to marry him. Watt married her on December 11, 1853.[12]

He took three more wives, all younger women. He began to court Elizabeth Golightly late in the 1850s. When it came time to propose to her, he wrote her a letter, in which he said, "I offer myself to you, if you can in return give me this love, and with it yourself, which offering would be prized by me above the glittering and perishable treasures of earth." She accepted his proposal, and they were married on July 23, 1859.[13] Seven years later Watt married Sarah Ann Harter, who had been abandoned by her previous husband, and was "imaciated with hard labor."[14] In 1863 he met twin sisters Martha and Mary Bench when he stayed at their parents' home in Manti, Utah. He talked to Martha and Mary, and after discussing many subjects that night, he felt good about both of them. He even asked them to think about a possible marriage with him. He told them that he had prayed, asking his Father in Heaven to bless them and "for guidance to myself and you relative to the proposal I made you when I was last near you." He concluded that "I can love you because you are good. I can trust you because you are faithful." Mary had no interest in marrying him. Martha fell in love with him. They were married in the Endowment House on November 8, 1867.[15]

The most charming love letter he wrote was to Asenath Richards, a proposal that was not accepted. "You know Asenath that the dashing devil may care young fellow with spurs and whip in hand and a cigar in his mouth and maybe a roll of tobacco in his cheek with a broad rimmed hat encircled with beaver and 3 or 4 tails flying behind has charms for some young woman that are not to be found in a sedate praying meeting going and half gray headed person like myself."[16]

On January 10, 1856, his first wife, Mary, only forty-six years old, died of consumption (tuberculosis), which she had contracted while working in the textile factories of Preston, England. In a letter to a relative in England eight years later he explained, "She died of consumption which she received by taking a severe cold that settled upon her lungs and which she could not have overcome." He told them, "She had crossed the great waters four times with me, passed with me through sickness, hardship, sorrow, and death; wandered with me over plains and sandy deserts, crossed the Rocky Mountains and then will be saying 'I will be your companion in heaven.'"[17]

Watt and Jane had difficulties from the first of their marriage, and they finally separated in 1863. He wrote her a letter desiring her to come back to him. He still loved her, and he wanted her to be a part of the family and not try to divide it. "I desire of you first to cease speaking evil of me and circulating falsehoods; second, I wish you to contradict those scandalous stories which you have circulated about Alice and seek her forgiveness." Finally he wished her to live "a humble and faithful life before the Lord, and strive to make a loving wife to me the rest of your days and all shall again be right between us."[18] In 1863 two missionaries from the Reorganized Church of Jesus Christ of Latter Day Saints converted her to their faith. With the help of a squad of General Patrick

Connor's soldiers from Fort Douglas, she left the territory, later marrying Adam Saladin, who was a soldier stationed at Fort Laramie. They moved to Nebraska, where she joined with a branch of the Reorganized Church of Jesus Christ of Latter Day Saints.[19]

According to family tradition, Watt was also an artist. At one time, using dark paper and scissors, he cut silhouettes of people. Nothing has survived to the present time of his paintings or his work with scissors and dark paper. Some drawings have turned up, though, in his shorthand notebooks. Presumably when he had time, he sketched the likenesses of some of the people sitting near him or in the audience. Altogether thirty-two sketches are in his notebooks. Many of them were drawn hastily, and some are cartoon-like drawings or caricatures. Very few are identified, but others are recognizable, including Brigham Young and Daniel H. Wells.

Because of his interest and his shorthand ability, he involved himself with almost all of the cultural and intellectual organizations in Utah. He joined the Universal Scientific Society, the Polysophical Society, the Deseret Theological Institute, the Deseret Typographical Association, and the Deseret Dramatic Association, even acting minor parts in several plays. Knowing that the Deseret Dramatic Association orchestra needed a viola player, Watt taught himself how to play the viola. He also joined the Deseret Musical Association in 1862, which during the 1860s performed Hayden's *Creation*, Mozart's *Twelfth Night*, and Handel's *Messiah*. He became the corresponding secretary to the Pomological Society, which later became the Deseret Horticultural Society and then merged into the Deseret Agricultural and Manufacturing Society (DAM), though it emphasized agriculture more than manufacturing. He also had a small library, but only a few titles are known to us. He ordered a few books through David Calder, a friend and a book dealer. He received a book by Robert Kemp Philip entitled *Inquire Within for Anything You Want to Know, or, Over Three Thousand Seven Hundred Facts Worth Knowing*. Another was entitled *Live and Learn: A Guide for All Who Wish to Speak and Write Correctly* to help him with his English grammar and transcriptions of the talks he reported.[20]

He began to grow a variety of crops in his garden and raise many animals, which he exhibited in the local DAM fairs. He grew some large cabbages, tomatoes, corn, parsnips, and other products, as reported by the *Deseret News*.[21] He brought some large peaches into the Historian's Office one day in 1855. In 1865 he also sold many varieties of seeds of crops he raised.[22] In January 1864 the fruit committee of the DAM visited Watt's gardens and found a large crop of strawberries. The committee reported that they found one strawberry with a circumference of six inches. In 1865 when the U.S. speaker of the house Schuyler Colfax visited Salt Lake City, his guides took him to Watt's garden. Colfax reported in his journal, "Strawberries abound, and we reveled in them in the garden of George D. Watt, who has the finest garden of all." He then noted everything he had there. He said that Watt "had made a garden where the sagebrush and gravel had reigned supreme, and had apricots, peaches, flax, *morus multicaulis* [mulberry trees], strawberries largely, plums, cotton, etc."[23] Watt preached self-sufficiency for the Latter-day Saints. He raised silk worms and produced silk cloth and finally clothes made of silk. He thought by raising silk, the people of Utah would not be dependent upon the cloth of the outside world. Thomas Stenhouse, the editor of the *Semi-Weekly Telegraph*, wrote that Watt had a factory in his home. "He has cotton spinning, woolen spinning, weaving of all the varied classes; then he has his thousands of silk worms producing in their department." He thought that Watt had many skills: "By the bye, George has mastered the violin, is a member of the Orchestra, wears home spun in the summer; home spun in the winter; eats his own bread, wears his own apparel and makes his own music."[24]

In 1866 Watt began to write about agriculture, at first anonymously, and wrote altogether eight articles. In the *Semi-Weekly Telegraph* he wrote an article titled "A Word in Season" in which he described the practice of planting a fruit tree. He advised that such trees should be planted in the month of March. He followed that up with an article entitled "Apple and Pear Seeds." He started out talking about Utah economics and said that men looking for precious metals have brought a demand for more products. Then he said that seeds of all kinds should be planted, and "when you are asleep, or following the avocations of life, the little rootlets of these plants may be working for you—may be helping you to that which you cannot get when money cannot be had." Another article he titled

"Asparagus." He advised that this vegetable should be harvested only sparingly the third year after planting. He said that asparagus was the first crop of the season and should be cut early in the spring. "After peas become abundant, asparagus should not be cut, but should be suffered to make top and gather vigor and strength of root for another year."[25] Watt also wrote an article entitled "Shade Trees," expressing his disgust with the cottonwood trees planted by the earliest pioneers. The locust and mulberry trees were better. "The locust in addition to being a very thrifty grower, forms, under proper training, a dense top, and produces a hard, tough and useful timber." The other tree he favored was the mulberry. "The mulberry forms a handsome top and is in many ways very useful and profitable."[26] He also published an article titled "Dip[h]theria," which was primarily about sanitation and cleanliness. He thought anything that was dirty or had decaying substances in it should be cleaned, especially a carpet. "It is often the case that carpets are allowed to remain on floors too long before they are removed and cleansed, and the floors under them swept and washed clean."[27]

In his longest and last report, a six-part serialized article, which Watt entitled "A Talk," he discussed raising sheep. Sheep should be given good sheds for the winter. The flocks should not be "huddled together in winter in dirty pens, without shelter, exposed to the rains and snows of the fall, winter and early spring, scantily fed." If treated well, the sheep produce good wool. To him, handmade socks were better than machine-produced ones. They were a better quality. He discussed how much wool would be needed for socks if there were a demand for them. He thought "Demand and Supply are the great foundations of commerce." He did not think, though, that the demand should drive up the price. An unfair higher price "strikes a blow at the best interests of our growing country, and spreads a gloom and discouragement over the portion of society affected by it, and over those interests which keep up an increasing demand to meet lively and active sources of supply."

He felt that everyone in the family should be industrious. "The true Mormon husband and father is a farmer, a mechanic, a manufacturer, a shepherd, or a stock raiser; he is valiant in battling the elements to produce what he needs." The same was true of the woman of the house. Watt wrote: "The true Mormon wife and mother is industrious, economical; managing her household with skill, seeking to save on all sides, rather than to recklessly consume and squander her husband's substance. She watches over her children with solicitude and care, as to what they eat, drink and wear."[28]

Beginning about 1855 the British Mission Office printed more volumes of the *Journal of Discourses* than it could sell. As a result Watt found himself in serious financial difficulty. The office cut the number being published, but it was impossible to bring the publication out of the red. George Q. Cannon, the mission president, recommended that the Church buy a press and take over the *Journal*'s publication. In 1865 the church took over the publication of the *Journal of Discourses*. Thereafter Watt was made an employee of the church and continued his work on the *Journal of Discourses* in that way.

This action diminished his income, and with added wives and more children, Watt needed additional income. In 1853 he had discovered the possibility that he might be in line for an inheritance in the British Isles that would provide him with a nice living. At that date he was only interested in fulfilling his responsibilities in Utah and taking care of his family. He decided not to even try for this inheritance then, but by 1867, needing money, he decided to go to England and pursue this possibility. He left with Brigham Young Jr. and traveled through the worst winter that had been experienced for many years.

They traveled by stage across Wyoming and finally arrived at North Platte, Nebraska, where they boarded the train, but before they arrived in Omaha they were held up by drifting snow for more than twelve hours. Afterward they continued their journey to New York City and even stopped at Niagara Falls. At the sight of the falls Watt wrote, "I was struck with awe and wonder when I viewed, as it were a world of waters leaping with a clear bound into a fathomless abyss, and breaking into a spray in their rumbling, gurgling, roaring, dashing downward course, as if they dreaded to meet the mysterious depths of the boiling caldron into which their foaming, raging floods have emptied themselves from the days of gray antiquity." In the same report he said, "They kiss you at a distance with their misty spray, but let no mortal creature within the

Fig. 14. Photograph of George D. Watt, 1867. Author's collection.

inevitable grasp of their rushing, angry, merciless cascades, for no power but that of Omnipotence could rescue."[29] They next journeyed to Washington DC and saw the sights there and then returned to New York. In that city they boarded the ship *Java* and arrived in England on March 20 and stayed until May 23.[30] It had been an eventful trip. He saw his sister and her husband but failed to obtain the Irish land. The English government had required that he live in England before he could obtain the land and the title that he sought. In a letter to the *Millennial Star*, he wrote: "If you believe that I have the faintest shadow of wish to leave my people with whom I have been connected for thirty years then you are deceived. . . . for were you to make me England's King and lay at my feet England's wealth without her debts, to forsake my religion and my people, to dwell with you, by the grace of God it would not amount to even a temptation. The wealth of the world cannot purchase the promise of eternal life which I possess through the Gospel."[31] He later wrote a letter to Brigham Young from New York, reporting new developments in the Pitman shorthand system. He ended his letter with the words, "I long to be by your side, and pray, if it can be so ordered in the Providence of God, that I may never again leave it in time nor eternity."[32]

Watt continued traveling with Young throughout Utah as he had done before, reporting his sermons in shorthand. He also wrote reports for the newspaper about these trips.

Needing additional money for his growing family, he decided to approach Brigham Young and ask for a raise. He had been receiving $3.50 a day. On May 15, 1868, he asked Young. His well-planned words did not work, and an argument ensued. Young felt that he was paying Watt too much, and Watt did not spend enough time in the office anyway. Watt laid down his notes before Young and said, "Brother Young, if George D. Watt does not earn every cent he gets, you had better get someone who can." Later, realizing that he needed to take notes at the School of the Prophets, a meeting of the priesthood brethren, he took another of his notebooks and pen to the meeting. He was stunned when Brigham Young told those assembled, "I do not want George D. Watt around me. I cannot get rid of him. He comes into the office when he darn pleases. [Then] he goes off and tends his cherry trees." Young told the meeting attenders that Watt did this week after week without asking his permission. "I do not want you George, why, because you won't do as I want you to."[33] Watt left the meeting never to serve Young again. He never returned to the office. He had been humiliated by a person whom he had looked up to ever since he joined the church in 1837. He left all of his shorthand notes and other papers in the office, never to see them again.

At first he stayed home tending his garden. Then the School of the Prophets asked him to visit the towns throughout Utah and talk on the sericulture: the raising of silk worms and making silk. He began preaching about it in his own Fourteenth Ward in September and by the end of December had talked in Salt Lake, Sanpete, and Davis Counties. In the midst of his travels he committed to Robert Sleater and William Ajax to become a business partner with them in a general merchandise store in Salt Lake City. While speaking for silk, he also began mentioning his opposition to the new Zions Cooperative Mercantile Association that Young had organized, and he refused to join with the other merchants in the new organization. Within a few months his store had gone bankrupt. He lost all his property in Salt Lake and decided to move to his farm in Kaysville.

After Watt moved to Kaysville, he for a time recommitted himself to the church. He wrote a letter to Brigham Young expressing some of his feelings. In thinking about his experiences with his business he said that he had tried to be a merchant and smash all "our enemies," but "the lesson was to short and light, so by the force of the intended blow I lost my balance and fell into the mud hole." He had asked no one's advice, "but on I went through mire and clay up to my eyes, asking no help from any man, bearing my own burdens, trusting in God alone for deliverance, and confessing all my folly and sins unto Him. It has been a hard road to travel, but I have found Him a sure help in time of need." What was most important to him was that he had "entered into solemn and grave covenants to stand by my brethren and the cause of truth, and I am going to do it, the Lord being my helper to the end of the chapter." He hoped his experiences of the recent past had given him a little more ballast to steady himself, "and that the latter part of my days may be spent more to the glory and honor of God than the former."[34]

While he was in Kaysville, he deviated from the church he had converted to many years before. He became involved with the Godbeite movement, which was founded in spiritualism, the contacting of spirits from the other world. He had problems with his bishop, the ecclesiastical leader of his congregation, Christopher Layton. One day he wrote to Brigham Young to lodge a complaint against the teachers that had been sent by Bishop Layton. To the teachers he admitted taking the *Salt Lake Tribune*, a Godbeite newspaper, but he did it to be informed what it was up to. He thought, "Its mineral department is an exaggeration and, used to flood the country with people from abroad, to rob the Mormon people of their municipal legislative rights. . . . The communication and editorial department appear to me to be full of snap snarl and fight. As a whole I think it is an ambitious, shallow pated, boasting, insulting, pugnacious, snarling, senseless sheet." Watt tried to hang on to the "Old Ship Zion," but his constant fight with Bishop Layton lessened his grip. He finally gave up and began speaking in public meetings for the Godbeite movement and spiritualism and against the church he had been associated with for so long. He wrote two articles in the *Salt Lake Tribune* entitled "Brigham's Enoch" and the "Gobbling Prophet" wherein he stated that even though cooperation was correct, Brigham Young had gathered all riches to himself. He wrote that he did not "write in bitterness of spirit towards Young or the Mormons, but with an uncompromising hostility to oppression and wrong."[35] On May 3, 1874, the *Deseret Evening News* announced that George D. Watt had been excommunicated from the Church of Jesus Christ of Latter-day Saints for apostasy. From March 1874 to April 1875 he gave a series of lectures against the economics of Brigham Young and Mormonism in general. One of his lectures was entitled "My Former Ideas of God. How I Became Possessed of Them and Why I Rejected Them." His last lecture to the Salt Lake Society of Progressive Spiritualists was entitled "The Phenomena of Spiritualism and Its Uses."[36]

After this he became more content to stay in Kaysville on his farm to take care of his family. He changed his views somewhat. He even asked twice for readmittance into the Church of Jesus Christ of Latter-day Saints but was turned down. In December 1878 through January 1879 he wrote a long letter to the president of the church, John Taylor. He again asked for admittance to the church, but he wanted Taylor to know what he believed. The letter is a philosophical treatise that, because of its language and concepts, is difficult to understand. It reveals a man who is able to grasp and explain complicated religious concepts, sometimes not clearly, not in simple terms, but in the words of a student of philosophical theology. He believed in an impersonal God, as he defined it, "in the unchangeable and infinitly extended God—the soul of universal nature." He felt that God was "the fountain of all truth, light life and intelligence, stamping himself in degrees, planes, and phases upon the infinite arcana of matter." He did not believe in the devil. "I can see no room or use for a personal devil," he stated. He did not believe in the atonement of Jesus Christ. To Watt, Christ was a good man and had saved mankind through his reforms, not through his atonement. "In this sense I understand Jesus Christ, as the Savior of men . . . which was enshrined in his pure mind and exemplified in his holy life." He did not believe in the fall of humanity. Each person had "steadily advanced . . . from the lowest point through the evolutions of matter and mind to his present attainments." He did not believe "in the efficacy of sacrificial blood." He did not see the Bible as an infallible guide. "To accept sacred writing as infalable guides and rules of faith is equivalent to confining infinite capacities to finite limits, which is an impossability." He thought that the Bible was "a very beautiful astroaligorical expression of the uncultured notions of primitive man regarding the wonderous mystery of creation around him."

Watt felt that his new, altered faith should not prevent him from associating with the church and his old friends. He did not understand how a person can be "justly severed from the association of his friends purely on account of a change of conviction and faith if it is his wish to be associated with them." The "presence of his family has been shunned with freezing persistency, and debarred from their usual social contact with neighbors and friends as though they carried with them the poison of the deadly Upas." He thought that after John Taylor had become president that these feelings had changed. "While love sings, and friendship pleads resistance dies." In his addendum he wanted Taylor to know that he was not blameless for his separation from former friends. He was suddenly "crushed, by a public charge of meanness and sly robbery, by one against whose affirmation I had no appeal." He continued, "I could only see my character as an honest man gone among my friends and brethren, my future efforts to do good defeated, over thirty years of labor and struggle a blank, and branded as a scoundrel to the end of my life." He thought he might have taken a more reasonable course, but "I was chagrined and insensed. I did not take time to reason, but in strict accordance with my impulsive nature kicked over the bucket and spilled the milk." After this, "My mind gradually lost its fixedness to the one purpose, and merged into a state of mobility. I have wandered over the arid and hopeless wastes of infidelity, I have wrestled with the ghostly mirage, and to me, unprofitable manifestations of modern spiritualism. . . . I have looked upon the hard cold and polished surface of exact sciense, to find at last some comfort and spiritual food in the more inductive revealments of true philosophy."

He said he had to write this letter to satisfy himself. He told Taylor, "If I am again permitted to enrole myself as a member of your church I may do so as an honest man, and not as a sneak and an embicile." He finally finished the letter and sent it off to Salt Lake City.[37] He never was rebaptized.[38] He died on October 24, 1881, at his farm in Kaysville and was buried in the Kaysville cemetery.[39]

5

Sermons Delivered by Orson Pratt On Board the *Ellen Maria*

The Lord is a being of great compassion
and mercy to all of his creatures.
—Orson Pratt, Sermon, March 9, 1851

Introduction to Orson Pratt Sermons

Orson Pratt, a member of the Quorum of the Twelve Apostles of the Church of Jesus Christ of Latter-day Saints, and his wife, Sarah Marinda Bates, traveled with George Watt and company on the *Ellen Maria*.[1] Their children Orson Pratt Jr. (13), Celestia Larissa (9), and Laron (3) are listed with Orson and Sarah Marinda Pratt as members of the James W. Cummings 1851 overland trail company and were almost certainly also on board the ship.[2] Another child, daughter Marintha Althera Pratt, died on board ship on May 24, 1851. Pratt had been serving as mission president of the British Mission. During the voyage Pratt spoke to the company of Latter-day Saints on board the *Ellen Maria* on at least three different Sundays, February 16 and March 2 and 9, 1851. George D. Watt reported these sermons in Pitman shorthand, but there is no indication that he ever transcribed them. This is possibly the only verbatim account of a sermon delivered on a Latter-day emigrant ship.

Shorthand written from dictation, reporting a speaker's words, is usually less carefully written than shorthand compositions, notes, journals, and drafts of letters, where the writer could take time to write the characters and to include the vowels, which were written as diacritics. A reporter often struggled to keep up with a speaker, and the poorer quality of the shorthand reflects that struggle. Watt's shorthand for these three sermons is more difficult to transcribe than his shorthand of the journal and letter, where he had more time to carefully form the shorthand symbols.

February 16, 1851[3]
[Sermon delivered to Latter-day Saint emigrants on board the *Ellen Maria* on Sunday, February 16, 1851. George Watt kept a detailed journal of this journey in a separate notebook. Date on notebook is Sunday, February 15, 1851, which is incorrect.]
[Image 1; cover of notebook]

Contents
4 discourses by Elder Orson Pratt upon the ocean.[4]
[Image 2]

Elder Toone[5] lost an infant child[6] this morning, <who died> about six o'clock, aged 11 weeks. [She was] feeble from birth, [and] unable to suck.

Sunday, February 15. The saints assembled at the usual hour, half past ten, minding to the ship time. Elder Toone opened the meeting by singing page 132 "Sweet is the Work, my God, my God, [*sic*] to Sing thy Praise, Give Thanks and Sing," etc. Brother Toone prayed as follows.[7] O God, our Father in Heaven, this morning we present before thee thanks giving [for thy] mercies unto us. Thou hast [got us?] in a privileged calling. We ask thee, in the name of Jesus Christ, whatever impediment [may be in us], please look over and grant, [that] we may find acceptation. Since we have been on board this vessel, we have been comforted and tried, yet thou hast always sustained us, and we thank thee for all thy goodness unto us. We say [to] thee this morn, whatever [has] been wrong among us, forgive us; find favor so that we may enjoy ourselves, and have the privilege [of the] communion of thy spirit. We are dependent upon and live through thy providence continually. In thy mercy, take us safely across this ocean and land us in New Orleans. Thou knowest the tediousness of this journey. We submit to thee. Take charge of this vessel, even the captain of this vessel, that they may have power and wisdom to take this vessel and any concerned. Bless Brother Orson before thee, and [that] all [may be] comforted and

Fig. 15. *Orson Pratt*. Created by Frederick Piercy. Courtesy of Church History Library.

edified thereby. Bless his family, and bless our president, Brother Watt. Grant, O Lord, [that] thy Spirit may dwell in him in all his counsel. Let a gracious blessing [be] through all. Let this company feel thou [hast] blessed us in all our circumstances. Thou knowest we have some little confidence in thy mercies past. Increase in us a greater hope, not to be over come with temptations, [that] evils [not] gain the ascendancy over us, [that the] Holy Ghost [will] preside over us, [and that we will] go forth in safety. Many prayers we desire to offer unto thee for our friends, but we sum up all with thankfulness, and ask thee to hear us, through Jesus Christ, amen.

Sung page 132 "O What Triumph Shall I Rise," remainder of the same hymn.

Elder Pratt spoke: I will endeavor, brethren and sisters, to speak to you for a short time this morning, inasmuch as [the] [Image 3] Lord [will] assist me so to do. I feel very unwell, in consequence of being tossed about upon the waves so, and in consequence of feeling in this way, I may not be able to call in my thoughts and my mind so as to speak to your edification, unless the Lord shall see fit, by his wisdom and goodness, to remove this affliction from me, and give me his Spirit to call in my thoughts. I feel truly thankful to the Lord this morning, that it is as well with us as it is. Notwithstanding we have been retarded in the forepart of our voyage, yet no accident has befallen us, and the Lord has, in a great measure, recovered us from our sickness, and the most of us are blessed with health. And for these favors we have reason to rejoice, and be thankful to the Almighty in whose hands we are, for we are constantly in his hands, and he is a very merciful and kind Being, [if?] it were not so, our many imperfections and faults would bring upon [us] great trouble and distress. But the Lord is a Being that knows how to succor those that are weak, and those that are imperfect, and he knows how to bear with our infirmities. And he has proclaimed himself, even in the earliest days of the world, as a God, and long suffering, full of compassion and mercy, and a God that pardons the transgressions of his people. It is because of his mercy, therefore, that we are placed as we are at this present time, for surely it could not be in consequence of our great righteousness that the blessings of heaven rest upon [us], for all of us, from the highest to the least, [are] more or less imperfect.

We have been surrounded by the traditions, the false and corrupt traditions, and a corrupt and perverse religion. These traditions have done more or less influence upon our minds, and when we think we are free from traditions, it is because we have not a very great portion of the Spirit to discern the real condition of ourselves. I presume there is not a man in the Church of Latter-day Saints that is entirely free of the false and corrupt traditions of his forefathers. We, all of us, are more or less subject to them, and they have power and influence over us, but we do not realize it. But the Lord intends, by degrees, to sanctify his people. And for this purpose he is gathering them together from the different nations of the earth, that they may be assembled [Image 4] in one body, and there have the privilege of being instructed, not by the wisdom of man, not by the learning of man, but by the inspiration of his Holy Spirit, by the same principle that the ancient saints received instruction, namely the spirit of revelation and prophecy. That is the principle, and the only principle, by which any people of God can be sanctified, can be purified, can be [principled?] and prepared to inherit the mansions of glory, and to dwell in the presence of those pure and exalted beings in heavens above. There is no other principle, no other medium of sanctification, independent of this. It is by the spirit of revelation that all the ancient saints, it was by the school of revelation, rather, that all the ancient saints were purified, inasmuch as they were faithful to the end.

And if it were not for the spirit of revelation, the church of God could have no existence upon face of the earth. It can only be continued by this principle, and when the principle of revelation ceases from among men, then the church of Christ ceases from among men. When prophets, and revelators, and inspired men cease from the earth, the [church?] of God ceases from the earth. According to this provision, there has been no church of God in existence on the earth for many centuries. This is the real belief of the Latter-day Saints. We believe that the church of God has been extinct from the earth for many generations, and we believe that ~~it has~~ ceased with the spirit of revelation, for surely there is no way by which we can distinguish the church of God from the churches built up by man, through his own wisdom, only[8] by this principle. The Bible, any way, gives us no information of a people called the people of God, unless [there are] prophets and revelators among them.

We might begin away back, to the very beginning of man, and trace the history of man and the history of the dealings of God with man, down for 4 thousand years and upwards, and during the whole of that period of time, we find [that when] God had a people upon earth, he spoke with them, [sent] angels to them, unfolded the visions of eternity to them, [and] had prophets and revelators speak by the inspiration of his Spirit among [them]. But for about 17 hundred years past, the people opined the Great Mover has concluded [his work, and the] gate is charged. They do not say it directly [but] indirectly, [Image 5] by telling the people [that] God has Christian churches on earth, and at same time tell the people those Christian churches have no visions, no revelations, any prophets unknown. All these these[9] occur[ed] [to] the people 18 hundred years ago. What right have we to believe such nonsense, to think, if we will think, the churches of God will have no accordance with the Bible, not agreed with the Bible, no importance for them to be the church of God.

Well, no, it is no small thing for people to prophesy, to be bound by revelations. Why? Because of the responsibility that people [are] placed under, before the heavens [and] before God. The people [who] have lived without prophets, [or the] visions of eternity, are not under the same responsibility as the church of God is. Why? Because the Lord will judge mankind according to the law presented before them. And when there is no message sent from God by living prophets and revelators, the people cannot reject any message [or] [remark?] unless it is sent. Consequently, those churches that call themselves Christian churches are not under the same responsibility as the church of God is. The Lord will not, on the day of judgment, will not condemn [them] for rejecting a message [that was not sent]. Consequently, [they are] not under condemnation, so far as that is concerned. The condemnation lies with this present generation. God has opened the heavens, [and] sent his angels from on high [with as] important messages to men that ever saluted the ears of mortals, namely, that book called the Book of Mormon, revealing the dealing of God with the people upon the great western hemisphere. This vast light and knowledge [has] burst forth upon this generation, and every soul that rejects this important message, they reject something that will prove their condemnation in the great judgment day. It could not be otherwise.

A great many people suppose the Latter-day Saints [to be] outside of [the] church, while we tell them the same as [the] ancients in their day, [the] same story they told the people in their day. The Apostles, when they were sent forth, had to tell the people of their generation that not a solitary individual could be saved and reject their message. All the prophets that lived before the [apostolic?] church was organized [gave] the same through revelations [of] life unto all, life to those [Image 6] who received them. Just so it is in our day: when God speaks from the heavens, he speaks for the benefit of all. If he would condemn one man for rejecting a message in the last days, [he would] condemn all the children of man upon the same principle. After all, though the Lord will condemn them, theirs will not be near so great as they [who] receive the message and [then] turn away from it. They are the individuals [who] [have had?] responsibilities placed upon them, of all people under the whole heavens.

The sectarian world may reject the Book of Mormon. [If they do], they will be condemned, yet in the eternal world their punishment will not be the same as they who have embraced the fullness of the gospel, and hardened their hearts against [it], and turned from its sacred and holy principles. I make these few observations in that the saint may have a [realizing?] sense of the responsibility placed upon them. There is no situation, no circumstance in which you can be placed, that will relieve you from the responsibility of the everlasting covenant which you have entered into at the time you were baptized, and came into the church. It matters not how trying your circumstances may be, what difficulties you may be surrounded with: there is nothing that will justify any of us in turning away from the truth, and rebelling against [it], and if we do so, our condemnation will far exceed the condemnation of those [who] never received the truth.

This is plainly revealed and set forth in one of the revelations that God gave to his servant Joseph Smith by vision in the year 1832.[10]

In this great vision that was made manifested, the Lord unfolded to Joseph Smith and Sidney Rigdon, both at the same time, different classes of people [in] different situations, who have passed from this life. And it was made manifest to them that those who received the fullness of the gospel and the gift of the Holy Ghost, [and] had their sins forgiven them, and after all this shall turn away from the holy covenant, and transgress, and deny the Holy Ghost, and do this willfully, [there is] no forgiveness for them. And that their punishment [would] exceed the punishment of all other beings: no other creatures [will] be exposed to as great [a punishment] as creatures of this description. The reason of this [however/way?] [behooves?]: it is because [of] the great light that men have, they can sin in perpetuity to this light. But, says one, [after?] a Latter-day Saint falls into transgression [is there] any forgiveness [Image 7] to that person? Yes, [if he will] repent with all his heart. If we through our weakness fall into transgression, and confess our sins and forsake [them], we can obtain forgiveness.

There are certain sins which are called the sins against the Holy Ghost, and there are other sins that are not sins against the Holy Ghost. Well now, supposing a person does not not [*sic*] repent, who has not sinned against the Holy Ghost, [but rather] continues to commit sins, and does this through the weakness of his nature, and will not repent. They will have to be punished in the eternal world, in the same manner as they who sin against the Holy Ghost. I might mention, for instance, David. We all know the great transgression into which he fell. He was a man who possessed light and knowledge. He understood the commandments of God. The Holy Spirit had been imparted to him. He had been filled with the spirit of prophecy, and yet, in the face, the eyes of all this, he fell through a temptation . It is was[11] not done maliciously. [He] fell through a temptation that did not expose him to the unpardonable sin, but he placed himself in a condition [that] he could not be forgiven in this life. No, for he not only committed adultery, but [he] also placed Uriah in a situation to be murdered. This placed David in a condition [that he] could not receive a forgiveness of that sin in this world; he had to be punished in the eternal worlds for that transgression. [We read in] 2 Acts a quotation concerning David: Thou wilt not leave my soul in hell, neither suffer thy Holy One to see corruption.[12] He assumes, then, that David's soul was to be cast down to hell, but saw that he would eventually be redeemed from hell. But if he had sinned against the Holy Ghost, there could not have been any redemption ~~from~~ for committing [that sin]. [The] Apostle Peter says that Peter[13] had not ascended unto heaven; his spirit had been separated from his body [for] more than a thousand years. Where was he all this time? He was suffering the penalty of his transgression. I want the Latter-day Saints to understand this: there are some sins, [that] if we do them, we [may may?] have to humble ourselves before the Lord, ever so much, in the eternal worlds. We have to be punished for those sins.

Says one, [do] you believe in redemption for man in an iniquity? [Image 8] Yes. The Lord is a being that constructs his plan upon a remarkably magnanimous principle. His plans extends into all worlds, and into all eternity. But there are certain creatures that the plan of redemption never can reach: the devil and his angels, and those that become his son by sinning against the Holy Ghost. Redemption never can reach these creatures throughout all the ages of eternity. But others, like with David, after they have been punished in the eternal world sufficiently long, redemption will reach them. Their souls will not be left in hell.

Another instance besides David, [but] before I refer to this, I will make a few remarks upon a certain principle that perhaps some of the Saints be ignorant of.[14] The sealing principle, being sealed upon unto the day of redemption. It is not every one that attains [to] this principle. There is a certain way, and a certain ordinance, and a certain authority that is necessary to be exercised by the restoration of the priesthood, that this may be secured unto men. In ancient times, some of the people of God attained this. The Corinthians and Ephesians had rendered themselves proved in the sight of God. They had kept his commandments [and] walked in obedience to his ordinances. They had attained to the sealing power of the holy priesthood, [which] had been placed upon their head by proper authority. Now, after a person has obtained this power, suppose they fall into transgression? After that, what [are] the consequences? They must be punished for it. Can you bring any example? Certain[ly; there is a] case in the Corinthian church. That church had obtained this seal, and after it had been placed upon [them], some of them fell into a gross transgression: they committed fornication. Paul writes an epistle to them: what [did he] say about that person? Did he say that such a person, if he repented, should obtain forgiveness? No, he says in the name of the Lord Jesus Christ, when you are gathered together, and my Spirit, to deliver such a one unto Satan for the destruction of the flesh, [that the] spirit [may be] saved in the day of the Lord Jesus.[15] [This is a] curious kind of doctrine. He had not much charity, according to the ideas of this generation. He knew that, after the sealing power was upon his head, after having been sealed, [there was] no [Image 9] forgiveness for him in this life. [He] exhorted that such a one be delivered to Satan etc. What [would] become of the spirit? Until the day of Lord Jesus, [it would] be in torment in [the] flesh. The devil [would] have power over him in this life., but at the same time to have power over his spirit when that day come, the day even spoken of by the prophet, a thousand years of rest, the day of the Lord. One day with the Lord is as a thousand [with man].[16] It is the seven[th] thousand years, the millennium period. When that day comes, the Corinthians that had been delivered over to Satan, their spirits [will] all [be] redeemed from the buffeting of Satan, because of the seal placed upon [them and they will] be saved in that day.

This ought to be a warning to the Latter-day Saint, lest they fall into these great sins. There is a responsibility placed upon [them] to be more strictly upright, honest, [and] obedient to the commandments of God than any other people upon the face of the whole earth. Suppose [that] after we have obtained some of the blessings of the everlasting covenant, which you will yet have to receive, for that is the object of Lord [in] gather[ing] his people together, which they never could receive scattered abroad through the nations, blessings that pertain to the last dispensation of [the] fullness of times, and ordinances that are to be revealed, in order to prepare a people for the day of the Lord, for the millennium period of glory and peace. When you become acquainted with these ordinances, if you should then turn away from righteousness and commit fornication, or any of those enormous sins, the Lord will deal with you very differently than he would with mankind [in general] for the same sins, after so much information and light has been given to the saints of the Most High.

There is a certain class of creatures that I will now mention, that are out of the church, that have no right to come into the church, the Lord would not receive them into his church. It is those that commit murder and shed innocent blood, against law and testimony, and [when?] wickedly and maliciously do it. As [an] example of this transgression, we may refer you to the murderers of Jesus Christ. They have no right to come into the church of God, [or] to be baptized. It was instituted for the remission of sins. Those wicked murderers could not have their sins remitted, [or] anything to do with baptism, as Peter said when he preached to them in the 3 or 4 [Image 10] chapter of Acts. He exhorts them in this manner: Repent ye therefore, and be converted, that your sins may be blotted out, when in the times of refreshing shall come from the presence of the Lord, and he shall send Jesus Christ.[17] What? Are we to wait until he sends Jesus Christ, before our sins can be blotted out? Yes, that is the language of Peter to those murderers: repent and be converted, that your sins may be be [*sic*] blotted out, when the times of refreshing shall come from the presence of the Lord; and he shall send Jesus Christ. It seems [that] they had to wait a long period before their sins could be blotted out. <Says one>, [what] would be the use of their repentance? It would be this: [to] get their sins blotted out when he send[s] Jesus Christ. If they did not repent and be converted, [they] could not be forgiven; [they would have to] wait a longer period. I thought ~~conversion~~ when a man was converted and [his] sins was forgiveness.[18] Forgiveness is one thing, and conversion another thing. Those persons were not to be forgiven, but to be converted. Whatsoever they had ~~done~~ that was evil, if he would repent, [he would] be forgiven when Jesus Christ came, if they had not, [repented, they would have to] wait 3 or 4 thousand years, until after the thousand years ended.

The Lord is a being [that] dwells upon principles, just the same as we do; and he dwells upon wise and just principles, and he has ordained laws and ordinances that will set the condition of all the human family, that have not committed the unpardonable [sin], to all [who would] be saints. He has given a law that [who/all?] has not committed that sin, says one of the revelations in the Book of Doctrine and Covenants. [There are] different bounds and conditions, according to the nature of the law and circumstances. All those laws pertaining to the people in the last days are to be made all acquainted to the saints. How could they understand the laws, and penalties, and bounds, and conditions, suited to the different capacities of the children of men, without revelation? No, they cannot; revelation is needed, and if the saints are to judge the world, they must become acquainted with the law. They must understand the penalties of the law, the conditions and bounds of the law, and administer it accordingly.

What more is it necessary for me to say this morning? My mind is full. I do not know of anything of greater importance than the nature of the law[s] which govern on the ship *Ellen Maria*, and its bounds and conditions, for if we abide in the conditions of these laws, we shall be prepared to abide in the conditions of greater law hereafter. [If we] cannot keep these laws, how can it be possible [for us to] keep greater laws. I do not see this. The saints are obedient. I do not think you could find any <company> [of] people in the nations of the old world, except the Latter-day Saints, more faithful. [Image 11] Should there be any individual who will not be faithful to the instructions of of [*sic*] Brother Watt and his counsel, I want them to put the coat on. I do not want anybody else to wear it. Understand, if you cannot abide the rules of the ship, and [the] laws given us, how can it be expected [that] you can abide the celestial law? In this, the bright region above, where all is strict harmony, we will find [that] we shall have a great deal of [*illegible*], and complain[ing], and aching, and knocking in the rough places, before we shall be able to abide that law. Take the very best of us: we have all got to trim ourselves, and throw away every thing that is corrupt, unholy, and impure, to sanctify our hearts, [and] to be perfectly honest before God and before one another, and to deal justly with our neighbor, with our brother, and with our sister. What says the scripture? He that is unjust in the least, is unjust in the greater things. If you see a person unjust in one farthing, and undertakes to cheat his neighbor even one farthing, though the farthing may not be of much consequence, he that will be unjust in the least, will be in greater things. So let every man be perfectly just in all of his dealings with his fellow Christian, [and] be perfectly just before God, that the principle of dishonesty may have no place in our heart. [This is] what we have got to come to, if we wish to enjoy those beings [who] inhabit the eternal worlds.

The Lord [will] have a people to do his will on earth, [the] same as it is done in the eternal worlds. In order to accomplish this, we have got to watch over every disposition of our mind, and [to] bring our own into subjection to the law of God, to subject our tempers, our angry feelings, and to seek the welfare of each other. We have started, all of us, to go to the mountains. We are on our way. Some of you may not have [sufficient] means to carry you through, but you have got your faces set Zionward. It is your intention to accumulate [the] means to pursue your journey farther. What is your object? It is to obey the commandments of heaven, to fulfill the requirements of any revelation, to fulfill the predictions of [the] ancient prophets, namely, to gather [out] from Babylon. That is a very laudable undertaking, to seek to fulfill the commandments of God. He [Image 12] has an object in view: he intends to have his people gather in one, in order that he may show himself to them in a marvelous manner, in power, emitting advice by the voice of prophets, inspired men, [and] angels sent from the eternal world. He intends to explain to you what his will is, that you may become more and more perfect in his sight, and [be] prepared for the glorious day of the advent in the heavens. Let all the Saints begin here, while on the ship *Ellen Maria*, [to] bring every feeling of their hearts in concert to counsels given to them from time to time.

Let me inquire: has all the saints been obedient to the counsels that brother has given you last Sabbath? Every one can reflect in their own minds, and ask themselves if they have been obedient or not. This was the captain's desire, that none but the second cabin passengers have the privilege of promenading upon this deck. Has this been complied with? Answer this for yourselves. Again, this was my desire [and] Brother Watt's desire that there should be prayers on the ship at specific times. Certain rules been appointed in order to carry out this [call?]. Do they all gather at the sounding of the horn, and leave minor circumstances, except some of those who are appointed to particular work? Or are there some who say it will do no good. [I will] let you answer this question. Are there some who creep into their beds and become careless.[19] All of these things. [I will] let you answer for your self, all of these things, [and the] rules and laws of the ship ~~little~~ *Ellen Maria*.

May the Lord bless you, brothers and sisters, and may he give you and all of us that meek and humble spirit that is willing to harken to good wholesome advice, and may he inspire our hearts with earnest prayer and supplication, that when we call upon his name, he may hear us. I want to live [so] that when I call upon [him], he will open his ears, and answer our prayers. When the Lord does not answer our prayers, some thing [is] out of the way, that is, if our prayers are reasonable. The revelations of God says: what so ever we ask, it shall be granted to us. Our prayers [are] not answered [if] we are not so diligent as we ought to be. I take these remarks home to myself: when my prayers ~~not~~ are granted something [*illegible*], I have myself to blame, and nobody else. Having said these few remarks, [I] give way for others.

Brother Toone administered the sacrament to the people. [Image 13]

Brother Watt spoke, after which Elder Pratt introduced the affair of the butter and cheese. He ordered 3 pounds of butter.[20] And 2 pounds of cheese, [but] they had got it reversed: 2 pounds of butter

and 3 pounds of cheese.[21] But the ~~butter~~ 3 pounds of cheese is not as good as 3 pounds of butter. I am indebted to the passengers of this ship 3 ½ <d>. This I can pay here to Brother Watt or another person or, when I get to New Orleans, I can get small change and give it to you individually. The way this mistake was made was this: I have sent out about 20 ships. In looking over the last 2 ships, I found they had made the same mistake. I note[ed] to them, and told them to put in the same amount of provisions as before. The mistake made by the line was made ~~by~~ with the other two ships. Brother Watt was mentioning that some of the passengers would not mind the 3 ½ or the whole amount of money for the benefit of some poor; [it] will be all the same to me. It was concluded by the unanimous vote of the company present that the four pounds seven shillings be consecrated to the poor who cannot help themselves up the river from New Orleans, except two pounds of it which was loaned by Elder Watt to the company for oil, which was to be paid to him out of this sum. 19 shillings Brother Pratt gave to the company, which was made out ~~by~~ for cordage to [hold?][22] the luggage. The meeting came to a close by singing "Praise God from whom All Blessings Flow" and a blessing[23] from Elder Watt. Elder Toone's child was buried after the meeting.
[Image 13]

Sunday March 2nd 1851 latitude longitude

Elder Toone opened the meeting by giving out the hymn on the 81st page, "Shepherd Divine"[24] etc. The saints are cheerful, all out in their Sunday habiliments. Elder Watt joined in prayer for the company. Sung again page 126, "Ye Sons of Man a Feeble Race Exposed to Every Snare"[25] etc.

ELDER PRATT

These brethren and sisters, perhaps, would feel better to seat themselves; that would give an opportunity to those that are the most [Image 14] distant to hear better. The Lord has favored us with another opportunity of assembling ourselves on the deck of this vessel. And we have reason to rejoice in his goodness in preserving our lives, and in bestowing that degree of health which the most of us are permitted to enjoy this morning. There is no [principles?] knowledge [or] mercy bestowed upon mankind, save it be that it comes from God. He is the great author of all blessings and goodness [which are] bestowed on man; but we do not always realize this as we ought. We are often times, when blessed with a long continuation of health, apt to forget that he is the bestower of health, and do not give thanks unto him for this blessing, until we are deprived of it, and then we are stirred up in the remembrance of the Lord, that is, if we have a disposition to serve him. There are some that do not remember him in sickness, [in] health, [in] prosperity, [or in] tribulation. But I am speaking of those that have a regard for the great Author of their existence: they are apt to be forgetful of his mercies. I judge this from the history of the people of God in all past ages.

We are apt to be forgetful, too, of our own weakness, of our own imperfections and follies, and not to honor the hand of God in all things. This seems to have been the case, in a peculiar manner, with the children of Israel, when the Lord stretched forth his hand to deliver them from their bondage, and bring them in a goodly land promised to their forefathers, which he had made a covenant with their forefathers, that they and children should receive for an inheritance, not only in this life, but in the life to come. When the Lord stretched out his arm in signs and in wonders and in mighty deeds, and delivered Israel from Egyptian bondage, they soon forgot that it was the hand of the Lord, [the] God of their fathers, that had delivered them. And their history has been handed down to us as [an] example, as instances of the frailty and weakness of man kind.

These things we ought often to meditate upon, lest we view with contempt, in our hearts, their conduct, [and] follow [the] same ourselves. It is true [that] we have not seen the hand of Lord made manifest as they did. We have not seen as many miracles [as] they did. We have not seen [Image 15] the Lord displaying his power in the destruction of our enemies, in dividing waters, in sending plague upon our enemies, and in showing forth his glory upon the earth, as he did in ancient times. We have not had the privilege of seeing it to the great extent [that they did]. What would we [do], if we should have this privilege? Would we do as they did? Well, perhaps, the most of us would not, but if we judge according to the weakness and frailty of mankind, there are many of the inhabitants of earth that would do as they did, place them under similar circumstances. We are apt to think and say, that if we could only see the Lord manifest his power as he did in ancient [times], that we should never forget him after that. If we could only see the water divided, and have the privilege of walking through [on] dry shod, if we could see our enemies overwhelmed in the waters, we ~~should~~ <think> we should never forget the Lord.

How was it with Israel? A few days after they came to the foot of Mount Sinai, the Lord displayed signs of [his] power in a remarkable, wonderful manner. He told them to put bounds round about, for he, himself, intended to descend upon the mount. He descended with a cloud, lightnings, [the] voice of [the] trumpet, and the whole mountain trembled, and shook to its center by the power of Jehovah. And he spoke by the voice of the trumpet, out of the midst [of the] burning fire, and out [of the] midst of [the] cloud from the top of [the] mount. And as the trumpet waxed louder, and louder, and louder, the children of Israel trembled and feared. And the Lord spoke in the audience ~~in~~ of all the congregation of Israel, and delivered ten commandments, so all heard his voice that were capable of understanding. They all heard it, and so great was the power that the children of Israel came before Moses to beseech that the Lord no more speak with them. [They] entreated that Moses [to] speak with the Lord, and then [to] come and speak with them. The Lord heard their entreaties, and no more spoke with them by his own voice. But he spoke with Moses: [he] called him on the mount [and] kept him there for many days. And Moses stood in the presence of God, [and] beheld the Lord write upon tables of stone, and delivered to Israel the [*illegible*][26] oracles. [Image 16]

The Lord continued on the mount. But in the presence of all this power and glory, the children of Israel gathered together their ear rings, and other jewels, and gold, and melted it together and fashioned it in [the] manner of [a] calf, after [which] they fell down and worshiped it, and said: This be thy gods, O Israel, that brought thee up [out of the] land of Egypt.[27] There [was] the glory of God upon the mount, they could behold it, and yet in the face and eyes of this, they fell down and worshiped a golden calf, and called it their god. Now, if the Lord had not been a long suffering Being, what [would he have] done on that occasion? Why, his anger [would have] waxed hot, [and they] would have [been] swept off, the whole of them that fell unto this idolatry. [He is a] jealous God; when he sees the people worship [an]other being, [he] feels angry with them. He was angry with 'em, and intended to destroy them: Let me alone, [that I] may destroy them.[28] [He] said to Moses [that] he would spare him, and raise up of his seed a great nation [that] would serve [him]. He did not like to have it, so he pled with the Lord that he would not suffer his anger to burn against his people, [that he would] remember them for his covenant sake. The Lord was entreated by Moses, although he sent upon them a severe affliction, because of their idolatry.

He [Moses] came out of the mount and saw them worshiping the calf. He partook of the same spirit [that was] in the bosom of Almighty: his anger waxed hot [and] burned in the bosom of Moses, and he considered them unworthy of the sacred articles in his hand. [He] threw them down, [and they] broke to pieces. That was the end of the first covenant [that God] made with Israel: it was broken. That was the end of certain blessing[s] made on behalf of Israel. They were taken away from them, and that generation and [the] generation following did not enjoy them. What were they? [The] plan of salvation in its fullness. What [was] given in its stead? For the Lord called up Moses [a] few days afterwards, [and] gave [him] another set of tables, [with] something written upon [them]. What was it? There was the ten commandments, written on the first. And [he] introduced, instead of the gospel, a law of carnal commandments, [because of the] hardness of their hearts. [Image 17] And, instead of having the same gospel Jesus preached, he gave them a law after their own hearts. Instead of showing mercy, as under the gospel, it was to be an eye for an eye, and very strict. [*illegible*][29] A law, Ezekiel tells us in [the] 20 chapter, law not good etc.[30]

Do you suppose all [were] lost and damned? No. The many yet that should not attain to the glory of those [who] embraced the gospel, [and] had manifestations, [but] because of their great transgression [they were] deprived of the highest glory, [which] comes by means of [the] fullness of [the] gospel. A law was given, [if] kept, that introduced them in to a partial degree of glory. How do we know in this matter? It is the Lord may dwell ~~in~~ with his kingdom, if not in the same manner, in some respects, resemble his dealing in ancient times. He may do it, for the Latter-day Saints are apt to harden their hearts [as did the] former people of God. [I] do not say this reproving[ly], for my brethren and sisters present. I do truly believe, since I [have] been on board of this vessel, [that the] great majority [of the] people are truly the sons and daughters of God. I believe they are faithful, [and] as far as they understand the counsel and law of God, so far I believe they will endeavor to perform the same. I have no feelings in my heart to chastise the Saints before me. There may be exceptions, there may be a few here and there [who are] not as faithful as [they] ought to be. Therefore, let in the Holy Ghost, that influences [us] to [be] pure, and striving to do right. Let them not think I chastise them in these remarks; I say it only that we may always bear these things [in] our heart [and] minds.

[Even] if we are ever so pure, we do not know: in time to come, we may be placed in circumstances somewhat similar [to] that children [of] Israel were. We have reason to expect this, because the Lord has revealed this to us in revelations given through the Prophet Joseph, [in the] Book [of] Covenants, that he intended to lead this people as he led them in ancient times. He says, in [a] revelation given in 1834: I will raise up a Moses, and that he would deliver his church and in the last days from bondage and oppression, as he delivered his people in ancient [Image 18] times.[31] The Lord did not say that Joseph Smith was [the] one he speaks of. One in future: I will raise up one like a Moses etc. Would this be one not known to us, when it will indeed come to pass? When it does, let us all be prepared to remember what took place when the Lord redeemed Israel in ancient times, by meditating while in our afflictions, or any circumstances whatever, that when that day shall come, we may not fall as they fell in ancient times.

The Lord is a being that has compassion upon people according to that[32] understanding. Where they did not understand much, he did not send upon [them] so severe chastisement. The Lord never has sent a plague, as he did upon the children of Israel, burn thousands of them in a few minutes, [if it] had not been of the great power of God having been made manifest. If the day shall come that the Lord shall manifest his power among the Latter-day Saints, as he did among in ancient times, then look out for the transgressor to fall, and that speedily, for [he] did not walk according to the law made manifest. There are indeed persons on board of this vessel, [who], if suffered to live [to be] old men and women, will see the revelations [given] through his servant Joseph come to pass. You are now gathering unto the inner portions of North America. [Do you] suppose [that] we are always going to remain there? And I should not be surprised if the Lord, in his providence, did not keep us there many years. How long, I know not, but I look for a fulfillment of [the] sayings of the Lord, and I believe they will come to pass in their times and seasons. He says, by the keys he has given, his people [are to] be led in last days, and no power shall stay his hand. This [was] told ~~in~~ us in Book of Covenants [in] 1831: by the keys he had given and bestowed upon the people in those days his people are to be led[33] and no power is to stay the hand,[34] and the wisdom in leading them.

Remember that we have been deprived of our rights, I mean the kingdom of God, the rights granted to us by the constitution of United States of America, to emigrate and settle where we please. [Image 19] We have been deprived of the free citizens [of the] United States, [of] lands we paid them for. We have been driven, as weasels in the mountains, when our enemies expect us to perish. Has the Lord forgotten all these things? No the[35] Lord has a [*illegible*] with that nation, and they cannot get from under the yoke. And [the] Lord has decreed and determined certain things in regard to that nation [that it] cannot escape. If they should repent, and many of them, it would not frustrate the decrees [of the] Almighty [*illegible*] [the] people of God. But what are they? He has decreed in the Book of Mormon. Three or four thousand years ago, he made certain decrees concerning every nation that should inherit the land of America, from that time hence forth and forever. The decree was this: that what ever nation should be brought upon the face of that choice land [that] we call America, should serve the living God or they should be swept off, when the fullness of his wrath comes upon them.[36] And[37] he tells [them that] the fullness of his wrath should come upon them when they [are] ripened in iniquity.[38] He has fore told there of the persecution we have endured in Missouri and Illinois, in print ~~before~~ for the nations to look upon. The Book of Mormon was in print, and it ~~was~~ is there decreed, that the blood of the saints should cry to [the] heavens for vengeance upon that nations [*sic*].[39] Now, according to that prediction, the church of the saints [was] established after the book was printed, and the blood of the saints has called for vengeance after the book was printed. How could a man, [who was] not a prophet, foretell an event of this kind, ~~and bring~~ and it come to pass? Where was there a nation so unlikely to do this as the United States, before the year 1830, their [*illegible*] sons have not suffered a martyrdom. Where is there a whole people that has suffered for their religion? And, according to the constitution of that nation, unlikely come to pass. And [it is] most remarkable that some of the weak saints could believe, and that suppose that a whole mass of thousands of citizens been exiled, and wrote down threats, and rendered them no protection whatever, notwithstanding all their petitions. [The] Book of Mormon [will] be fulfilled. Woe unto them by whom those persecutions came, [Image 20] they have got to suffer. How [will they] suffer? [They will] fight among themselves, while the saints be minding their own business. Not a long [while, and] you will see the south and north states in war with each other, civil war, what will ruin [the] rest [of the] country. This will just as surely come to pass as the Lord God reigns, and rules, and lives in the heavens above: they will destroy each other. That nation, that is now such a flourishing nation, whose fame [has] gone abroad, they are to be brought down exceeding low, and humbled in the dust.

What about the saints inheriting their lands? When the Lord destroys that nation, it will be time enough for them to go back, and enter upon their peaceable possession. When that takes place, then [will] be the time of the Lord's power. The day of the Lord's power has not yet arrived. True, you have seen the sick healed. You have seen the power of God made manifest in the case of this cholera. You have seen all manner of sickness and diseases cured, and truly this is a great mercy to the saints, [and] reason to rejoice, that he has made manifest his power in this way. What is this, compared with the power [that is] promised to be [made] manifest? The day of the Lord's power will come after the times of the gentiles [are] fulfilled. The Lord says that Jerusalem [is] to be trodden down under the feet of [the] gentiles, until their times come in. [He] tells all Israel [will] be saved after the times of [the] gentiles come in.[40] When that day comes, when the servants in this church are now to go and hunt up Israel, etc., when that day comes, but not until then.

The day of the Lord's power will come that you will, Israel, see the hand of the Lord made manifest, and the Latter-day Saints also numbered with Israel, as conspicuously and in glory and manner was brought up their fathers in land of Egypt. [They will] bring [the] same testimony. [I] refer you to 11 chapter prophecy of Isaiah, [which] you are now well [acquainted] with: it should be in years well for them. He has predicted [that they will] lift up an ensign for the nations.[41] [The] next sentence "quoted"[42] "four corners of earth".[43] You presume by this that he is going to raise an ensign first. Where will he raise it? He [Image 21] yet tells [us that in] 18 chapter, here. Reads, quoted.[44] Thus we learn [that] there is an ensign to be lifted upon the mountains, before the Lord gathers an assembly [of] Israel. We might judge from this [that] it is not Israel [that] raises it, [as] they are not yet gathered. A few may take part in this, [but] it is to be reared by those of the gentiles. He says, in another place, "[I will] lift up mine hand to the gentiles. Kings shall be their nursing fathers, and queens nursing mothers."[45] From this we learn that this ensign is to be a work performed among the gentiles; they are the ones to lift an ensign that all the nations of the earth [are] called upon to see.

The work has already commenced: the saints [have] been driven into the mountains. What for? In order that the stone might be cut out of the mountains, without the assistance of uninspired men, or, as the prophets says, without hands.[46] The very thing the gentiles supposed [to] crush, the saints, is the very thing [that will] deliver them in the last days. They will lift an ensign upon the mountains. A standard will be reared, and when that time comes, the voice of the Lord from the heavens will be, from the heavens: Go forth, and hunt up my people Israel, assemble the outcasts etc.[47] Then will be the day of the Lord's power. Recall [what the] psalmist says: "Thy people be willing in the day of thy power."[48] [Who] will [be willing] in the day of his power? The children of Israel, [who have] been unwilling for something like 1800 years, will be willing, because they will see the Lord God of their fathers stretching out his hand. Then they will be willing. They will see his glorious miracles, and will turn to the Lord with all his hearts.[49] These [will] bow to the Lord God of the heavens, [who] rules in [the] heavens, and controls the destinies of nations. These [will] bow to him, that [laid] the foundation of this work, [and] commenced to prepare a people for the day of his power.

We have got to be prepared for it, as the children [of Israel] was. They had been in bondage. They were not instructed, so that the day of the Lord's power, manifested by Moses, caused thousands to perish. We have reason to hope that, through the process the Lord is carrying his saints through in these days, to be prepared for the ~~days~~ day of his power. We have reason to suppose [Image 22] trials, etc., prepare them, so [when] the day of the Lord's power comes, [they will be] prepared, and not bring down the Lord's vengeance, as the children of Israel did. There will be exceptions, for the Lord has told, in the 20 chapter of Ezekiel, there will be exceptions. I will repeat the passage: with fury poured out, will I rule over you: and I will bring you out of the nations with an out stretched arm, and I will bring you in the wilderness of the people and there, as I pled with your fathers, there will I plead with you, saith the Lord God.[50] Do not you see, then, that it is the day [of the] Lord's power? Do not you perceive [that] they are to be gathered with a mighty hand, and with an out stretched [arm], ere a fury poured out? What [does] that mean these exceptions? I expect that they do not all keep his commandments. [See the] next verse: [And I will] purge out the rebels [from] among you, but they shall not enter in into the land of Israel, etc.[51] He will get them assembled in the wilderness of the people, and [he] begins to plead with them, like [he] pled with their fathers. Those rebels will rebel against counsels delivered, [and] the consequence will be: I will purge out the rebels among you etc.[52] They did not enter in, in ancient times. When they rebelled, all that generation except Joshua [and] Caleb perish[ed]. Just so, in the last days, when the Lord begins to plead with Israel, thousands of them [will] perish.

Let the Latter-day Saints, then, keep this in remembrance; let them remember the Lord God of Israel. We should. We have [remembered him] to day. Call upon his name. Put aside every thing. Sanctify their hearts, and purify their affections. [Be] virtuous and upright in all of their doing. If [they] do not do this, the day of the Lord's power [will] find them out. If not, [if they do not] cleanse it before then, then they will not be able to stand, and endure, and receive the blessings promised. The Lord is a being not to be mocked: when he speaks, he means what he says. His word is not to be trifled with, especially by those who have entered into a covenant to keep his word, by being buried in the water, [by being] baptized. When they have done this, if they will give way to their passions and feelings, the Lord will hold them strictly to that covenant, [and they will] be purged out, unless they repent. We need to repent, to purify [Image 23] our hearts, [and to] pay more respect to the revelations of God than we have done in days gone [by].

The saints that have gathered into the valleys of mountains; [they have] passed through a great many scenes. How many more [they will] pass [through], I do not know. ~~We have~~ This we have to pray for: if he sees no other way to sanctify ~~them~~ and purify his people, but [through] afflictions continue to chasten them, it is better to be chastened than to lose our glory. The Lord says: I will plead with Zion and with her strong ones.[53] This [he] told them before [they were] driven away from their lands. I will plead with them by sword, plague, [and] by devouring fire, until they shall become sanctified before me. What a glorious promise! If he had not made this promise, I do not know [but] some of the honest hearted [would] become faint hearted, lest the Lord should leave them to themselves and forsake them. Here is promises, [that] instead of the Lord forsaking the latter-day kingdom of God, it is to be pled with by pestilence, by sword, plagues, [and] devouring fire, until they are sanctified before [the] Lord, and purified and prepared to inherit the great blessings [of the] last days.

When the Lord sees [that] we get lifted up, and despise counsel, and not do right in the valley, and not bring up our children, when we get there, he will plead with us. He will not suffer us to go on as the gentile world does; he lets them go on in their own way, and does not chasten them. They are not his people. [With] the Latter-day Saints, not so. [If they] do wrong, the Latter-day Saints [will] be visited with plagues [and] some awful judgments, and in this way he will plead with the strong ones of Zion, until they are prepared to accomplish the purposes of God in the last days. When I get to reflect upon these things. I feel my bones to quake and tremble within me, realizing the greatness, and majesty, and power of the latter-day work that is to roll forth among the nations, and then to look upon our own helplessness. But when I reflect upon the mercy of heaven, [and the] long suffering [of the] Almighty, I take courage. I sit up. Be merciful and bring many to glory to inherit the mansions prepared for them. [Image 24]

We have been a long time tossed upon the mighty deep. What is the reason? Shall we say it is the transgressions of the majority of the Saints upon this vessel? I do not believe it is. If there are individual[s] upon board of this ship that will do wrong, and will not repent, I pray that the [judgment of the] great God [will] rest upon those, and not upon the innocent. I pray he may have compassion on the innocent, and let the judgment come upon them that merit it, and inasmuch as there are those who do wickedly, and fail to repent, I pray the Lord deal with them according to his great mercy, [and] that [he] will deal with [them] according to the merits and mercies of his [Beloved?] Son, if he will repent, and do right before the Lord. These are the feelings of my heart.

And I feel, in the name of Jesus Christ, to bless the saints, and all those who desire to [do] right upon this ship. May the blessings of health rest upon [you]. May the Holy Ghost invigorate your minds, and make you healthy and strong. And whenever the Lord sees fit to send us on our voyage, we will be thankful, [and], if he keep us here tossing about, believing this scripture that all things work together for good to them that will do right. Consequently, [we have] no cause for complaining, or uneasiness, [or] worry. If we are kept here from week to week, why not rejoice in it? But to go further: if he should see fit, [that] we should all perish, and suffer many things before we perish, would not this be a cause of rejoicing? ~~What a happy~~. If he [should] say: [How are/Hour?] be done, what a happy thing, [to be] wafted to his bosom. I feel that I should like to be spared, to do a good work. What [would] I feel about, knew be translated[54] like old father Enoch? I want [that] not to be accomplished. Why? Because I desire to live to see the gospel sent forth to the nations of the earth, that they have no excuse, that it may be a witness to all people in the last days. Consequently, [I have] no desire to be translated, until I can bring many souls to repentance, and bring them to the knowledge of the truth. I view that the Lord will grant me this desire, [that] we may all get through this voyage. The Lord's will be done. I am willing to leave this world when the Lord will, and this [is] [Image 29][55] the desire of every true hearted saint. Having said so much, I will not detain you any longer.

Brother Toone presided over the sacrament. Brother Toone spoke upon the necessity of the saints reading the works and [sparing/storing?] up only from the books of the saints. Elder Watt addressed the meeting quoting some of the precepts of Christ from the ~~2d~~ 5 chapter of Matthew and applying them to our case. A good spirit reigned in the meeting to the end. Blessing by Brother ~~Pratt~~ <Watt>.

Sunday March 9th

Brother Toone opened the meeting by giving out the 209 hymn, 212 page. The morning is fine, and the ship is pressing her way through the briny ocean under a full press of sail, <furled>, from a southeast wind. We have this morning two births. Sister Spicer, whose little son was buried in the ocean yesterday, has received another son this morning. Brother Toone prayed unto the Lord. Sung again the hymn on the 213 page "What Wondrous Things we now Behold, which Were Declared from Days of Old," etc.

ELDER PRATT SPOKE AS FOLLOWS:

Through the great providence of our Heavenly Father, we, all of us [are] blessed with the privilege of beholding another Sabbath day, and are permitted to assemble on this deck for the purpose of worshiping God. I arise to speak a few words, although I, at the present time, do not feel able; my bodily health is such that I do not scarcely feel able to stand before you. But note [that] it is a joy to me, at all times when circumstances will permit, to speak to my fellow mortals upon the great plan of life and salvation. I know that, without the assistance of the Spirit of God, no man living can impart that necessary instruction to the children of men. It matters not how talented he may be, how much wisdom of this world he may have obtained, [or] how much education [and] science he may have treasured up in his heart; all these will avail him nothing unless he has the spirit of truth, the gift of the Holy Ghost, to give utterance to the great and important truths necessary to be communicated to the people. [Image 30] And it is my desire: that the

Lord will at this time pour out his Spirit upon me, or some other that may be present, that we may be enabled to edify one another, and give such instruction and counsel to those who may be present, as shall be beneficial to them to receive, as shall strengthen them in the way of righteousness, build them up in the most holy faith, and increase their confidence towards God, their love towards one another, and their desires to do that which is right.

The Lord is a being of great compassion and mercy to all of his creatures; his hand is ever stretched out over them for their good. He delights in their happiness, although we cannot always understand his ways and his thoughts concerning us, [because] he frequently works in a mysterious manner with the human family. His ways are not as our ways, [as] the ancient prophet says, and his thoughts are not as our thoughts, for as the heavens are higher than the earth, and more glorious than the earth and the things contained therein, so are the ways of the Lord, so are his designs.[56] When compared with the thoughts, the designs, and ways of man, they are infinitely superior to our ways. And doing that which we think is ~~our~~ not for our good, is frequently intended for our good, [and] that which we suppose is a chastisement to us, results in the end as our greatest good. Perhaps it may be a chastisement for the time being, but the Lord designs it for good.

We read in scriptures of truth, that God chastens those whom he loves.[57] We find this to be the case especially concerning the saints [of the] last days. They have been severely chastened, many of them, but this is not a sign that God is displeased with them, because they have been greatly afflicted. It is not because God has forsaken his people, that they are thus in tribulation, for the Lord has told his people in the last days, that after much tribulation cometh the blessing.[58] Some may be overcome by these tribulations. [They] may not be able to endure them. [They] may fall victims to the power of persecution. [They] may be destroyed by their enemies. [They] may perish in their afflictions, so far as their bodily and mortal life is concerned. But notwithstanding this, the Lord loves them, and he will bestow upon them the reward, though they may be called to lay down these mortal bodies, to slumber in the dust, or to slumber in [Image 31] the mighty ocean, until the morning of resurrection. This is not a sign that the Lord is displeased with his people, but he suffers these things to prove his people, to see whether they will be faithful in all things, even unto death.

Well, as yet, there is not many of us that are [here] that have suffered very greatly. Our sufferings are not worthy to be compared with the suffering of many of the ancient saints. Read the history of the ancient people of God, where tens of thousands of them were murdered for their religion, and suffered all manner of cruelties, which were inflicted upon them by their enemies. Well now, there is not many of the saints [that have] suffered martyrdom in these latter days. And if hundreds have fallen victims to the persecutions that have been heaped upon by their enemies, why the great majority of the people have been spared, and [have] been permitted to overcome, and endure, and have been delivered, from time to time, from all their tribulations. We have seen, it is true, some very dark times in our persecutions, when, to all natural appearance the saints of God seemed to be overcome for a moment. Death and destruction seemed to threaten them on every side: the sword on the one hand, and starvation ~~on the~~ on the other, and the cold winter blasts, and the deep snows, threatened them with perishing. But they have overcome all these tribulations, and each time that they have been thus persecuted, the Lord has brought them into better circumstances than what they were formerly in.

When we were driven from the city of Nauvoo, people considered, or it was considered by many, that it would be almost impossible for the church to survive that great tribulation, to be driven out in the cold month of February when the thermometer was some 20 degrees below zero, to be driven out with no inhabitants,[59] to wander upon the bleak, snowy prairies, and to pitch our tents upon the drifts of snow. [Our] children [were] crying for bread. Looked at the hand of the Lord, and he has brought us through it. And the situation we are now placed in in the valleys of mountains is [Image 32] one hundred fold better than any situation we have been placed in since rise of this church. That which our enemies intended for our overcome, proved [to be] one of the greatest temporal blessings upon the people of God. If we ~~have~~ <had been> permitted to have remained in Nauvoo, what [would have] been the consequence? I will tell you, that was not the land where the poor saints, that are gathered from among the nations, could find a home, for the resources were not there. [They] could not find land without paying a great price, for the principal portions of land [were already] taken up by settlers. Consequently, if the saints from different nations had come to Nauvoo in their distressed circumstances, what [land] could [they] have had? [We continually?] find they would have scattered abroad again, in order to seek a living. The Lord saw all this. He only intended [that] we should tarry there for a season, until we got recruited from our Missouri persecution, and after that to bring us forth in a greater country, where there is an abundance of land, free for all, without paying the least sixpence. Go and inherit it, and it brings forth in its strength, and yields ~~in~~ its [*illegible*] to the saints of God. In this respect, we are better [off] where the poor can be gathered, and when they get there, they have an abundance of means to subsist upon. [The] land gives abundance. All they bring forth from the earth has, as yet, brought a good price, and been the means of enriching thousands [of] poor saints. Here we see the hand of the Lord in this. [Our] enemies supposed, [that] when they got us among the Rocky Mountains, [it would] not [be] possible for us to subsist. They supposed [that] we should perish, be killed of starvation. [They] supposed [it would] be the end of the church. It has has [*sic*] been our salvation, temporally speaking.

Again, the Latter-day Saints are better off in regard to another thing: [Image 33] as [laws/loss?], that of [property/priority?]. While in Nauvoo, [though one?] incorporated in one of the states of union, they were constantly vexed [by] law suits inflicted upon us by our enemies, in order to persecute us under [the] pretense of [the] law. And in this way, our prophet suffered year after year some scores of law suits, but each time came off victorious; yet, it was harassing [and] perplexing to be thus vexed by his enemies. This would have continued, had not our enemies drove us out from their midst, but now we are planted by ourselves, more than a thousand miles from the United States. Furthermore, the government of the United States has been moved upon to grant unto us a territorial government, to grant unto us a governor of ourselves, to appoint the President of this church [as] the governor of the territory, and [given us] power to elect our own officers and make our own laws. This is a great benefit. [It is] better to make our own laws and to be distanced from our enemies, than it would have been had we tarried in Nauvoo. [We are] much more blessed [than we] would have been in our former position. I consider this as the hand of God.

We can see the hand of God in another thing, in relation to this last movement of the church to the mountains. At the same time that we were moved to the mountains, it would have been very difficult, indeed, to have obtained raiment, though we might have obtained food, had not the Lord at the same time discovered what is termed the gold rush. This having been discovered, the gentiles who worship gold, that considered it as their greatest and most precious thing here upon the earth, flocked away by tens of thousands. And they had to pass through the valley, and this made a market for all of their surplus provisions, and this brought in clothing, farming utensils. and every thing needful for the benefit of saints, The hand of the Lord was in this. And he had told us years before [that] we would [~~*illegible*~~] [get] the riches of [the] gentiles. He has been doing this years past. Many of our [Image 34] that[60] they drive have had to crave a morsel of food, and were glad to give a dollar [a] pound. Those who have tried to starve us have had to come bounding to us [to] get a little food to eat. [The] hand of God [was] in all these things. If it had not been for something of this kind, unless the Lord performed a miracle, how we should obtain these things? But the Lord told us in the Book of Covenants, his business to provide for his saints.[61] His ways are mysterious: ~~we~~ that which we thought to be one of our greatest afflictions turned out [to be our] greatest blessing.

[I] do not know what our next affliction may be. I could hope that we might have no more persecutions from the gentiles, if [it] be the will of the Lord, [but I] do not know his will regarding this matter. I do not know. He may suffer us to have another persecution. We have been persecuted by towns, governors, and officers of states; we have not yet been persecuted by the United States in a national capacity. I do not know; we may have to be. And I think when that times [*sic*] comes, [it will] be the last persecution the saints endure, when they are persecuted by the nation as a nation. [I] do not know [if] this [will] be the case, but should it be the case, let [not?] the saints be found [*illegible*], for you may depend upon it, that the same God that has upheld us hitherto, and has bestowed upon us great blessing after the persecution, will bring us through, and we shall find our blessings be enlarged hundred fold [to] what they are now.

You know, Daniel has told us some very glorious things about the saints possessing the kingdom and dominion, and [the] greatness of [the] kingdom under [the] whole heavens,[62] glorious promises [tended?] organization of town [in city?] of Nauvoo, county, territorial government?[63] But it will be the dominion and the greatness of domain under the whole heavens, immense kingdom that be not like [petty?] government in modern Europe, like that of Queen Victoria, [or like that of the] people [of the] United States. It will be a [Image 35] domain expanding to the ends of earth, the earth possessing. The Lord God has declared by the mouth of his ancient prophet that the latter kingdom should be a real empire, that all nations [and] kingdoms [are] to serve him. [It will] come to pass, and there is no power on earth [that can] hinder [what] the Lord God sets his hand to perform, [or] his arm. But let's not despise the day of small things, for out of them proceedeth that great. Well, the Lord laid the corner stone of earth [same/some?] it first, and made a large world. After a while he had to bind by forming a [whole?] nucleus, around which [he] gathered together scattered elements. And [he] organized it into the form of [a] great globe, and filled it with man, and animals, [and] all living creatures. Thus, so the Lord begins in a corner, as it were. His work [is] apparently small, [and] looked upon with disdain by those who call themselves the great of the earth. Like our Savior [done?], he who is King of Kings. He was despised [on] behalf of the children of men. [He] was born in a manger. [He] was not looked upon with respect by the children of men, [but was looked upon as] a poor, despised, uncertain [man]. He descended below all things, that he might ascend above all things, and fill all the heavens with his glory, and with his power and with his greatness, and with his majesty, and sway a kingly scepter over all the creations he has made. Well, he began very small: he came down in a very humble position. And so the saints, the kingdom of God established in the last days, begins very small, [but it will] roll like a stone cut out of the mountains. It rolls from the mountains, and as it rolls from the mountain heights, he gathers strength, force, [and] power, until it becomes a great mountain and fills the whole earth.

We are then looking for something worthy of the children of God. We are not looking for small things, [but] for eternal life, eternal priesthood; for eternal power, eternal creation, [and] to sway an eternal scepter over eternal kingdoms [that the] Lord has organized, [Image 36] and will organize, for the benefit of his sons and daughters. We have a great many things to overcome, before we can be entrusted with all this power, dominion, happiness, [and] honor. We have got to show ourselves proved in this day of small things. If we cannot do this in the days of our mission, poverty, [and] tribulation, we shall not be counted worthy to reign as kings and priests, and sway a righteous scepter over the creations of God, [which] he has designed for his people. [If] man [is] not faithful in the days of his tribulations and poverty, how [can] God make him ruler over ten cities or over five cities?

Most of the religious world conclude that the next life [is] a kind of idolatry: a life occupied with writing [and] singing, with no thing particular to do or perform. [That is] not the case: it is to be a very active life. It is [supposed] to be a rest, true, [but a] different kind [of rest]. People [are] supposed to rest from all sin, sorrow, tribulation, and persecution, and all the evil that inflict mortal man in this life.[64] But you will find out in the next life [that] man has got a great work to perform, which is prepared in the next world, to do that great work. We are not prepared to do much in this life; our capacity so small, have weak strength, [and our] mortal infirmities [are] so great, [that] we cannot perform that we would desire sometimes, [because] we are so hemmed in on every side by the infirmities of flesh. Well, the time will soon come [when] we shall be freed from all of these infirmities. We will have bodies of immortal flesh and bones. We will have that power and glory that God has designed for his people, that will enable us to enter upon an active life, into a life, not a life that will only endure for a few years, but for ever. We are looking, then, for another life. We are not limited in our desires and capacities to the vain and transitory things of this [Image 37] life; we are seeking for the kingdom that is to be eternal. If [we] will seek for a kingdom [and] for power in the eternal worlds, let us seek for it lawfully, with correct principles, [such as] the instructions [that] Brother Watt imparted to us last Sabbath: [to be] meek [and] pure in spirit, to be ever merciful, to do unto others as we would they should do to us. Seek to do all those things [that] Jesus pointed out, as far as our circumstances will permit. And, by doing good, and being very humble, and meek, and keep[ing] the commandments and sayings of Jesus, we will be prepared to receive this kingdom, and enter unto all that power that the Lord has in the resurrection for us.

A great many people in the religious world are seeking very earnestly to save the spirit; [they] think little about the body. The Latter-day Saints differ from them in this; [in the] resurrection we are looking not only for the salvation of the spirit, but the body also. We know that no man can be perfect in happiness, no man can receive a kingly power and glory in the eternal worlds, unless he has a body of flesh and bones. But [what does] that scripture mean, that flesh and blood cannot inherit the kingdom of God?[65] [It] means just what [it] says: flesh and blood. Neither can [it], but did you ever read any scripture [that] says flesh and bones cannot inherit the kingdom? For Jesus himself, when he rose from the tomb, rose with immortal flesh and bones, and was quickened by [the] immortal spirit, and ascended with that immortal body to the right hand of his Father, to receive majesty, and power, and dominion, not only in heaven, but on earth. He inherit[ed] the kingdom of God with flesh [and] bones, but no blood.

When you come up from your graves, [you will] have no blood, [for] blood is natural life. As to immortality, what [will] supply the place of blood, which is necessary now, to sustain the natural life? If it were not for the blood that circulated in the veins, [Image 38] our bodies could not survive. But the very thing that preserves us in life for a few years here is very thing that tends eventually to death: blood tends to mortality, to change the system, to bring disease, and death, and sickness, and pain, and sorrow. What [will] supply the place of this? Ezekiel has told us, in the 37 chapter, he had a view of resurrection. He says [that] the hand of the Lord was upon him, and carried him out in the spirit, [and] set him down in the midst of valley full of bones. The Lord asked him a very curious question: son of man, can these bones live? Well, to all natural appearance, if he had been a person not having faith in God, he would have said, No, [they are] dry [bones]. [He was] ignorant upon the subject. Hence, he says: O Lord God, thou knowest. Then says the Lord: Prophesy, son of man; say unto them, O ye dry bones, hear the word of the Lord. Thus saith the Lord, and he prophesied, and as he prophesied, there was a noise, and shaking bones came to itself, bone. Flesh, and sinews came upon [them], and skin covered them above, [but there was] no breath in them. The flesh had come upon, the sinews came upon, then skin covered flesh and sinews, but no breath in them. Then the lord told Ezekiel to prophecy again to the winds. So he prophesied, and breath entered into them. And here, then, is life: they lived, [and] stood upon their, feet an exceeding great army.[66]

What [does] all this mean? O, says the Methodist, that means the scene when he is overwrought at our camp meeting, [and there is] great shaking. [That is the] mean[ing of] the saying: bone comes to bone, or, in other words, the sinner raised to newness of life. [That is the] sectarian interpretation. The Lord says, son of man, these bones are the whole house of Israel.[67] [They have a] different interpretation: they say our bones is dry, etc. Therefore, say unto them: Behold, O my people, I will open your graves, and cause you to come [up out of your graves], [Image 39] and bring you unto the land of Israel.[68] The Israelites had got ~~an idea~~ Israel ~~had not~~ not understand the resurrection; [they] did not know how this [was] to be fulfilled to their fathers. Hence, they say: Our hope is lost. [We are] cut [off from] our fathers of [old], without giving us a [hint?] of it. We are cut off from our [parts/parties/purpose?]. The Lord, in order to explain this great matter to them, says: O my people, I will open your graves, and cause you to come up out of your graves, and bring you to the land of Israel, bone to bone, skin cover [flesh and sinews]. [In all/Know of?] this the immortal spirit [will be] enabled, [and] after he rises up in that manner, they are brought unto the land of Israel.

How different [are] these views to that of [the] sectarian world, that, after they are arise from their graves, they are wafted away off under the starry skies, after the bounds of times and space, [and], as [a] general rule, cease. Not so with the ancient prophets. They looked ~~faith~~[69] <forth> to the times that the fathers come up out of their graves, with immortal flesh, skin, [and] bones, [and] take possession of [the] land promised to their fathers. They will be prepared to inherit the earth. We are so full of infirmities, and thus we are not prepared to inherit the earth. All [of] our temporal days [are] mingled with grief and sorrow. Not so with the immortal bodies: no more death, pain, [or] sickness. And the land of Canaan [will] be purified from all the curses [that have been placed] upon [it] because of the sins of the people. The just [will] be adopted [and obtain an] inheritance [as] immortal beings. Jesus [will] be there. If the Lord would not do all this, he sit away off, beyond the bounds of time and space? No, he will inherit the earth, as our Elder Brother. We shall be just like him. Paul says he will fashion our bodies like unto his,[70] glorious bodies, made like [unto his]. Consequently, [he will] be in our midst and fulfill that saying in David, Give unto you the heathen for thine inheritance, and uttermost parts of earth for [Image 40] for[71] thy possession.[72] All the uttermost parts of earth, as well as the lands of Israel, [*illegible*] be in possession of Elder Brother, divided out among his brothers, [who will] be made joint heirs with him.

We [are] looking for a greater inheritance [than] the gentile[s] [are] looking for. They will pass through [a] great deal [to] heap up gold to buy [a] quarter mile of land. We will [comprehend?] [that] this is beneath our dignity, to labor all [our] life to buy us this much land. [The] uttermost parts of [the] earth [will] be given to our Elder Brother, and [he] will make us joint heirs with him. This is one of the best promises [that] can be given, as far as landed inheritance is concerned. [It is] better than those [*illegible*] [dudes?], [who, in] times of war, trample upon them, good for nothing. He declares [that those who obey him] shall have it [for an] everlasting inheritance. You know that [in the] Sermon on [the] Mount, glorious teachings [are] given us: Blessed are the meek, for they shall inherit the earth.[73] ~~Sectarian tell us~~ [The] sectarian tells [us that] tens of thousands wandered about in sheep skins etc., never to return again to the earth. [They] would not give much for Jesus' promises: they acknowledge they did not inherit the earth, and [not] a solitary foot of it. Do you suppose Jesus' promise [will] not be fulfilled? Those who have kept the sayings of Jesus will come up out of the grave. [Those who have] fought the victory of faith with all intelligent faculties [will be] prepared to inherit the earth in truth, and in great glory. [They will] be prepared to live.

You see, brethren and sisters, the Latter-day Saints are looking for the salvation of [the] body as well as salvation of [the] spirit, for an inheritance of body as well as spirit, of glory after a resurrection, as well as glory between death and resurrection. There is a great many things, [that] if mankind only understood, they would not be so exceeding anxious to get rid of their bodies, and never take them [up] again. They do not realize [what] Paul told us. He says, after [he had] spent this life in usefulness, and suffered all manner of things, [he] says: I have kept the faith, and there is hence forth laid up for me a crown of glory, which the Lord, the righteous judge, shall give me at that day.[74] [Image 41] What? Has old Apostle Paul not got his glory yet? Why? [He has] not got his body yet. Before any one can be crowned as king, [they must first] get [an] immortal body of flesh and bones. Paul says: The crown was laid up for [him], which the Lord, the righteous judge, [shall] give him at that day.[75] Why? Because then the old Apostle Paul [will] receive [an] immortal body and be prepared to wear a crown, and not until then.

Yet before any one [can] get that crown, [they have] got to secure it in this life. Here is the place to secure a kingly power. [We] cannot secure it if we neglect it here, and [neglect] the means God has ordained [for us] to secure [it]. What are those means? The Lord has ordained laws to bind every thing, certain laws, from the foundation of this world, that has a bearing upon man, from the days of Adam, as long as there shall be a mortal man upon the face of the earth. Among other things, he has ordained a certain medium through which a man can receive a crown, and ~~obtain~~ become a king, and a priest, through certain ordinances, [when they are] administered by proper authority. You know [that] in ancient times, when King David received power, [it was] by a certain authority. Samuel was commanded to anoint him king; [it] could not be conferred without an ordinance. If it could not be conferred without an ordinance in this life, how [so you] suppose [that] the kingly power and authority in [the] eternal [is] received without an ordinance? It cannot be done. This ordinance must be administered by revelation of Jesus Christ, [by the] proper administrator, [in the proper] place and manner, and in the way ordained from the foundation of world. And when you obtain it this way, it cannot be rent out of your hands, if you comply with the laws God has given. Well, all these things the Latter-day Saints must learn. They will hereafter understand.

We hardly yet understand the a b c of our religion, though we think, [as] some say, we are very wise concerning God, [and] even [our] future state, not compared, and which is not yet made manifest. We hardly know the first two letters of our religion. We have got to learn them all [Image 42] by grace. You that have children think it impossible to learn them algebra, etc., before you learn them some of the first principles of the alphabet. The Lord has children here. [He] created them, etc. If we get a little careless, we must have our minds bent down.

Let us be patient in all of our tribulations, realizing, in some measure, those things that God has in store for his people. The Lord had a great many kings in ancient days. Did you ever realize that the 7 churches, to whom John directed his revelation, had been made kings and priests to God? Read [the] first chapter [of] Revelation: God declares he had made them kings and priests.[76] He was writing to [people] living on the earth, that had been made kings and priests to God. Perhaps the females might inquire [if] they [are] to be made kings. No, [they will] not be made kings. [Even] if they are faithful of receiving glory? No, they will be made queens. They will inherit glory with their husbands [and] children. What? Are they going to have social circles in [the] next world? Why not? Are you going to lose your affections when you get out of this world, or [will they be] strengthened? What faculty, of those that he has instituted, [will we lose?] Point out one thing that will not be eternal. I am speaking of the original faculty of the Lord. Where is there one power or faculty that will ever cease to exist? Do you have love here for your children, [that] God implanted in your bosom? For your wife, [or] she for her husband? Who has planted it there? God. He declares to be love himself, possessing affections, kindness, and mercy. Consequently, you [will] love your wife in [the] next world. [If you are] faithful in this world, and keep the law of righteousness, your wife [will] enjoy with you all the kingly power [that I am] speaking of. Should you be appointed ruler over ten cities, [your] wife [will] enjoy it with you.

You will just have as much [affection] for your wife, father, mother, brothers, [and] sisters in the next world. [It will] increase a thousand fold. How [will it] increase? [A] man's affection increases just in proportion to his intelligence, just in proportion to his knowledge. Incidentally, [Image 43] look at God, who comprehends all knowledge. Look at his boundless love: is it not in proportion to his knowledge? Look at little children, [who have] not much notion of loving their brothers and sisters. Knows something about [itself maybe]. As they grow up and know something about their brothers and sisters [and] neighbors, [they] love them. And by and by, as they get acquainted with the human family, thousands of people, [and], if they are good persons, [they] love them and have anxious [feelings] for their welfare and finally persons desire for the happiness. Their bosom[s] yearn for the happiness of all the human family, as they get acquainted with the nature of happiness. When we arise from the grave, the same human spirit [will] possess the same affection. Love [will be] enlarged a thousand fold in proportion to the knowledge that is in our hearts. [We will] not confine our love to this world, [but also] think of other worlds and have power, in their love, to waft off themselves from world to world, and enjoy an intercourse with other intelligent beings, and impart instructions to them. And thus the fold of their intelligence [will be] greatly enlarged, [and their] reflections and their happiness [will] increase in proportion as this increases.

God is a happy being, because he looks abroad upon all the vast kingdoms he has made, and sees life, and happiness, and immortality reigning in their midst, if they have not fallen, and if they have [fallen], he has a [sphere?] opened for them. But, says one, I have always thought [that when we] got in [the] next world, every body [would] be like to us. Is every body like to you here? [Take the/talk of?] love to your father, mother, etc.; who planted [it] there? God, in the eternal way, instead of loving everybody else [with the] same kind of love, [the] family circle love [will be] stretched out to other worlds. Yet there will be that peculiar love to your own wife, etc., that does not extend to distant worlds. There will be your home, mansion, palace, head quarters of family circle. What, my brethren, would [be] more inconsistent than [Image 44] that God planted these in our bosom for a few years, and then entirely cast them away? [It] would look more inconsistent to the man of love [for the] family circle to be broken up and [to] have no more love to them than anybody. [It would] look gloomy [and] dreary to me, to have ideas of this kind.

Now, a great many people suppose [that] to set our affections upon [our] wife [and] children [is] wrong. Not so; never has [there] been a man or woman love their wife or children too much. Some of those whimsical notions: the parent that loves his children most, will correct his children because he loves [them], and he chastens the children. Those who do not correct them when they need it, do not love them. I have heard it preached up in the sectarian world: [you can] love them too much, [which is] all folly. If the Lord took all children away, I should think I did not love them enough, did not chasten them enough. [There is a] medium to be taken. Parents sometimes strike them in anger, [and are] too strict; [there is a] certain medium to be taken in all things. We should always endeavor to correct them in mildness, not in passion, lest they get angry and faint to follow after the same footsteps of their parents.

I will leave this for Brother Watt, and what ever the spirit put into his heart. I was much delighted to hear Brother Watt last Sunday upon the subject of of [*sic*] bringing up children. Husband and wife: a good lecture on this subject would do us good. I will go away, praying you may be blessed and prospered, all of you. ~~Be obedient. The sacrament was~~

The sacrament was administered by Brother Toone.

Appendix 1

Style Guide for Transcriptions from Pitman Shorthand

< > indicates material inserted above or below line.

All content written in longhand is in **bold**.

[*illegible*] or [*words illegible*] indicates a word or words are illegible.

[word] A word or word enclosed in [ ] indicates a word or words added for clarity.

[word?] A word or words enclosed in [?] indicates some uncertainty about the transcription.

[word/word?] Words separated by / and enclosed in [?] are alternative transcriptions for the symbol when it is not possible to determine the intended meaning; many shorthand symbols have multiple meanings. Examples: [if/for?] [one/no?] [further/farther/father/if there/for their/if their /for there?].

~~word or words crossed out~~ Words that are crossed out in the original. Illegible crossed out words are silently omitted.

Punctuation and capitalization have been added to aid readability. Pitman shorthand has symbols for punctuation, and while these are rarely used when reporting a speaker, Watt included extensive punctuation in his journal. Any nonstandard punctuation or capitalization that is indicated in the shorthand journal is included and footnoted.

Vowels in Pitman shorthand are written as diacritics; they are considered optional, and usually omitted, especially when a reporter is trying to keep up with a speaker. Watt occasionally included a vowel that gave a shorthand word an unusual meaning in that particular context; these vowels are footnoted.

Paragraph breaks have been added to transcripts for readability.

Where the shorthand symbol for a contraction can be read both as contracted and not contracted, such as *can't* and *cannot*, *didn't* and *did not*, etc., the full form is given. If a contraction is written in such a way that it can only be read as a contraction, it is given as such, as in *won't*.

All underlining in a transcript is in the original.

Words that are obvious shorthand errors are silently omitted.

Words written as two words though they would normally written as a single word (no where, to day, any thing) are transcribed as written.

Numbers are transcribed as they were written: numbers written as words are transcribed as words, and numbers written as digits are transcribed as digits.

None of the shorthand items in this book are paginated in the original. To clearly identify each page, we give the image number from the scanned images of the George D. Watt Papers in the Church History Library, Salt Lake City.

The original, unedited transcript of George D. Watt's shorthand journal is available in the Church History Library public catalog, collection CR 100 912, https:// catalog .churchofjesuschrist .org /assets /29dfdd82-69cb-47b0-88a8-3e2bc28e96fb/0/0.

Appendix 2

Third Company of Ten of the John Brown Company

We have listed every name that the official "John Brown Emigrating Company Journal" had as being a part of George D. Watt's ten. If the Pioneer Database included a middle name, we have inserted that into the list.[1] We have also put in last names where the journal and database did not list the wife's and children's names. If we found birth and death dates from the Pioneer Database, we inserted them. If the database differed in the spelling of the name, we have put those names in brackets. At times, the database will differ regarding the age of the individual. Most times this age difference is owing to when it was recorded. The database lists the individual's age when he or she left the first camp in Nebraska. The age for the individual in the "John Brown Emigrating Company Journal" is the age of the person when the event was recorded in the diary. If the ages were drastically different, we have noted this. In the "John Brown Emigrating Company Journal" the names are arranged by those traveling together, the first one having the number of oxen, cows, wagons, and dogs by his or her name. If the Saints by Sea BYU Database contained the names of those in Watt's ten, we have included the ship they traveled on for the first family member listed.[2]

George Darling Watt, Captain, age 39, 12 oxen, 1 cow, 2 wagons, 1 dog. Came on the *Ellen Maria* in 1851. May 18, 1812–October 24, 1881.
Mary Watt, age 40. About 1811–January 10, 1856.
George Darling Watt Jun., age 9. June 10, 1843–June 15, 1928.
Mary Ann Brown, age 59. April 23, 1791–September 23, 1884.

Jane Brown, age 22. June 8, 1828–May 6, 1891.

Samuel Patterson, age 35. Pioneer Database records his age as 22. Came on the *Ellen Maria* in 1851.

Robert Williams, age 35. September 16, 1815–January 1, 1882.

Alford Williams, age 9. Pioneer Database spelled his name as *Alfred*. June 29, 1842–unknown.

Thomas Lorenzo Margetts Sen., age 31, 6 oxen, 1 cow, 1 wagon. November 19, 1820–September 6, 1856.

Susanna Bayliss Margetts, age 28. June 2, 1822–May 15, 1918. Pioneer Database lists her as age 29.

Ann Margetts, age 4. December 27, 1846–July 31, 1913.

Thomas Cicero Margetts Jun., age 2. November 19, 1848–January 28, 1898.

Lorenzo Erastus Margetts, age 9 mos. October 6, 1850–August 23, 1904.

Esther Kimpton [Kempton] age 50. Esther Kimpton died July 20, 1851, and was buried in a large mound near the ford of the Loup Fork. About 1801–July 20, 1851. Came on the *George W. Bourne* in 1851.

Benjamin Votaw, age 25. About 1826–unknown.

Joseph Allen [Allan], age 30, 6 oxen, 3 wagons, 0 buggies, 4 dogs. Came on the *Ellen Maria* in 1851. December 24, 1820–June 14, 1896.

Lullah [Zillah] Allan, age 26.

Charles E. Allan, age 4. August 4, 1847–July 24, 1925. Age 3 in 1851.

Joseph William Allan. June 8, 1851–November 24, 1937.

John Marshall Yardley, age 35. July 24, 1817–October 10, 1884. Came on the *Josiah Bradley* in 1850.

Mary Yardley. Age 27. March 15, 1824–April 30, 1874. Came on the *Josiah Bradley* in 1850.

Joel Terry, age 39, 6 oxen, 1 cow, 3 horses, 3 wagons, 1 buggy, 1 dog. May 23, 1812–September 4, 1891.

Marian Terry, age 33.

Jane Terry, age 16. August 20, 1837–August 16, 1866.

William Anderson Terry, age 9. November 9, 1842–March 11, 1922.

John Parshall Terry, age 3. February 11, 1848–March 29, 1931.
Joel T. Terry, age 1½.
Omnah Terry, age 39. About 1812–unknown.
Amandah Terry, age 18.
Sabila [Savilla] Terry, age 16.
Ruby Terry, age 13. About 1838–unknown.
Tabotha [Tabitha] Terry, age 11. 1840–62.
Lucinday [Lucinda] Ann Terry, age 9. April 5, 1842–unknown.
James Angus Terry, age 3. March 10, 1848–May 25, 1924.
Mary Child, age 36, 4 oxen, 2 cows, 2 horses, 2 wagons. November 15, 1814–June 1, 1872.
Seth Child, age 15. January 19, 1836–June 19, 1898.
Amanda Child, age 12.
Joel Haskins Child, age 1. April 1, 1840–January 21, 1912.
Jason Child, age 9. About 1842–unknown.
Mary A. Child, age 2. April 17, 1849–July 27, 1918. Pioneer Database lists her middle name as *Hannah*.
Mary Ann Simmons, age 23. About 1828–unknown.
John Lynden, age 20. About 1831–unknown.

The following are Oregon emigrants (with the Third Company of Ten)

Edmund Judkins, age 23. About 1828–unknown.
Adam Meek, age 48. May 15, 1803–unknown.
Sophrona [Sophronia] Meek, age 35. August 5, 1825–unknown.
Sidney or Sydney Meek, age 18. About 1833–unknown.
Rachel Meek, age 16. December 31, 1835–unknown. Pioneer Database lists her age as 15.
John Meek, age 13. About 1838–unknown.
Robert Meek, age 5 years. December 12, 1845–unknown.
Amos Andrus [Andrews], age 41.

Appendix 3

George D. Watt's Wives and Children

Listed here are the wives and children of George D. Watt. Marriage dates are in parentheses.[1]

Mary Gregson, 1812–56 (1835)
James, 1837–43
Willard Richards, 1840–43
George Darling Jun. 1843–1928

Jane Brown, 1828–91 (1852)
Joseph, 1852–1917
Robert, 1854–unknown
Margaret Elizabeth, 1857–1923
Jane Brown and George D. Watt divorced in 1863. Brown later married Adam Saladin, 1839–98 (1865).

Alice Longstroth Whittaker, 1824–1909 (1853)
Alice Longstroth Whittaker was previously married to Moses Whitaker, 1818–52 (about 1838).

Elizabeth Golightly, 1841–1930 (1859)
Richard, 1860–1933
Isabella, 1862–1902
Alice, 1865–1920
Georgenia, 1869–1948
John Golightly, 1870–1948

Andrew Kennon, 1873–1902
Jane, 1875–1952
Julia Ann, 1878–79
Rachel Layton, 1880–1948

Sarah Ann Harter, 1850–1932 (1866)
Ermina Elizabeth, 1868–1945
Mary Ann, 1870–1946
Jennet Darling, 1872–1938
John Harter, 1874–1956
Eliza Elizabeth, 1877–1963
Minerva, 1879–81
Cora, 1881–1940

Martha Bench, 1846–1925 (1867)
George William, 1869–1937
Grace Darling, 1871–79
James Arthur, 1873–1945
Annie, 1875–1949
Mary, 1877–1933
Ida Mariah, 1880–1967
Martha Bench later married Francis Kilfoyle, 1829–88 (1882).

Appendix 4

Two Reminiscent Accounts from Early Latter-day Saint Missionaries to England

Heber C. Kimball, speaking about George D. Watt:

> In [18]37, that is the time I went to England, I went and Brother Hyde with me and Brother Willard Richards. The world supposed the church had gone over the dam, they had not the least idea but what Mormonism was done, and a great many that believed it turned away, supposing Mormonism was done with them, and it would never rise again. Still, I with others went to England and preached. . . . Here is Brother George Watt, writing right here. He had not been in the church not to exceed ten days before he began to prophesy. Says he, "Brother Kimball," he had been reading the Book of Mormon and the Spirit of God came on him. Says he, "Brother Kimball, as Lord God lives, we have got to be gathered to America, and that is the land of promise." Says I, "Brother George, prophesy away. You know I did not say much about that."[1]

John Taylor on the gathering:

> Well, mixed up with that has been other things, we have been gathered together here. And what for? What for? What did we come here for? Who knows? Well, we came here because God said he would build up his Zion in the latter days, and because those same elders, under the teaching of Joseph Smith and President Young, said, Gather the people together. It is a gathering dispensation. . . .

I remember a circumstance in Liverpool that transpired years and years ago, some 30 years ago. We were told by Joseph Smith, at that time, not to preach the gathering, for we had been driven from Missouri and thought it wise, as there was no particular, specific place [to gather at that time]. It was [thought it would] not [be] well to say anything until a place should be prepared, and we should have instructions, and then teach it. That was all well enough, but you could not keep it from the people. Why? Why, they had got the Holy Ghost, and the Holy Ghost took the things of God, and showed it to them, and you could not hide it from them. I remember a sister coming to me on one occasion. Says she, "Brother Taylor, I had a curious kind of a dream the other night." "What was it?" [I asked]. "Well," says she, "I dreamed there was a whole lot of Saints standing at the pier head down below in Liverpool, and that there was a vessel there, and it was going off to America, and we were going to some place they called Zion. I was going, you were going, and the saints all going. I thought I would ask you the meaning." <Said I>, "I will tell you, one of these times." We could not keep it away from the people. If we had been told not to baptize and lay hands on the people, we could have kept it from them, but when we baptized and laid hands on them, they received the Holy Ghost, [and] that Spirit showed the things of God to them, and we could not hide it from them.[2] (John Taylor, May 26, 1872; transcribed from David Evans's shorthand record by LaJean Purcell Carruth)

Appendix 5

Yearly Numbers of People Traveling the Overland Trails

Research for table 1 has been ongoing for the past fifty years. Some travelers kept journals that included the number of people in the company, sometimes with names. The John Brown Company of 1851 had such a list. But a number of companies had no number or list. The numbers in this table have been compiled by the staff of the Church of Jesus Christ of Latter-day Saints History Department by using these diaries and other sources. However, it is not possible to have a definite number of travelers because of the lack of records. This list is based on known counts in companies and projected estimates for companies where numbers were not given. It is also possible that some pioneers traveled to Utah in California-bound companies; there is no source or company name for these people. As far as total numbers for immigrants to Utah, it is reasonable to state that the number of Latter-day Saints who crossed the plains was about 60,000.[1]

Table 1. *Latter-day Saint pioneers coming to Utah before the railroad*

YEAR	NUMBER OF TRAVELERS
1847	1,919
1848	2,444
1849	1,598
1850	4,035
1851	1,735
1852	5,543
1853	3,060

1854	3,149
1855	2,048
1856	3,597
1857	1,373
1858	385
1859	1,703
1860	2,061
1861	4,408
1862	5,158
1863	4,021
1864	2,517
1865	973
1866	3,489
1867	560
1868	4,192
Total	59,868

Created by the authors.

Table 2 is taken from John D. Unruh Jr.'s *The Plains Across: The Overland Emigrants and the Trans-Mississippi West, 1840–60*. These are estimates as compiled by Unruh, who studied this question for many years. He included the number of travelers for the Oregon Trail and the California Trail in separate columns.

Table 2. *Oregon and California pioneers, 1849–60*

YEAR	OREGON TRAIL	CALIFORNIA TRAIL
1840–48	11,512	2,735
1849	450	25,000
1850	6,000	44,000
1851	3,600	1,100

1852	10,000	50,000
1853	7,500	20,000
1854	6,000	12,000
1855	500	1,500
1856	1,000	8,000
1857	1,500	4,000
1858	1,500	6,000
1859	2,000	17,000
1860	1,500	9,000
Totals	53,062	200,355

The year span is taken from Unruh, *Plains Across*, 119–20. The numbers of pioneers are estimates. Created by the authors.

Glossary of Nautical, Steamboat, and River Terms

The following terms refer to a ship/the sea or to a steamboat/river, or in some cases to both. If it is unclear in which setting a term applies, it is labeled either *nautical* or *river.*

about: to go about is to change the course of a ship by tacking.
afore: in, on, or toward the front of a vessel.
aft: the portion of the vessel behind the middle area of the vessel.
ahoy: a cry to draw attention; used to hail a boat or a ship.
alee: on the side of the ship away from the wind.
aloft: in the rigging of a sailing ship, above or overhead.
anchor: an object designed to prevent or slow the drift of a ship, attached to the ship by a line or chain.
arm: the spoke of a paddle wheel.
as the crow flies: a direct line between two points which is the way crows travel rather than ships, which must go around land.
ballast: heavy material that is placed in the hold of a vessel to provide stability.
bar: large mass of sand or earth, formed by the surge of the sea. They are mostly found at the entrances of great rivers and often render navigation extremely dangerous.
barrelman: a sailor who was stationed in the crow's nest.
batten down the hatches: to prepare for inclement weather by securing the closed hatch covers with wooden battens so as to prevent water from entering from any angle.
beam: the width of a vessel at the widest point, or a point alongside the ship at the midpoint of its length.
beam ends: the sides of a ship. *on beam ends* may mean the vessel is literally on its side and about to capsize; more often the phrase means the vessel is listing 45 degrees or more. In the second storm, Watt mentioned that he had to lash himself and his family in their berth because the ship had been thrown on its "beam ends."

becalm: unable to move due to lack of wind.

below: on or into a lower deck.

berth: a fixed bed or bunk on a ship or boat.

bilge: the compartment at the bottom of the hull of a ship where water collects and must be pumped out of the vessel.

board: to step onto, climb onto, or otherwise enter a vessel.

boiler: metal tank filled with water that is heated to produce steam that then powers the engine. The water level within the boiler was critical and usually was the contributing factor in boiler explosions. The largest steamboats had as many as eight boilers.

boiler deck: the second deck; the one above the boilers. The cabin and staterooms were located on the boiler deck.

bonnet: a strip of canvas secured to the foot of the course (square sail) to increase sail area in light airs.

boom: a pole along the foot of a fore-and-aft rigged sail that greatly improves control of the angle and shape of the sail.

bow: the front of a vessel.

bowsprit: a large mast or piece of timber that stands out from the bow of a ship.

bridge: a structure above the weather deck, extending the full width of the vessel, which houses a command center.

broadside: one side of a vessel above the waterline.

bucket: a wooden blade, or paddle, of a paddlewheel.

cabin: an enclosed room on a deck. Watt was in the second cabin, which was just below the poop deck. On a steamboat, an elongated, central room, running fore and aft, on the boiler deck, which served as a social hall and dining room for the cabin passengers.

capsize: when a ship or boat lists too far and rolls over, exposing the keel.

captain: the person in command of a vessel.

channel: the deepest part of a river bed, not always in the middle of the river.

chimney: sheet-metal tube used to carry smoke away from a steamboat and create a draft in the furnace.

condensing engine: a type of steam engine, normally of low pressure, that condenses the steam in the cylinder.

colors: the national flag flown on a ship.

come about: to tack.

course: the direction in which a vessel is being steered, usually given in degrees.

crank: the bent part of a shaft or axle through which reciprocating motion is transformed into rotary motion, or vice versa. River term.

decks: the top of the boat. A deck is a permanent covering over a compartment or a hull of a ship. The primary or main deck is the principal deck in a vessel extending from bow to stern. Ships have more than one deck, above and below the primary one.

depth of hull: on a steamboat, the distance from the bottom of the keel to the underside of the deck beam.

displacement: the weight of water moved aside, or displaced, by the hull of a boat.

dock: in American usage, a fixed structure attached to shore to which a vessel is secured when in port.

draft: the depth of a boat's hull under the waterline.

fair wind: a wind favorable to the direction a ship is sailing.

firebox: located beneath the boiler, heated the boiler water. River term.

first mate: the second-in-command of a commercial ship. According to Watt, the first mate was in charge of how much sail to put up or take down.

flue: one or more pipes extending through the length of a boiler, carrying hot gases from the firebox to the breeching, and aiding in heating the water within the boiler.

foot: the lower edge of any sail, the bottom of a mast.

fore: the forward part of the ship.

forecastle: a partial deck, above the upper deck and at the head of the vessel; traditionally the sailors' living quarters. It was this area of the ship that Watt needed the captain's permission to enter in order to find, he thought, an errant female of his party. On a steamboat, the portion of the main deck extending forward of the superstructure and housing the anchors, capstan, spars, stage plank, and hawsers.

foremast: the front mast of the ship.

fore-topsail: the sail above the bottom sail of the mast. Watt used this term when he said to "furl the fore top sail." *See* sail plan for further detail.

frigate: a navy sailing ship of a size and armament just below that of a ship of the line and built for speed and maneuverability.

full-rigged ship: a sailing vessel with three or more masts, all of them square-rigged.

furling the sail: rolling the sail up underneath the yard and quickly passing the gaskets around the furled sail.

furnace: the space under the boilers where the fire is built. River term.

galley: the kitchen of a ship.

genoa (or genny): a large jib, strongly overlapping the mainmast. Nautical term.

hail: to call to another ship.

hammock: canvas sheets, slung from the deckhead in messdecks, in which seamen slept.

helm: the wheel and/or wheelhouse area. *Take the helm* means take over the steering of the vessel.

helmsman: a person who steers a ship.

high-pressured engine: a steam engine powered by the expansive force of high-pressure steam injected into the engine's cylinder.

hog chain: an iron rod passing over braces, used to prevent the hull from hogging or sagging. River term.

hogging: the tendency for a hull to hump in the center and droop at the ends. River term.

hold: the interior space of a hull, used for cargo.

hull: the outer shell of a vessel exclusive of masts, yards, sails, and rigging.

hurricane deck: the third deck, located above the boiler deck. The name was derived from the ever-present wind on the deck, which made it a favorite viewing place on warm evenings.

jib: a triangular staysail at the front of a ship. More specifically, one mounted between the bowsprit and the head of the mainmast, a triangular sail set by sailing ships on the boom, which runs out from the bowsprit.

keel: the lowest and principal timber of a wooden ship, the single strongest member of the ship's frame. On a steamboat, the longitudinal timber that extends the length of the bottom of the vessel, forming its backbone.

knot: a unit of speed: 1 nautical mile (1.852 kilometers or 1.1508 miles) per hour. As a measure of speed the term is always knots, and never miles an hour. At least once in the essay Watt used miles per hour, and thereafter knots per hour.

knuckle chains: an iron rod used to hold up the sides of the hull. River term.

ladies cabin: the back of the cabin. On some boats the ladies cabin was partitioned off from the main cabin. It was not the exclusive domain of women.

lee shore: a coastline to which the wind blows directly. It can be dangerous as the wind tends to force the sailing ship down on it.

lee side: the side of a ship away from the wind. The side of the boat furthest from the wind, always the low side.

leeward: with the wind; toward the point to which the wind blows.

lighter: a barge or old hull used to carry a portion of a steamboat's cargo.

light sail: *see* sail plan.

lower deck: the deck of a ship immediately above the hold.

low-pressure engine: an engine type powered by a low pressure of steam, the driving force coming from the application, a partial vacuum formed in the cylinder.
main deck: the lowest external deck, which covers the hull.
mainmast (or main)**:** the tallest mast on a ship.
main sail: the center sail of the ship.
make all sail: the actions of letting out all the sail. This would only be done with a full breeze. The actions that follow this order include letting out the reefs, which had shortened the sail, squaring up the yards, tightening halyards, attaching sails.
mast: a vertical pole on a ship that supports sails or rigging.
masthead: a small platform partway up the mast, just above the height of the mast's main yard. A lookout is stationed there.
midship: the middle section of a ship.
mizzenmast (or mizzen): the third mast, or mast aft of the mainmast, on a ship.
nautical mile: a unit of length corresponding approximately to one minute of arc of latitude along any meridian arc.
pitch: a vessel's motion, rotating about the beam/transverse axis.
planter: a snag that is fixed to the riverbed.
point of sail: the boat's direction relative to the wind. There are eight commonly used points of sail.
poop deck: a high deck on the aft superstructure of a ship. The deck forming the roof of a poop or poop cabin, built on the upper deck and extending from the mizzenmast aft. When Watt left his cabin, he mentioned about going to the poop deck. They also held their meetings on that deck.
port: the left side of the boat.
quarter deck: that part of the upper deck of a boat abaft the mainmast, or approximately where the mainmast would be in the case of vessels without one.
reef: to temporarily reduce the area of a sail exposed to the wind, usually to guard against rigging. To reduce a sail's area by lashing a fold in it. Watt used this term when a storm came up and the sailors were sent up the masts to reef in the sails. In regard to steamboats, a submerged ridge.
royal sail: a small sail flown immediately above the topgallant on square-rigged sailing ships. It was originally called the topgallant royal and was used in light and favorable winds. Watt used the term *royals set* when he wrote the letter to the second mate and said that after the mate joined the Church of Jesus Christ of Latter-day Saints he would "sail through life with unreefed topsails and royals set."

sail: a piece of fabric attached to a vessel and arranged such that it causes the wind to drive the vessel along. It may be attached to the vessel via a combination of mast, spars, and ropes. The order for setting sail is from the largest and lowest on the masts to the smallest and highest. This is the order for all the masts.

sail plan: the light air sail plan is for a "light breeze." For this breeze the ship would need a set of huge, lightweight sails to keep the ship underway in a light breeze. A working sail plan is for sails that are much stronger than light air sails, but still lightweight. A storm sail plan is a set of very small, rugged sails flown in a gale, to keep the vessel underway and in control.

saloon: the large hallway that runs the length of the boiler deck; another name for the cabin. It also serves as a dining room.

sawyer: a snag whose upper end moves up and down in the water column.

second cabin: an enclosed room in a better location of the ship than steerage. These passengers generally had their food provided by the ship, whereas steerage passengers provided their own food.

second mate: the third officer on board, who eats and sleeps in the cabin but at the second table. The second mate is neither officer nor seaman and is expected to go aloft to reef and furl the topsails. The second mate furnishes the crew with supplies and works with the crew, but is not respected much as an officer. Watt wrote a letter to the second mate.

set sail (or "make sail"): Begin a voyage on water.

setting sails: all sails up on the ship. This is an idiom that Watt used in his letter to the second mate. He had used the terms *unreefed topsails* and *royals set* before. The top sail was the first sail put up, and presumably the royal sails are next. These may be the only sails that are up on a ship most of the time, but with a strong wind behind them, they would set or unfurl the other sails. Thereafter all the other sails are "set," or unfurled, which meant that the ship would have the winds to blow it rapidly through the ocean waters. On March 11, when there was little wind, Watt talked about "all sails set but it is light." He meant that the ship had all its sails up, but the wind was not blowing very much.

ship: a three-masted vessel square-rigged on all three masts, or on three masts of a vessel with more than three. Originally ships were personified as masculine, but by the sixteenth century they were almost universally expressed as feminine.

side-wheeler: type of steamboat in which a paddle wheel is located on each side of the hull.

snag: a tree in the riverbed forming an obstruction or hazard to navigation.

snag boat: a shallow-draft, double-hulled steamboat designed to remove snags from the river channel.

snag chamber: a sealed chamber within the bow used to prevent the entire hull from flooding in the event of a rupture by a snag.

spanker: a fore-and-aft or gaff-rigged sail on the aft-most mast of a square-rigged vessel. Nautical term.

speak a ship: to hail another ship and speak to the captain or someone on board. Watt used the term *spoke*.

spencer: known as a trysail. A small triangular or square fore-and-aft rigged sail hoisted in place of a larger sail when the winds are very high. Watt used this term.

stage (plank): the walkway, or gangplank, extending from a boat's forecastle to the shore.

starboard: the right side of the boat, facing forward.

staterooms: sleeping rooms located on either side of the cabin. River term.

steerage: a lower deck of a ship. The section of a passenger ship providing inexpensive accommodation with no individual cabins. In a storm the captain would lock the steerage so that no water would get down into the ship. That act and the fact that there was little light, only about five lamps, brought terror into the hearts of many people there. On the *Ellen Maria* a Welshman lit a candle while in steerage, and he was put into irons for his actions. The captain had a great fear that a candle or another type of light might cause a fire and burn up the ship. Watt did not have too much tolerance or sympathy for the Welshman.

stern: the back of the ship. Anything toward the back is "aft" or "astern."

stern-wheeler: type of steamboat in which a single paddle wheel is located at the stern.

tack: to change the direction of a sailing ship by turning the bow toward the wind so that the direction from which the wind blows changes from one side to the other, allowing progress in the desired direction.

tall ship: a large, traditionally rigged sailing vessel.

Texas: a series of cabins located above the hurricane deck.

topgallant sail: the square sail or sails immediately above the topsail on a square-rigged sailing vessel. Also known as a gallant or garrant sail.

top sail: a sail set above another sail on a square-rigged vessel. Farther sails may be set above the top sail. In the nineteenth century these were the principal and largest sails of the ship, the first sails put up and the last taken down. Watt used the term in his letter to the second mate.

tweendeck: a deck located between the main deck and the hold space, often where steerage was located.

under way: the description of a ship as soon as it begins to move under canvas power after an anchor has been raised from the bottom.

unfurling: this is accomplished by the crew laying out the yard and taking the gaskets off the sail.

unreef: during a storm the captain of the ship directed the sailors to reef in the sails in order to reduce the area of a sail, usually by folding or rolling one edge of the canvas in on itself. The converse operation, removing the reef, is called "shaking it out." Watt used the terms *unreef* and *unreefing* for the "shaking it out" process, which was probably the nineteenth-century term used on the *Ellen Maria*.

wharf: a structure on the shore of a harbor or on the bank of a river or canal where ships may dock to load and unload cargo or passengers.

white squalls: a sudden and violent windstorm at sea that is not accompanied by the black clouds generally characteristic of a squall. The name refers to the white-capped waves and broken water. A squall is caused by a sudden, sharp increase in wind speed that is usually created by active weather, such as rain showers, thunderstorms, or heavy snow. Watt used the terms *white squalls* and *black squalls* in his letter to the second mate. Presumably, he had heard the terms from the sailors. Black squalls are the opposite of the white squalls. On March 10 Watt wrote that because of a squall the night before, they had lost sixteen hours of sailing time.

windward: the weather side, or that direction from which the wind blows. It is the opposite side to leeward.

wooding: the act of loading fuel wood onto a steamboat, usually lasting about an hour and taking place twice a day.

woodyard: independently owned refueling sites along the river.

yard: a large wooden spar crossing the masts of a sailing ship horizontally or diagonally, from which a sail is set.

yawl: a rowboat serving as an auxiliary craft on nearly all steamboats.

Sources

American Sailing Association, "Sailing Terms Everyone Should Know," https://asa.com/news/2012/11/27/sailing-terms-you-can-use/.

Dana, *Seaman's Manual.*

English Language and Usage Stack Exchange, "What's the Sailing Ship Equivalent for 'Full Speed Ahead!'?," last modified May 16, 2020, https://english

.stackexchange.com/questions/290678/whats-the-sailing-ship-equivalent-for-full-speed-ahead.

Gillespie, *Wild River, Wooden Boats.*

Kane, *Western River Steamboat.*

Los Angeles Maritime Institute, "Setting, Dousing and Furling Sails," https://pdf4pro.com/amp/view/setting-dousing-and-furling-sails-los-angeles-maritime-5aac49.html.

Macquarie University, "Glossary of Nautical Terms (As Used in the Late 18th and Early 19th Centuries)," Journeys in Time website, "Ships" page, updated November 17, 2011, https://www.mq.edu.au/macquarie-archive/journeys/ships/glossary.html.

Wikipedia, s.v. "Royal (sail)," last modified October 24, 2017, https://en.wikipedia.org/wiki/Royal_(sail).

Notes

Note: The Pioneer Database was recently incorporated into the Church History Biographical Database, https://history.churchofjesuschrist.org/chd/landing?lang=eng.

Preface

1. The *Ellen Maria* was an American-built ship. It sailed on February 1 from Liverpool and arrived in New Orleans on April 5, 1851. For more information on the *Ellen Maria*, see chapter 1.
2. For a more complete history of George D. Watt's life, see Watt, *Mormon Passage*. Chapter 4 details his experiences on board the *Ellen Maria* crossing the Atlantic Ocean.
3. It is unknown what motivated him to learn Pitman shorthand.
4. See Watt, "Sailing 'The Old Ship Zion.'"

Introduction

This chapter has been revised and expanded from Fred E. Woods, "Gathering to Zion," in *The International Church*, edited by Donald Q. Cannon and Richard O. Cowan (Salt Lake City: Deseret Book, 2003), 43–58. It is also laced with additional books and articles the author has written on Latter-day Saint immigration/emigration over the past two decades.

1. The Church of the Latter-day Saints was organized as the Church of Christ in Fayette, New York, on April 6, 1830, under the direction of Joseph Smith. To avoid confusion with other churches, the name was changed in 1834 to the Church of the Latter-day Saints. The current name of the church, the Church of Jesus Christ of Latter-day Saints, was adopted in 1838. See "Name of the Church," https://www.churchofjesuschrist.org/study/history/topics/name-of-the-church?lang=eng.
2. "And ye are called to bring to pass the gathering of mine elect; for mine elect hear my voice and harden not their hearts. Wherefore the decree hath gone forth from the Father that they shall be gathered in unto one place upon the face of this land, to prepare their hearts and be prepared in all things against the day when tribulation and desolation are sent forth upon the wicked." *Doctrine and Covenants* 29:7–8.

3. The Quorum of the Twelve Apostles (often referred to as the Twelve) is the second-highest governing body in the Church of Jesus Christ of Latter-day Saints. Members of the Quorum, some other Church leaders, and missionaries were given the title *elder*.
4. Allen and Leonard, *Story of the Latter-day Saints*, 127; note that the other missionaries were Willard Richards, a dear friend of Heber C. Kimball's, as well as four Canadian missionaries, Elders Joseph Fielding, John Goodson, Isaac Russell, and John Snyder.
5. J. Smith, *History of the Church*, 2:492. However, Watt and some other British converts to this new religion learned about the gathering to America on their own. See appendix 4 for two reminiscent accounts by early Latter-day Saint missionaries to England.
6. Allen, Esplin, and Whittaker, *Men with a Mission*, 53. Apostles Kimball and Hyde left England on April 20, 1838.
7. J. Smith, *History of the Church*, 4:119. By this time the total membership in the Church in the British Isles was reported as 1,631, including 132 priesthood leaders. See Whitney, *Life of Heber C. Kimball*, 278.
8. J. Smith, *History of the Church*, 4:134. This maiden voyage ended in New York. The migrants then traveled by rail and steamboat to Nauvoo, Illinois. For an overview of Latter-day Saint emigration history from the port of Liverpool in the nineteenth century, see Woods, "Tide of Mormon Migration."
9. Priscilla Staines, "Reminiscences of Priscilla Staines: Liverpool to New Orleans, 23 Jan 1844—7 Mar 1844," Saints by Sea, https://saintsbysea.lib.byu.edu/mii/account/423. Priscilla Staines, in Edward Tullidge, *The Women of Mormondom* (1877; repr., Salt Lake City, 1975), 288. Jane C. Robinson Hindley, who experienced the challenge of leaving her home and gathering a decade later than Staines (1855), also seems to have experienced the magnetic pull of the gathering and therefore left England with, as she noted, "the fire of Israel's God burning in my bosom." See Hindley, "Jane C. Robinson Hindley Journals," 1:11–14.
10. Moon, "Letter of Francis Moon."
11. M. Hamlin Cannon asserts that 4,733 British Saints gathered to Nauvoo during 1840–46. Andrew Jenson puts the figure at an even 5,000. Cannon, "Migration of English Mormons," 441; Jenson, "Church Emigration," 441.
12. "Emigration."
13. J. Smith, *History of the Church*, 4:186, 5:296; *Doctrine and Covenants* 124:25–27.

14. "Epistle of the Twelve."
15. Woods, *Gathering to Nauvoo*, 84–87. Joseph Smith was killed on June 27, 1844.
16. Cowan, "Church Growth in England," 202.
17. The First Presidency is the leading governing body in the Church of Jesus Christ of Latter-day Saints.
18. Clark, *Messages of the First Presidency*, 2:108.
19. Zobell, *Under the Midnight Sun*, 48–49.
20. On St. Louis as a gathering place, see Woods and Farmer, *When the Saints*, 5–57; Farmer and Woods, "Sanctuary on the Mississippi."
21. Woods, "Perpetual Emigrating Fund," 910.
22. Arrington, *Great Basin Kingdom*, 64. John D. Unruh Jr. maintains "at least 10,000 forty-niners detoured via the Mormon oasis." Unruh, *Plains Across*, 253.
23. Young, "Letter of Brigham Young to Franklin D. Richards" (1855).
24. Hafen, "Handcarts to Zion," 316. Although nearly two hundred died in the Willie & Martin handcart companies, the other eight handcart companies were very successful.
25. Hulmston, "Mormon Immigration in the 1860s."
26. Sonne, *Saints on the Seas*, 69, 126.
27. Sonne, *Saints on the Seas*, 139. For more information on the voyage across the Atlantic, see Woods, "Sea-Going Saints"; Madsen and Woods, *I Sailed to Zion*. A list of the Latter-day Saint chartered voyages during 1840–90, coupled with passenger lists as well as over 1,300 first-person immigrant accounts, is found at Saints by Sea, https://saintsbysea.lib.byu.edu/, of which the author of this introduction is the chief editor and compiler.
28. Young, letter of Brigham Young to Elder Franklin D. Richards [1854].
29. For an overview on the role of the Church agents at the New York immigration depot, see Woods, "Knights at Castle Garden." See also Woods, "Gifted Gentleman."
30. George Q. Cannon to Brigham Young, April 23, 1859, 1–2, Church History Library.
31. Bitton, *George Q. Cannon*, 100.
32. Thomas Taylor to Brigham Young Jr., May 30, 1866, in the New York Emigration Book, 22 March 1866–10 July 1866, 34, Church History Library, quoted in Woods, "Two Sides of a River."
33. Woods, "Norfolk and the Mormon Folk."
34. For excellent studies on the story of Latter-day Saint emigration from Great Britain and Scandinavia, see Taylor, *Expectations Westward*; Mulder, *Homeward to Zion*.

The Process of Transcription

1. For this reason it was often called *phonography*, meaning "sound writing."
2. As I have written elsewhere, he followed contemporaneous practice in rewriting the content of his shorthand as he transcribed. See Dirkmaat and Carruth, "Prophets Have Spoken."

1. The Atlantic Ocean

1. The president of the group on board the ship called the members together for church meetings and special prayers and took care of all problems with the church members.
2. Orson Pratt (1811–81) was an original member of the Quorum of Twelve Apostles of the Church of Jesus Christ of Latter-day Saints. He was returning to Utah Territory after serving as the president of the European Mission of the Church of Jesus Christ of Latter-day Saints. "Pratt, Orson," The Joseph Smith Papers, https://www.josephsmithpapers.org/person/orson-pratt?highlight=orson%20pratt.
3. Pitman shorthand was first published by Sir Isaac Pitman in 1837 and soon gained broad acceptance. Pitman, *Manual of Phonography*, 37.
4. For a history of the British mission, see Allen, Esplin and Whittaker, *Men with a Mission.*
5. Even before 1840, when the apostles who were in Britain began to preach gathering to America, Watt had known that linking his fortunes to the church would take him from his native land to the United States. Two weeks after he was baptized, he prophesied that they would all go and be gathered to America. See Heber C. Kimball discourse of July 16, 1854, Church History Library. Historian's Office general Church minutes, 1839–1877, 1851–1855, 1854 June–July, Salt Lake City, Church History Library, https://catalog.churchofjesuschrist.org/assets?id=766fd499-f118-4583-b845-4bea214e3215&crate=0&index=0. In 1859 Kimball again told about that same event; see Church History Department Pitman Shorthand transcriptions, 2013–2020; Addresses and sermons, 1851–1874; Heber C. Kimball, 1852–1868; Heber C. Kimball, August 7, 1859, Church History Library, https://catalog.churchofjesuschrist.org/assets?id=64531491-4f46-4a19-8769-410a7745b4a8&crate=0&index=0 .
6. The height of membership in the Church of Jesus Christ of Latter-day Saints, the Mormons, in Britain in the nineteenth century came about 1851, when the official 1851 census of Britain listed the total membership as being over 30,000. For a recent study of the Latter-day Saint population and the

1851 census see Doxey, "Church in Britain." Her primary purpose is to list the congregations throughout the British Isles. An older British study by Owen Chadwick lists the membership according to the census records as 16,628 members. Chadwick admits, though, that according to church membership records (probably the *Millennial Star*), membership in 1850 was over 30,000 people. See Chadwick, *Victorian Church*, 436–39.

7. James Willard Cummings (1819–83), age thirty-one. He was the captain of the James W. Cummings Company (1851), which left Kanesville, Iowa, in June and arrived in Salt Lake City the end of September. See "James Willard Cummings," Pioneer Database, https://history.churchofjesuschrist.org/overlandtravel/pioneers/7527/james-willard-cummings.
8. For transcriptions of Pratt's sermons, see chapter 5. For an excellent description of the emigrant's ship experience, see David H. Pratt and Paul F. Smart, "Life on Board a Mormon Emigrant Ship," *World Conference on Records, Preserving Our Heritage*, Series 418, August 12–15, 1980.
9. "Journals of George Henry Abbot Harris: Liverpool to New Orleans, 10 Jan 1852–19 Mar 1852," Saints by Sea, https://saintsbysea.lib.byu.edu/mii/account/789?netherlands=on&europe=on&scandinavia=on&keywords=George+Henry+Abbot+Harris&mii=on&sweden=on.
10. In the early years of Latter-day Saint emigration, steerage passengers supplied their own food. The year 1851 was an early year, and most of the Latter-day Saint ship's passengers were in steerage. George Watt and his family, Orson Pratt and his family, and a few others were not. See Sonne, *Saints on the Seas*, 54.
11. Fifty-nine other emigrant vessels sank between the years 1847 and 1853. Sonne, *Saints on the Seas*, 139.
12. Hartley, "Atlantic Crossing."
13. J. R. Baker, "Diary of Jean Rio Baker," Saints by Sea, February 26, 1851. Her name is given as both Jane and Jean Rio Griffiths Baker; the most reliable sources give her name as Jane Rio Griffiths Baker.
14. "Journal of John Woodhouse: Liverpool to New Orleans, 8 Jan 1851–14 Mar 1851," Saints by Sea, https://saintsbysea.lib.byu.edu/mii/account/325?netherlands=on&europe=on&scandinavia=on&keywords=john+woodhouse&mii=on&sweden=on.
15. "Journal of Thomas Day: Liverpool to New Orleans, 18 Feb 1850–18 Apr 1850," Saints by Sea, entry for March 30, 1850, https://saintsbysea.lib.byu.edu/mii/account/755?netherlands=on&europe=on&scandinavia=on&keywords=%22thomas+day%22&mii=on&sweden=on.

16. "Diary of William Stuart Brighton: Liverpool to New Orleans, 27 Nov 1854–12 Jan 1855," Saints by Sea, https://saintsbysea.lib.byu.edu/mii/account/244?netherlands=on&europe=on&scandinavia=on&keywords=William+Stuart+Brighton&mii=on&sweden=on.
17. Mandal, *Ship Construction and Welding*, 21–24.
18. Adams, *History of the Town*.
19. George D. Watt, journal, Church History Department Pitman Shorthand transcriptions, 2013–2020; Addresses and sermons, 1851–1874; George D. Watt, 1851, 1867; George D. Watt, January 28–August 14, 1851; Church History Library, https://catalog.churchofjesuschrist.org/assets?id=29dfdd82-69cb-47b0-88a8-3e2bc28e96fb&crate=0&index=0.
20. Watt, journal, March 1 and 18, 1851.
21. The transcription of names in Pitman shorthand is very difficult; the transcription of "John Curtis" is close but may not be exact. There is no other information on this person. See March 1, 1851, entry for the captain's attitude toward his crew.
22. Watt, journal, March 18, 1851.
23. Dana, *Two Years before the Mast*, 9–14.
24. See "How many people does it take to operate a historical sailing ship?," Quora, answered February 21, 2021, https://www.quora.com/How-many-people-does-it-take-to-operate-a-historical-sailing-ship.
25. Watt, journal, February 10, 1851. See Dana, *Two Years before the Mast*.
26. Watt, journal, undated entry between January 31 and February 7 entries.
27. These are some preliminary notes of a church service held February 9, 1851, on board the *Ellen Maria*, which Watt wrote before the start of his chronological journal. As noted in the style guide in appendix 1, the journal is not paged, and image numbers from the scanned copy of the journal are used to identify separate pages. For more details in transcription, see appendix 1.
28. Watt gave more details on her death in his entry of February 11, 1852.
29. The remainder of this page contains notes and numbers not related to the journal; we have chosen not to include the information here.
30. Watt traveled with a group who were all members of the Church of Jesus Christ of Latter-day Saints, commonly referred to as *saints*.
31. See the glossary for all terms related to the ship.
32. Communion; commonly known as the sacrament in the Church of Jesus Christ of Latter-day Saints.
33. For an excellent explanation of the Latter-day Saint migration through Liverpool, see Woods, "Tide of Mormon Migration," 60–86.

34. Orson Pratt (1811–81) was born in Hartford, New York, the son of Jared Pratt and Charity Dickenson. His younger brother, Parley P. Pratt, baptized him into the Church of Jesus Christ of Latter-day Saints on his nineteenth birthday. He later became a member of the Quorum of Twelve Apostles. He served countless missions. Before leaving Britain he was the mission president of the British Mission. *Encyclopedia of Mormonism*, 4 vols. (New York, Macmillan, 1972) 3:1114–15.
35. Probable intent is *own*.
36. A reference to the William Davies incident on Friday, January 31; see entry for that date, below. William Daviesage thirty-seven, was a laborer in steerage. He had a wife, Jane, age thirty-one, and three children. See also *European Mission Emigration Records*, 1849–1925, 1849–1851, Church History Library, https://catalog.churchofjesuschrist.org/assets?id=38b87d5b-7d50-48b0-969f-3b213d784175&crate=0&index=0. Hereafter cited as *European Mission Emigration Records*. We can find no other information about William Davies except what Watt provides in his journal. Later, Davies was put into irons when he lit a flame in steerage, and later he was excommunicated while he was on the ship, as Watt explains; see entries for March 27 and 30, below.
37. This is the verso of the previous page.
38. See *Doctrine and Covenants* 27:2.
39. John Toone (1813–92), age thirty-seven, was a counselor in the ship's presidency to George D. Watt. He had a wife, Emma, age thirty-one, and four children when he came on board. His daughter, Ann, who was nine weeks old, died on board the ship. *European Mission Emigration Records*, https://catalog.churchofjesuschrist.org/assets?id=38b87d5b-7d50-48b0-969f-3b213d784175&crate=0&index=0.
40. James Stratton, age twenty-six, was a tailor traveling in steerage. See "Stratton, James, Liverpool to New Orleans, 1 Feb 1851–7 Apr 1851," Saints by Sea, https://saintsbysea.lib.byu.edu/mii/passenger/54475?netherlands=on&europe=on&scandinavia=on&keywords=James+stratton&mii=on&sweden=on.
41. Francis Clark, age twenty-three, is only mentioned as Mrs. Stratton in the *European Mission Emigration Records*.
42. *The* is written twice, once at the end of the line and again at the beginning of the next line. Such repetitions were not unusual in shorthand reporting.
43. A prayer.
44. The next page is blank.
45. In 1842 Watt sailed from Liverpool to New Orleans on his journey to Nauvoo, Illinois. He sailed back to Liverpool in 1846.

46. The difference between the U.S. system and the British system centers on two terms, a short ton (U.S.) and a long ton (British). A short ton is a unit of weight equal to 2,000 pounds. The term is mostly used in the United States, where it is known as the ton. The long ton is equal to 2,240 pounds. See Wikipedia, s.v. "short ton" and "long ton," accessed August 24, 2021, https://en.wikipedia.org/wiki/Long_ton; Wikipedia, s.v. "English units," accessed August 24, 20212, https://en.wikipedia.org/wiki/English_units.
47. There were 378 Latter-day Saint passengers on board the ship. There were other passengers as well. "A Compilation of General Voyage Notes: Liverpool to New Orleans, 1 Feb 1851—7 Apr 1851," Saints by Sea, https://saintsbysea.lib.byu.edu/mii/account/330?netherlands=on&europe=on&scandinavia=on&keywords=Ellen+Maria+1851&mii=on&sweden=on.
48. William Dunbar (1822–1905) was born in Scotland and was a missionary in England and France from 1846 to 1852. He immigrated to Utah Territory in 1852. See "William Cameron Dunbar," Pioneer Database, https://history.churchofjesuschrist.org/overlandtravel/pioneers/10686/william-cameron-dunbar; "Dunbar, William C.: Liverpool to New Orleans, 10 Jan 1852—19 Mar 1852," Saints by Sea, https://saintsbysea.lib.byu.edu/mii/passenger/15593?netherlands=on&europe=on&scandinavia=on&keywords=william+dunbar&mii=on&sweden=on.
49. This is the same William Davies who was put in irons because he exposed an open light in steerage and was later excommunicated.
50. See Genesis 19:26.
51. Asterisk is in original. An asterisk in Pitman is written as an X with a dot in each corner and usually indicates that the material is either continued elsewhere or continued from elsewhere, though that is apparently not the case here. All but one of Watt's asterisks are in this section, February 1–16, 1851; perhaps he was marking the beginning of a new entry.
52. Punctuation is in original.
53. Directly into the wind.
54. Punctuation is in original.
55. Punctuation is in original.
56. See Judges 16.
57. Punctuation is in original.
58. The Roman god of fresh water; the counterpart of Greek god Poseidon.
59. Punctuation is in original.
60. Punctuation is in original.
61. He is writing about the difficulties of the passengers the night before, having vomited most or all of their food. Watt was always concerned about

cleanliness. Most people writing a journal would not mention this, but he did. Punctuation is in original.

62. Treacle could be molasses, but it is probably a blend of molasses, sugar, and corn syrup used as syrup at the table.
63. Quotation marks are in original.
64. Punctuation is in original.
65. There is no Isaac listed in the *European Mission Emigration Records* of the *Ellen Maria*; however, this could have been a nickname. See *European Mission Emigration Records.*
66. Punctuation is in original.
67. Punctuation is in original.
68. Punctuation is in original.
69. Punctuation is in original.
70. Punctuation is in original.
71. Punctuation is in original.
72. Punctuation is in original.
73. Philip Baker, age twenty-nine, was a laborer. He was assigned to the second cabin where Watt was also assigned. *European Mission Emigration Records*. See also "Philip Baker," Pioneer Database, https://history.churchofjesuschrist.org/overlandtravel/pioneers/51112/philip-baker.
74. David Jones, age fifty, was from Merthyr, Wales, and was in steerage. *European Mission Emigration Records*.
75. See chapter 5 for a complete transcript of Pratt's sermon. Punctuation is in original.
76. Punctuation is in original.
77. Talked to someone on another ship. Dana, *Two Years before the Mast*, 8.
78. Only opening quotation marks are in the journal.
79. Punctuation is in original.
80. Punctuation is in original.
81. Punctuation is in original.
82. Punctuation is in original.
83. Cape Clear is an island off the southwest coast of Ireland, eight miles off the coast of West Cork. "Cape Clear Island," www.capeclearisland.ie/index.
84. Punctuation is in original.
85. Richard Preece (1806–51), FamilySearch, https://www.familysearch.org/tree/person/sources/LLQD-J7D. Susannah Pritchard Preece (1806–82) traveled with the John Tidwell Company to Salt Lake City in 1852. "Susannah Preece," Pioneer Database, https://history.churchofjesuschrist.org

/overlandtravel/pioneers/44802/susannah-preece; FamilySearch, https://www.familysearch.org/tree/person/sources/M45C-SG4.

86. Punctuation is in original.
87. The side of the ship facing toward the wind.
88. Punctuation is in original.
89. Punctuation is in original.
90. Punctuation is in original.
91. Punctuation is in original.
92. Punctuation is in original.
93. Punctuation is in original.
94. Placement of inserted phrase is as indicated in shorthand. Obvious intent is "useful to our friends" <who intend to emigrate>.
95. Anne Toone, born November 23, 1850. FamilySearch, https://www.familysearch.org/tree/person/details/KWVM-4WC.
96. See chapter 5 for complete transcript of Pratt's sermon.
97. Punctuation is in original.
98. Punctuation is in original.
99. Punctuation is in original.
100. Punctuation is in original.
101. Punctuation is in original.
102. *And* is written twice, once at the end of one line and again at the beginning of the next line.
103. Punctuation is in original.
104. Punctuation is in original.
105. Punctuation is in original.
106. A nautical term meaning that the ship is heeled so much on one side that the deck is practically vertical. See the glossary for other nautical terms.
107. Punctuation is in original.
108. Punctuation is in original.
109. Amos Fielding was born in 1792 in England and died in Salt Lake City in 1875. He immigrated to the United States in 1811 and returned to England by 1829. He was baptized into the Church of Jesus Christ of Latter-day Saints in the fall of 1837. In 1842 he led a group of Latter-day Saints to Nauvoo, Illinois. He returned to England by 1844 and served as a church agent from 1844 to 1846. Amos Fielding, age fifty-two, was traveling with June Fielding, age twenty-nine. See "Amos Fielding" in The Joseph Smith Papers, https://www.josephsmithpapers.org/.
110. Punctuation is in original.
111. Punctuation is in original.

112. Quotation marks are in original.
113. There were eleven lanterns, six furnished by the ship and five by the emigrants. This man lit his own candle, thus endangering the ship, if it had caught fire. Sonne, *Saints on the Seas*, 54. Punctuation is in original.
114. Words in bold are in longhand in the original journal, throughout. David Jones, age fifty, was a miner in steerage. He had a wife and two children. See *European Mission Emigration Records.*
115. Edward Williams, a miner, was traveling in steerage. See *European Mission Emigration Records.*
116. Llanelli is a town just west of Swansea, Wales.
117. Carmarthenshire is a county in the southwest of Wales. The largest city is Llanelli.
118. Ann Morgans, age twenty-five, was from Wales. See *European Mission Emigration Records.*
119. Aberdare is a town in the Cynon Valley in Wales at the confluence of the River Dare and the River Cynon. It is four miles southwest of Merthyr Tydfil. Cwmbach is today a tiny hamlet between Llanelli and Timsaren. It is about thirty-five miles from Aberdare. The branch would have been closer to Llanelli. Glamorganshire is a county situated in the south of Wales and has as its largest towns Swansea and Cardiff, which is now the capital of Wales.
120. John Harris, age thirty, was a miner from Wales. See *European Mission Emigration Records.*
121. William Williams, age thirty-seven, was from Wales, traveling in steerage, and a laborer. See *European Mission Emigration Records.*
122. Thomas Phillips, age thirty, was from Wales. *European Mission Emigration Records.*
123. Punctuation is in original.
124. Punctuation is in original.
125. The ship *Ellen* sailed January 8, 1851, from Liverpool and arrived March 14, 1851, in New Orleans with 480 passengers. *European Mission Emigration Records*; "Read Accounts of This Voyage: Liverpool to New Orleans, 8 Jan 1851—14 Mar 1851," https://saintsbysea.lib.byu.edu/mii/voyage/120?netherlands=on&europe=on&scandinavia=on&keywords=Ellen+1851&mii=on&sweden=on.
126. This is the *George W. Bourne*, which sailed from Liverpool on January 23, 1851, and arrived in New Orleans on March 20, 1851, with 289 passengers on board. *European Mission Emigration Records*; "Read Accounts of This Voyage: Liverpool to New Orleans, 23 Jan 1851—20 Mar 1851," Saints by Sea,

https://saintsbysea.lib.byu.edu/mii/voyage/151?netherlands=on&europe=on &scandinavia=on&keywords=bourne+1851&mii=on&sweden=on.

127. From this point on, Watt wrote the words *latitude* and *longitude* as if he expected to come back and write in the numbers when he found out that information, but he never did. We have left the words in the text.
128. The Madeira Islands, 540 miles southwest of Lisbon, Portugal, are a Portuguese archipelago positioned about 360 miles directly west of Morocco, Africa, in the north Atlantic Ocean.
129. Punctuation is in original.
130. Punctuation is in original.
131. Punctuation is in original.
132. Punctuation is in original.
133. Punctuation is in original.
134. Watt wrote *the* twice, at the end of one line and again at the beginning start of the next line.
135. Watt wrote *which* twice, at the end of one line and again at the beginning start of the next line.
136. Watt reported this sermon in Pitman shorthand; for transcription, see chapter 5.
137. Marintha Althera Pratt was born December 21, 1849, in Liverpool, Lancashire, England, and died May 24, 1851, on board the *Ellen Maria*, in the Atlantic. Her body was preserved in treacle (molasses) and taken to Missouri for burial. She was buried in the cemetery in Kansas, Jackson County, Missouri. See FamilySearch, https://www.familysearch.org/tree/person/sources/K23V-VLX; Watt, journal, May 10, 1851.
138. I.e., there was a new moon; see "Moon Phases Calendar," March 1851, Catalina Sky Survey, Lunar & Planetary Laboratory, College of Science, University of Arizona, https://catalina.lpl.arizona.edu/moon/phases/calendar?month=3&year=1851.
139. Phoebe Bromley, age fourteen, was the daughter of John Bromley. Her mother's name was not listed, but the clerk put her age as forty-one. *European Mission Emigration Records*.
140. Punctuation is in original.
141. Sarah Spicer, age thirty-two, was traveling in steerage. She is listed with three children. *European Mission Emigration Records*.
142. This is Grantham, Lincolnshire, England. Watt wrote this name in longhand. He probably pronounced it as "Grantum."
143. Watt reported part of this sermon in shorthand. See chapter 5 for transcription.

144. Punctuation is in original.
145. Punctuation is in original.
146. Punctuation is in original.
147. The center of the deck had better circulation, thus it was not so hot. The boxes were all piled in the center. Punctuation is in original.
148. There are many whales that live in the North Atlantic. It would be difficult to speculate as to what type it was. Punctuation is in original.
149. Punctuation is in original.
150. Punctuation is in original.
151. The *Millennial Star* (often abbreviated as the *Star*) was a periodical published by the Church of Jesus Christ of Latter-day Saints in England from 1840 to 1970.
152. Punctuation is in original.
153. This John probably intended to be baptized when he got to the valley. Punctuation is in original.
154. Punctuation is in original.
155. Could also be read: *walk of the man.*
156. Sarah Marinda Bates (1817–88), FamilySearch, https://www.familysearch.org/tree/person/details/LKY2-LNQ.
157. James Turnbull, age thirty-four, was a ploughman and traveling in steerage. He had no wife or children. He traveled to Salt Lake City in 1859 with the George Rowley Company. *European Mission Emigration Records*; *Pioneer Database*, https://history.churchofjesuschrist.org/overlandtravel/pioneers/21701/james-turnbull/.
158. Torphichen, Scotland, a town between Glasgow and Edinburgh.
159. Punctuation is in original.
160. FamilySearch gives her name as Mary Mickle; see https://www.familysearch.org/tree/person/9VRC-96P.
161. John McPherson, age forty-five, was in the second cabin and was a master mariner. He had a wife, age thirty-five, and ten children ranging from nineteen years to eleven months old. *European Mission Emigration Records.*
162. Name as given on the *European Mission Emigration Records* is Hugh McLeod. He was a stonemason, age thirty-four, and was traveling in the second cabin with his wife, Jane, age thirty-four. *European Mission Emigration Records.*
163. Punctuation is in original.
164. An alternate name for Marian Pratt; see "John Brown Company (1851)," *Pioneer Database*, https://history.lds.org/overlandtravel/companies/75/john-brown-company-1851.

165. This is Maria S. or L. Maddison, age thirty-nine, traveling with three children ages eighteen, sixteen, and seven. *European Mission Emigration Records.*
166. There are two women by the name of Emily on the *European Mission Emigration Records*: Emily Robins, who was the wife of Henry Robins, and Emily Wood, age twenty-three, who was traveling with Rebecca Wood, who may have been her mother. *European Mission Emigration Records.*
167. Watt wrote *on the sail* twice, at the end of one page and again at the beginning of the next page.
168. Underlining indicated in shorthand.
169. The island of Hispaniola was formerly known as Santo Domingo.
170. Probably Jamaica. It lies south of the two islands, but more to the south of the east side of Cuba.
171. Vowel is indicated in shorthand.
172. *7* written over *8*.
173. Cape de Cruz is on the south shore of Cuba, often called Cape Cruz.
174. This is the same William Davies who left the ship while it was in the harbor. He was convinced to come back. Then he was put into irons for having a lighted candle on the deck.
175. Sarah Wilde, age thirty, was traveling in steerage. Her husband, Henry, age forty, was an oil maker. They had five children ranging from ten to two years old. Jane Wilde, age eighty-one, and Martha Sparks, age sixty-seven, were also traveling with them. *European Mission Emigration Records.*
176. *£* and *s* are written above the numbers.
177. Evan Howells, age twenty-nine, was traveling in steerage with his wife, Mary, age twenty-six. *European Mission Emigration Records.*
178. John Lane, age thirty-four, and his wife, Sarah, age thirty-five, traveled in steerage with one son, Thomas, age five. *European Mission Emigration Records.*
179. Written *krngkrr*.
180. The bar of the river is the point where the river dumps all its excess soil into the ocean. It makes a small island that the ship has to traverse. At high tide enough of the island is underwater that the ship sails over it.
181. John Richards, age twenty-five, was traveling in steerage. *European Mission Emigration Records.*
182. See the glossary for terms related to the boat and rivers.

2. The Rivers

1. John Fitch and James Rumsey developed steamboats prior to Fulton, but these boats were too expensive for commercial traveling. See Robert O. Woods, "The Genesis of the Steamboat," American Society of Mechani-

cal Engineers, December 28, 2010, https://www.asme.org/topics-resources/content/the-genesis-of-the-steamboat.

2. Kane, *Western River Steamboat*, 11.
3. Kane, *Western River Steamboat*, 12–13; Wikipedia, s.v. "Steamboats," https://en.wikipedia.org/wiki/Steamboat; "About Steamboats: tools/implements," accessed August 24, 2021, http://www.museum.state.il.us/RiverWeb/landings/Ambot/TECH/TECH4.htm.
4. Kane, *Western River Steamboat*, 15.
5. Kane, *Western River Steamboat*, 15.
6. Encyclopaedia Britannica online, s.v. "Steamboat," accessed May 3, 2021, https://www.britannica.com/technology/steamboat; "Steamboats," American Studies at the University of Virginia, https://xroads.virginia.edu/~Hyper/DETOC/transport/steamboats.html.
7. Henry Miller Shreeve was the first person to use the high-pressure steam engine. Sandy Moulton, "Steamboat: Definition & History," Study.com, https://study.com/academy/lesson/steamboat-definition-history.html.
8. For information concerning the construction and history of the steamboat, see Kane, *Western River Steamboat*.
9. "Helpful Hints for Steamboat Passengers," Explorations in Iowa History Project, https://iowahist.uni.edu/Frontier_Life/Steamboat_Hints/Steamboat_Hints2.htm.
10. Gillespie, *Wild River, Wooden Boats*, 65–67; Chappell, *History of the Missouri*, 83–84.
11. She uses the term *hurricane deck* for the second deck, which was usually called the *boiler deck*. Perhaps on the *Concordia* it was called the hurricane deck. J. R. Baker, "Diary of Jean Rio Baker," March 29, 1851, Saints by Sea.
12. "A History of Steamboats," U.S. Army Corps of Engineers, https://www.sam.usace.army.mil/Portals/46/docs/recreation/OP-CO/montgomery/pdfs/10thand11th/ahistoryofsteamboats.pdf.
13. Hartley and Woods, *Explosion of the Steamboat Saluda*, 19.
14. Hartley and Woods, *Explosion of the Steamboat Saluda*, 19.
15. In order to give the reader continuity, we have duplicated the last entry of the previous section of the journal.
16. Bury is a mill town located just north of Manchester.
17. Alexander Scott Entwistle.
18. "Baton Rouge, April 10, P.M. Steamer St. James passed up yesterday evening; Savanah this morning at 1 o'clock; General Scott at 8½ this morning, and Aleck Scott, 3 this evening. River has fallen 7 inches since 30th. This place is now 4 inches below high water mark of '49. Innumerable crevasses

have occurred above and below, causing immense destruction of crops. The sugar crop in some Parishes will be entirely cut off. Weather for last three days has been cold, but to-day is quite warm." *Daily Nashville Union*, April 11, 1851, 2.

19. Watt wrote *the* at the end of one page and again at the beginning of the next page.
20. "Vicksburg, April 12, . . . The Aleck Scott and General Scott up yesterday," *Nashville Republican Banner*, April 14, 1851, 3.
21. Not everybody onboard the *Aleck Scott* was a member of the Church of Jesus Christ of Latter-day Saints.
22. Punctuation is in original.
23. Elizabeth and James Shelley had eleven children ranging from twenty-eight years to six months old. John was fifty-six years old. For information on Elizabeth Bray Shelley, see FamilySearch, https://www.familysearch.org/tree/person/details/KWJB-P25.
24. Words written: n; shts.
25. "One of the emigrants, a woman named Shelby, fell overboard near Island Twenty-one, and was drowned. She was drawing a bucket of water at the time the accident occurred. She leaves a family of fourteen children and a husband to mourn her loss, on their advent in this land of their adoption. Elder Orson Pratt arrived with the company.—Mo. Rep., April 17," *Alton Telegraph*, April 25, 1851, 1. The location is somewhere south of St. Louis, Missouri.
26. See Matthew 7:24.
27. "St. Louis, April 16, P.M. . . . Steamboats. The *Aleck Scott* arrived this morning. The Pacific leaves this evening," *New Orleans Times-Picayune*, April 18, 1851, 2. "Arrival of Mormons.—The *Aleck Scott*, which arrived from New Orleans yesterday morning, had on board a number of Mormon families, in all about 370. They are in care of Austin Pratt, a Mormon leader, and are direct from England.—St. Louis [undecipherable]," *Louisville Courier-Journal*, April 21, 1851, 3. "English Mormons, to the number of three hundred and seventy, arrived at St. Louis on the 16th," *American Telegraph*, April, 29, 1851, 1.

    Watt was in St. Louis in 1842 when he first emigrated to the United States and was traveling to Nauvoo. The entire party had to winter in the area. Watt and many of the group lived just across the Mississippi from St. Louis in Alton, Illinois. St. Louis was a very important place for the Latter-day Saints during this period. Many stopped here for a season and worked until they were able to obtain enough money to go to their new Zion, Salt

Lake City. In 1851 Thomas Wrigley served as president of the St. Louis Conference with approximately three thousand members. They held their devotional services twice each Sunday. The *Missouri Republican* reported, "Our city is the greatest recruiting point for Mormon Emigrants from England and the Eastern States, and the former especially, whose funds generally become exhausted by the time they reach it, generally stop here several months, and not infrequently remain among us a year or two pending a resumption of their journey to Salt Lake." Quote is from the *Missouri Republican* as quoted in Woods and Farmer, *When the Saints*, 36–37.

28. Watt wrote *of* at the end of one line and again at the beginning of the next line.
29. Punctuation is in original.
30. A British pound was worth $4.35 USD in 1850. Thus Hardy loaned Watt about $130.50. "How Much Was the English Pound Worth in American Dollars in 1850?," CoinSite, https://coinsite.com/how-much-was-the-english-pound-worth-in-american-dollars-in-1850/.
31. Punctuation is in original.
32. See Matthew 6:28–29.
33. "Bound for Utah.—The *St. Louis Republican*, of the 23d ultimo, says: 'Yesterday a number of gentlemen connected with the territorial government of Utah, and the Indian department in that quarter, Elder Pratt, and a number of Mormons, and several persons connected with the commerce of the valley, left on the Robert Campbell for Council Bluffs, en route for the Salt Lake." *Washington D.C. Republic*, May 1, 1851, 2. "Utah Territory.—On the 22d ultimo a number of gentlemen, connected with the Territorial Government of Utah and the Indian department in that quarter, Elder Pratt and a number of Mormons, and several persons connected with the commerce of the Valley, left on the steamer Robert Campbell for Council Bluffs, en route for the Salt Lake." *Washington DC Weekly National Intelligencer*, May 10, 1851, 2.
34. The *Aleck Scott* was a Mississippi steamboat and did not go up the Missouri River. Its probable route was from St. Louis to New Orleans and return.
35. Watt wrote *of* as the last word on the previous page and again as the first word on this page.
36. There is no proof of any Missourians being in Nauvoo when Joseph was assassinated.
37. When the Latter-day Saints were driven out of the state of Missouri in the fall of 1838, a group of Missouri state militia attacked the small settlement of Haun's Mill, where Jacob Haun owned a small mill on Shoal Creek and

had been joined by about thirty families. Altogether seventeen Saints were killed, and many were wounded. Ten-year-old Sardius Smith was killed in the blacksmith shop, where he and other men and boys had taken refuge. His murderer later bragged, "Nits will make lice, and if he had lived he would have become a Mormon." Allen and Leonard, *Story of the Latter-day Saints*, 128. The original quote is in Roberts, *Comprehensive History*, 1:482.

38. Jane Wilde, age eighty-one, traveled on the *Ellen Maria* in steerage with Henry Wilde and his wife, Sarah Wilde. *European Mission Emigration Records*.
39. She was buried in the Kansas City, Jackson County, Missouri, cemetery.
40. Alexander Robbins (1818–1902), age thirty-three, had served as the president of the St. Louis Conference. "Alexander Robbins," Pioneer Database, https://history.churchofjesuschrist.org/overlandtravel/pioneers/7877/alexander-robbins.
41. "More Mormons.—The *St. Louis Republican* of the 9th says: The steamer Atlantic, which reached our port yesterday, brought up from New Orleans two hundred and forty English Mormon emigrants, who, with the exception of some twenty-five, have been left for a day or two at Quarantine Island. Mr. Thos. Wrigley, the Elder in this city, gives us the following account of these emigrants:—The party, under the charge of Mr. Hallowell, Mormon Elder, left Liverpool on the 4th of March last, in the company of quite a large number of other passengers. The passage across lasted some nine weeks, during which time there occurred little sickness and but two deaths, the deceased in both instances being children. It would appear that the journey was not prosecuted in an idle spirit so far as the propagation of the Mormon creed is concerned.—Fifty of the other passengers, we learn, embraced the doctrine before the vessel reached her place of destination. Of the two hundred and forty emigrants, twenty-five will proceed immediately to Council Bluffs, thence to Salt Lake City, with the company in charge of Elder Robbins and Little.—The steamer Statesman, which had been detained beyond her regular time, started up with them yesterday afternoon." *Buffalo Daily Republic*, May 23, 1851, 2. "Mormons. . . . The *Statesman* did not leave yesterday, as was stated, but is expected to leave to-day, having on board two hundred passengers. These are mostly Mormon emigrants, who arrived here a few days ago from the New England States, and the remainder are from this city, among whom is Alexander Robbins, the late President of this city.—Organ and Reveille, May 9th, 1851." *Frontier Guardian*, May 30, 1851, 3.
42. Punctuation is in original.
43. Punctuation is in original.

44. "Arrivals . . . The Robert Campbell arrived on Wednesday the 21st, at the same place with a large company of Saints from England Scotland, &c., under the watch care and direction of Elder George D. Watt, our able Phonographic Writer, and Lecturer. A goodly number of both companies are destined for the Valley of the Great Salt Lake this season, and the balance will remain in this, and surrounding counties of Western Iowa for the time being. . . . All the Saints who have got this far on their journey, seem to be anxious to get to the end of it; but the weather being so very unfavorable for the last ten days, they are compelled to lie on their oars a short time much against their will; but they believe that all will work together for good to those who love God." *Frontier Guardian*, May 30, 1851, 2.
45. Kanesville, Iowa, is the present city of Council Bluffs, Iowa.
46. In order to enable the emigrants through each point of their experience, the First Presidency had what was called an agent in each of the important places. This person was responsible for meeting the ship or boat and helped them get on their way to the next point. New Orleans was the first point since it was the port city. In 1851 Watt mentions no agent meeting them. Watt disembarked from the *Ellen Maria* and found a steamboat that would carry them to St. Louis. Often times St. Louis was the second place for a church agent. Watt mentions no one there either. The third place was Kanesville, Iowa. The agent here was Orson Hyde, a member of the Quorum of Twelve Apostles. Watt appealed to him for financial assistance. Hyde would have been responsible for getting the new arrivals off to a wagon train and on to Utah. The year 1851 was the last year that the Latter-day Saints used this as a center of emigration. The First Presidency asked Hyde to come to Salt Lake City, which he did. Kanesville shortly after was renamed Council Bluffs.
47. See Robert Williams, Autobiography, 1859, Church History Library, 120–21.
48. See "Rebus," *Frontier Guardian* 3 (June 11, 1851): 4.
49. See "Answer to Rebus in Our Last," *Frontier Guardian* 3 (June 27, 1851): 4.
50. See George D. Watt, letter to editor, February 25, 1867, *Deseret Evening News*, April 3, 1867, 109. For more information on his struggles with oxen, see transcription of his Pitman shorthand draft of his letter to John M. and Margaret Brandreth in chapter 3.

3. The Trail

1. "How Much Was the English Pound Worth?," CoinSite.
2. Watt, journal, no date. This is written just before the July 4, 1851, entry.

3. Preston F. Thomas (1814–77), "Preston F. Thomas," Pioneer Database, https://history.churchofjesuschrist.org/overlandtravel/pioneers/7934/preston-f-thomas.
4. Alexander Robbins (1818–1902), age thirty-three in 1851. "Alexander Henry Robbins," Pioneer Database, https://history.churchofjesuschrist.org/overlandtravel/pioneers/7876/alexander-henry-robbins.
5. "John Brown Emigrating Company Journal, 1851 July–September," Pioneer Database, https://history.churchofjesuschrist.org/overlandtravel/sources/4892/john-brown-emigrating-company-journal-1851-july-september. We cannot be sure that Thomas included all of the wagons for the Oregon pioneers.
6. Watt, *Mormon Passage*, 102–3.
7. Watt, journal, July 17, 1851; Williams, "Robert Williams Autobiography."
8. Watt, journal, July 22, 1851.
9. "John Brown Emigrating Company Journal," July 5, 1851.
10. "John Brown Emigrating Company Journal," July 5, 21, 1851.
11. "John Brown Emigrating Company Journal," July 27, 28, 1851.
12. "John Brown Emigrating Company Journal," July 27, 28, 1851.
13. "John Brown Emigrating Company Journal," July 29, 1851.
14. The Morris Phelps Company left Kanesville on June 9, 1851. They must have split apart near the end of the journey since they did not arrive in Salt Lake City until between September 26 and October 1, 1851. The Harry Walton/Garden Grove Company left Garden Grove, Iowa, on May 17, 1851. They crossed the Missouri River about July 1 and arrived in Salt Lake on September 24 or 25, 1851. The journalists called the John G. Smith Company the Shurtliff Company. The Smith Company arrived between September 15 and 23, 1851. The different dates of arrival for the other companies meant that they had broken up, and several groups were pursuing their own quest for the Salt Lake Valley. See "Morris Phelps Company (1851)," Pioneer Database, https://history.churchofjesuschrist.org/overlandtravel/companies/235/morris-phelps-company-1851.
15. Watt, journal, July 29–30, 1851.
16. Watt, journal, July 28, 1851.
17. J. R. G. Baker, "Jane Rio Griffiths Baker Diary," August 2–3, 1851, Pioneer Database.
18. "Elias Smith Journals, 1836–1888, Journal, 1851 May–1854 October, 13–35 [images 14c-36]," Pioneer Database, August 26, 1851.
19. In order to give the reader continuity, we have duplicated the last entry of the previous section of the journal.

20. Kanesville, Iowa, is the present city of Council Bluffs, Iowa.
21. "Arrivals. The steamer Statesman, from St. Louis, thirteen days out, arrived at Kanesville Landing, on Tuesday the 20th inst., having on board a company of Saints, under the care of Elder Alexander Robbins, late President of the St. Louis Conference. Among the number of passengers were President Orson Pratt from the British Isles, his lady and family, en route for the Valley, in good health and spirits; Silas P. Barnes Esq., from Boston, lady and family, Elder James McGaw, one of our missionaries from Texas, and our celebrated French missionary, William Howell, and family. The latter is the gentleman who was so very successful in making converts crossing the Atlantic on board the ship Olympus, while on their way from Liverpool to New Orleans. We are informed that there were only fifty-two passengers on board the Olympus, who did not belong to the Church, with exception of the Captain and Crew, and out of that number fifty were baptized into the Church before they arrived at New Orleans." *Frontier Guardian*, May 30, 1851, 2. Punctuation is in original.
22. Mary Ann Wood Watt Brown, born April 23, 1791, died, September 25, 1884, age sixty in 1851. Baptized in England with the first baptisms in Preston on July 30, 1837. "Mary Ann Brown," Pioneer Database, https://history.churchofjesuschrist.org/overlandtravel/pioneers/7731/mary-ann-brown. Punctuation is in original.
23. He is very insistent that he needs two wagons: one for his wife, Mary, and their son, George D. Jr., and another wagon for his mother and his half-sister, Jane. Other families had used one wagon to transport more people than the number he wanted to transport in his two wagons. Later events hint that Mary would not have Jane in the same wagon with her. George married Jane as a plural wife on January 5, 1852. They had two sons and a daughter, the last being born in 1857. Difficulties arose soon in their marriage, and Brigham Young granted Jane a divorce on October 28, 1863. Shortly thereafter she converted to the Reorganized Church of Jesus Christ of Latter Day Saints and left Utah. She married Adam Saladin at Fort Laramie. They moved to Nebraska and later Kansas. For more information, see Watt, *Mormon Passage*, 161–70.
24. The Latter-day Saint emigration pattern was to have an emigration agent in the places that were needed to help the emigrants on their journey. The first place of importance was Liverpool, where the mission president designated which member would emigrate and when. He also booked the ships. The second place was at Kanesville, Iowa. Orson Hyde, a member of the Quorum of Twelve, was the emigration agent there. Hyde, upon request of the First Presi-

dency of the church, returned to Salt Lake City in 1851, thus ending Kanesville as the jumping-off place for the Latter-day Saint emigration to Salt Lake.

25. Punctuation is in original.
26. I.e., unless.
27. The Perpetual Emigrating Fund made loans to enable Latter-day Saints to emigrate to Utah. See "Emigration," Restoration and Church History, Church of Jesus Christ of Latter-day Saints, https://www.churchofjesuschrist.org/study/history/topics/emigration?lang=eng.
28. *In* is written twice, once at end of the line and again at the beginning of the next line.
29. Punctuation is in original.
30. Punctuation is in original.
31. Watt did not write the closing quotation marks. Punctuation is in original.
32. Punctuation is in original.
33. Punctuation is in original.
34. Watt wrote the word *cattle* in two different ways, connected by longhand *or*.
35. Punctuation is in original.
36. Altogether he had borrowed $466 from various men. Record keeping of those types of transactions was poorly maintained.
37. Punctuation is in original.
38. Watt described this incident and other experiences of his journey in a letter to his sister and brother-in-law, Margaret and John M. Brandreth. Watt's Pitman shorthand draft of this letter is extant; for transcription, see the end of this chapter.
39. Punctuation is in original.
40. *Of my* is written twice, once at end of one page and again at the beginning of the next page.
41. Punctuation is in original.
42. *Was* is written twice, once at end of the line and again at the beginning of the next line.
43. A Scottish word for *butcher*.
44. Punctuation is in original.
45. Albert Carrington (1813–89), "Albert Carrington," Pioneer Database, https://history.churchofjesuschrist.org/overlandtravel/pioneers/355/albert-carrington.
46. Punctuation is in original.
47. James W. Cummings (1819–93), "James Willard Cummings," Pioneer Database, https://history.churchofjesuschrist.org/overlandtravel/pioneers/7527/james-willard-cummings.

48. Punctuation is in original.
49. Punctuation is in original.
50. Lyman Omer Littlefield (1819–93), "Lyman Omer Littlefield," Pioneer Database, https://history.churchofjesuschrist.org/overlandtravel/pioneers/21812/lyman-omer-littlefield.
51. Punctuation is in original.
52. John Brown (1820–96), age thirty in 1851, crossed the plains six times, twice as the captain of a company. "John Brown," Pioneer Database, https://history.churchofjesuschrist.org/overlandtravel/pioneers/350/john-brown. Watt was appointed as the captain of ten not because of his skills in handling oxen, but because of supervisory skills, being a leader on the ship.
53. Watt incorrectly dated this entry and several following entries *eighteen fifty*.
54. The John Brown Company was organized near the location of Winter Quarters. Storms caused the first Latter-day Saints to leave Nauvoo for the west in 1846, having much difficulty as they crossed Iowa, and many of their wagons bogged down in the mud. Brigham Young realized that most of the journey to the Rocky Mountains lay ahead of him and the others who were in Winter Quarters. Organizing the Saints was a problem that seemed to him insurmountable until January 1847, when he received from the Lord what was called the "Word and Will of the Lord concerning the Camp of Israel in their journeying to the West." He was told to organize the people into companies with captains of hundreds, fifties, and ten. Also the revelation commanded them that they should be organized "with a covenant and promise to keep the commandments and statutes of the Lord our God." This revelation made the journey of the Latter-day Saints a spiritual trip as well as a physical one. The John Brown Company was organized the same way as those very first companies. They traveled together under their leadership as designated in the revelation given to Brigham Young and also had their spiritual meetings. See *Doctrine and Covenants* section 136; Orton, "This Shall Be Our Covenant," 119–51.
55. "Preston F. Thomas," Pioneer Database.
56. Punctuation is in original.
57. Joseph Chatterley (1807–53), age forty-four in 1851. "Joseph Chatterley," Pioneer Database, https://history.churchofjesuschrist.org/overlandtravel/pioneers/7743/joseph-chatterley.
58. Punctuation is in original.
59. Joel Terry (1812–91), age thirty-nine in 1851. "Joel Terry," Pioneer Database, https://history.churchofjesuschrist.org/overlandtravel/pioneers/21293/joel-terry. John Warren Norton (1810–63), age forty-one in 1851. "John War-

ren Norton," Pioneer Database, https://history.churchofjesuschrist.org /overlandtravel/pioneers/7850/john-warren-norton.

60. Ferryville was northeast of Winter Quarters, on the east side of the Missouri River. Plewe, *Mapping Mormonism*, 77.
61. Possible intent is *individuals*.
62. Punctuation is in original.
63. The Elkhorn River is one of the largest tributaries of the Platte River. It joins the Platte just south of present-day Omaha, Nebraska. It is not known where they crossed the river. They must have decided to cross the Elkhorn River at another place, rather than the usual place.
64. Punctuation is in original.
65. Punctuation is in original.
66. Edwin Rushton (1824–1924), age twenty-seven in 1851. "Edwin Rushton," Pioneer Database, https://history.churchofjesuschrist.org/overlandtravel /pioneers/7881/edwin-rushton.
67. Punctuation is in original.
68. Punctuation is in original.
69. William Clayton in his *Emigrants' Guide* notes that Pappea Creek is "ten feet wide, high banks. Some timber on the creek, but it is difficult to water teams. After this the road is crooked and uneven to the Elk Horn." See Clayton, *Latter-day Saints' Emigrants' Guide*, 5. Stanley B. Kimball, editor of Clayton's guide, states, "Properly this was the Big Papillion or Butterfly River, so named from the masses of butterflies once found on its banks." See Kimball, *Latter-day Saints' Emigrants' Guide*, 42.
70. We cannot find a Brother Hall in the Pioneer Database.
71. Wood and coal did not burn hot enough to make iron malleable enough to shape wagon tires and other wagon parts. Blacksmiths obtained a better and more efficient fuel by cooking the wood or coal, which released the impurities from it. They would then use this more pure fuel, coke, to make the fire hotter. With a hotter flame, the metal was able to be shaped correctly. Here, Brother Hall was cooking the wood or coal.
72. *Who however was* is written over illegible shorthand.
73. Punctuation is in original.
74. Punctuation is in original.
75. Punctuation is in original.
76. Benjamin Votaw or Vantow, born about 1826. "Benjamin Votaw [or Vantow]," Pioneer Database, https://history.churchofjesuschrist.org /overlandtravel/pioneers/7940/benjamin-votaw-or-vantow; *European Mission Emigration Records*.

77. Thomas Margetts, age thirty-one. "Thomas Lorenzo Margetts," Pioneer Database, https://history.churchofjesuschrist.org/overlandtravel/pioneers/7830/thomas-lorenzo-margetts.
78. Almon W. Babbitt (1812–56), prominent in the early affairs of the Church of Jesus Christ of Latter-day Saints. "Babbitt, Almon Whiting," Joseph Smith Papers, https://www.josephsmithpapers.org/person/almon-whiting-babbitt.
79. Vowel is given in shorthand, but probable intent is *men*.
80. Punctuation is in original.
81. The wagon trains would assign one or more men to watch at night for possible Indian attacks. Punctuation is in original.
82. For an explanation of the making and use of coke, see note 70, above.
83. Punctuation is in original.
84. Adam Meek (born 1803), age forty-eight in 1851. "Adam Meek," Pioneer Database, https://history.churchofjesuschrist.org/overlandtravel/pioneers/7834/adam-meek.
85. Punctuation is in original.
86. Clayton calculated that Shell Creek was about thirty-nine miles from the Elkhorn. Watt calculated that this creek was about thirty-six miles from where Brown's Company crossed. Because of the weather they probably crossed the Elkhorn at different places. Clayton wrote that Shell Creek was twelve feet wide and three feet deep. "The creek is bridged, and a few rods lower is a place to ford. Plenty of timber on it. After this you will probably find no water for twelve miles." See Clayton, *Latter-day Saints' Emigrants' Guide*, 5.
87. Brown's journal written by Preston Thomas stated that the company camped by the side of Looking Glass Creek. See Brown, July 13, 1851. Clayton wrote that Looking Glass Creek was sixteen feet wide and two feet deep. "There is a poor bridge over this creek. It is, however, not difficult to ford. Plenty of timber on and near it." See Clayton, *Latter-day Saints' Emigrants' Guide*, 6.
88. James Cooper Holt (1824–56), age twenty-seven in 1851. "James Cooper Holt," Pioneer Database, https://history.churchofjesuschrist.org/overlandtravel/pioneers/20519/james-cooper-holt.
89. Clayton wrote that Plum Creek was five feet wide and at the altitude of 1,090 feet. "On this creek the old Pawnee mission station stands, but is not a very good place to camp, being near the Pawnee cornfields." See Clayton, *Latter-day Saints' Emigrants' Guide*, 6. Of the four journalists of the Brown party, only Elias Smith commented on this being near the old Pawnee mission. Kimball said that the name of Plum Creek came from the wild

plums growing on its banks. He also wrote that the Pawnee mission was abandoned in 1846 and the missionaries were transferred to Bellevue on the Missouri River. See Kimball, *Latter-day Saints' Emigrants' Guide*, 45. Punctuation is in original.

90. Punctuation is in original.
91. Punctuation is in original.
92. Clayton, *Latter-day Saints' Emigrants' Guide*, 6, reads: "8 rods, 2 feet deep. Some timber, and plenty of willow. After this, the road runs on the bottom through high grass for some distance, and gradually rises to higher land." On some maps this stream is named Willow Creek. See Kimball, *Latter-day Saints' Emigrants' Guide*, 46.
93. Edmund Judkins (born about 1828), age twenty-three. "Edmund Judkins," Pioneer Database, https://history.churchofjesuschrist.org/overlandtravel/pioneers/7798/edmund-judkins.
94. He is referring to Clayton's guide.
95. Punctuation is in original.
96. Esther Kempton (about 1801–51), age fifty in 1851. "Esther Kempton," Pioneer Database, https://history.churchofjesuschrist.org/overlandtravel/pioneers/7808/esther-kempton.
97. George Darling Watt Jr. (1843–1928), age eight in 1851, son of George D. Watt. "George Darling, Jr. Watt," Pioneer Database, https://history.churchofjesuschrist.org/overlandtravel/pioneers/7942/george-darling-jr-watt.
98. The other journalists identify this as Loup Fork.
99. Prairie Creek, "12 feet wide 1 ½ feet deep. Plenty of water and grass, but no timber. Banks some soft and miry. By taking a south west course from this creek, you would strike Wood river six or eight miles above the old crossing place, and thence crossing to the Platte, by a course a little west of south, the road may be shortened at least five miles." Kimball, *Latter-day Saints' Emigrants' Guide*, 49. Kimball noted that the name of the creek was Americanized. It is French for "meadow." Clayton, *Latter-day Saints' Emigrants' Guide*, 7.
100. Joseph Allan (1820–96), age thirty in 1851. "Joseph Allan," Pioneer Database, https://history.churchofjesuschrist.org/overlandtravel/pioneers/7709/joseph-allan.
101. In cattle a condition attributed to the hollowness of the horn. Punctuation is in original.
102. Brown recorded that they camped on the banks of the Wood River in order to repair one of Robbins's wagons, which had a broken wagon wheel.

See "John Brown Emigrating Company Journal," July 23, 1851. Clayton mentioned that the Wood River was twelve feet wide and one foot deep. "Plenty of timber, and a good place to camp." Clayton, *Latter-day Saints' Emigrants' Guide*, 7. Kimball, in his edition of the guide, said that the original Brigham Young exploring party crossed the Wood River about 2.5 miles southeast of present-day Alda. See Kimball, *Latter-day Saints' Emigrants' Guide*, 49.

103. Ft. Kearny was established by the army in 1848 to protect the emigrant trains along the Oregon Trail from Indian attacks. It is situated along the Platte River, about nine miles southeast of Kearney, Nebraska. It was disbanded in 1871 and later became the site of the Ft. Kearny Historical Park. Ft. Kearny was named by the War Department for Gen. Stephen Watts Kearny, who died in 1848. See Hartley and Anderson, *Sacred Places*, 284–85.
104. James Madison Monroe (1823–51) traveled that year in the John Reese Freight Train. Monroe was killed by Howard Egan on September 30, 1851, on the Bear River for seducing Egan's wife, as Monroe was returning to Salt Lake City. "James Madison Monroe," Pioneer Database, https://history.churchofjesuschrist.org/overlandtravel/pioneers/7980/james-madison-monroe; Hartley, *Faithful and Fearless*, 260–62.
105. Punctuation is in original.
106. "A wide creek, with deep banks, but no timber except a few willow bushes. The road runs alongside this creek for three and a half miles." Clayton, *Latter-day Saints' Emigrants' Guide*, 8. "This site is about two miles east of Overton. The creek may have been named by Heber C. Kimball." Kimball, *Latter-day Saints' Emigrants' Guide*, 51.
107. This could have been Thomas Bateman (1808–52), who traveled in 1850 with the Livingston and Kinkead Freight Train. "Thomas Bateman Jr.," Pioneer Database, https://history.churchofjesuschrist.org/overlandtravel/pioneers/5794/thomas-jr-bateman.
108. This was possibly David Wilkin (1819–91), who traveled to the Salt Lake Valley in 1851 with the Wilkin Freight Train. See "David Wilkin," Pioneer Database, https://history.churchofjesuschrist.org/overlandtravel/pioneers/21302/david-wilkin.
109. He was referring to the James W. Cummings Company, in which Orson Pratt traveled. He called it the Pratt Cummings [Company]. See "James W. Cummings Company (1851)," Pioneer Database, https://history.churchofjesuschrist.org/overlandtravel/companies/97/james-w-cummings-company-1851.

110. This is Orson Hyde whom Watt mentioned as being in Iowa. He was with the Orson Hyde Company.
111. The Garden Grove Company is listed in the Pioneer Database as the Harry Walton/Garden Grove Company, https://history.churchofjesuschrist.org/overlandtravel/companies/313/harry-walton-garden-grove-company.
112. They had mistakenly learned that a man had been killed in the Garden Grove Company, but it was a thirty-year-old woman named Elenor Kingsley, aka Elenor Young. On July 22, 1851, she was killed in a stampede. "We started about eight o/clock when a terrible catastrophe happen[e]d, which chills my very blood to write it. The Captain thought it best for each ten to travel some ways apart for fear the cattle would run away with the wagons[,] they were so wild: But notwithstanding all this precaution, we had not proceeded more than three miles before some of the teams took a fright and ran away. A Young woman by the name of Kingsly jumped out of the hind part of the wagon and before she could get out of the way, another team and wagon ran over her; her sister ran to her and asked her if she was hurt much, when she exclaimed 'I do not know'[;] these were the only words she uttered, for she instantly expired, leaving her only sister without a relative in the company. It was sad to see how bitterly she wept and no wonder she could not be comforted, to have an only sister killed in so shocking a manner; knowing that she must be left to sleep alone in this desolate place which probably her grave will never be passed, by white men again to her knowledge, for we are as much as an hundred miles from the main road." "Ossian F. Taylor Journal, 1851 April–September," Pioneer Database, https://history.churchofjesuschrist.org/overlandtravel/sources/10951229984542879854-eng/ossian-f-taylor-journal-1851-april-september?firstName=Ossian%20F.&surname=Taylor.
113. Elias Smith said that they camped on Skunk Creek that evening. Smith, "Elias Smith Journals," July 31, 1851. "Skunk Creek, six feet wide. Crossing of Skunk creek. Banks some soft, but not difficult. No timber." Clayton, *Latter-day Saints' Emigrants' Guide*, 8. "Skunk Creek. This name was given by Heber C. Kimball and is probably today's Pawnee Creek, near Brady's Island." Kimball, *Latter-day Saints' Emigrants' Guide*, 51.
114. L. A. Shirtliff was a member of the John G. Smith Company, which arrived in Salt Lake City a few days before the John Brown Company in 1851. "L. A. Shirtliff," Pioneer Database, https://history.churchofjesuschrist.org/overlandtravel/pioneers/46368/l-a-shirtliff.
115. Clayton also mentioned this cold spring: "Good spring of cold water. At the foot of the bluffs, north of the road, and at the head of the Pawnee swamps." Clayton, *Latter-day Saints' Emigrants' Guide*, 8.

116. "Carrion creek, 10 feet wide, one foot deep. Good place for grass, but no timber near." By that time the company had traveled 297 miles. Clayton, *Latter-day Saints' Emigrants' Guide*, 8.
117. Emily Smith Hoyt also commented on this stranger: "One of the Oregonians traveling with them rose and complimented them on their good order, good feeling, and brotherly kindness toward each other." Watt, *Mormon Passage*, 104. Baker also wrote about this stranger: "One of the strangers in our company spoke at our meeting this afternoon and pleased us very much, by his testimony in our favor." J. R. G. Baker, "Jane Rio Griffiths Diary," August 3, 1851, Pioneer Database.
118. *Spoke* is written twice, once at the end of one line and again at the beginning of the next line.
119. The journalists all agree that the road along the bluffs was sandy, which made it hard on teams, very slow, and very difficult.
120. There were a number of small creeks along the bluffs, which Elias Smith named. Preston Thomas in the official "John Brown Emigrating Company Journal" did not name them but said that they passed over a number of small creeks on this day. Smith named the streams Petite, Picanninni, Goose, and Duck Creeks. Clayton named them as Petite, Picanninni, Goose, Small Spring, Small, Duck-weed, Shoal Stream, and Rattlesnake Creek. See Clayton, *Latter-day Saints' Emigrants' Guide*, 9–10.
121. The companies sometimes left messages on the skull of an oxen for other companies behind them.
122. Punctuation is in original.
123. This was probably James Field (1830–1907), who was in the James W. Cummings Company. "James Field," Pioneer Database, https://history.churchofjesuschrist.org/overlandtravel/pioneers/7542/james-field. Even though the John W. Brown Company was the last one that left in the year 1851, they had taken a shortcut and got in front of the Cummings Company. It was also possible to pass companies on the plains in Nebraska and in Wyoming.
124. Clayton mentioned a "lone tree" on the north side of the river. See Clayton, *Latter-day Saints' Emigrants' Guide*, 10. The tree in Watt's journal was in the right spot for Clayton's description. According to Kimball, the tree described by William Clayton "was one of three trees so named along the Mormon Trail. It was a Cedar Tree and stood three miles east of present-day Lewellen. Some Pioneers, including Young, carved their initials on its trunk, thereby contributing to its demise." Kimball mentions that there were three lone trees on the Mormon Trail. See Kimball, *Latter-day Saints'*

Emigrants' Guide, 55. Hartley and Anderson in *Sacred Places* mention a "lone tree" farther down the river near Prairie Creek about 150 miles away from the one that Clayton and Watt describe. According to them this lone tree was a large cottonwood with a trunk ten to twelve feet in circumference. See Hartley and Anderson, *Sacred Places*, 5:273. None of the other journalists of 1851 talk about this tree.

125. Watt wrote *of a* twice, on the same line.
126. This might be Crab Creek.
127. Elias Smith labeled the bluff as "Cobble Hills" and passed the "Ancient Bluff Ruins." Smith, "Elias Smith Journals," August 9, 1851. Clayton mentioned that after Cobble Hills, "you will find it mostly sandy for ten miles." He described the Ancient Bluff Ruins as "resembling the ruins of ancient castles, fortifications, &c. but visitors must be cautious, on account of the many rattle-snakes lurking round, and concealed in the clefts of the bluffs." His mileage calculation is 419 miles from Winter Quarters and 612 miles to Great Salt Lake City. See Clayton, *Latter-day Saints' Emigrants' Guide*, 11. Kimball wrote about Cobble Hills: "These gravel bluffs, so difficult for oxen to negotiate, were named by the Pioneers and located between Indian Lookout Point and the Ancient Bluff Ruins." In describing the Ancient Bluff Ruins, he wrote, "These magnificently eroded formations were named by English Pioneers who thought they resembled ruined castles in their homeland." Kimball, *Latter-day Saints' Emigrants' Guide*, 57.
128. He is referring to the Harry Walton Company, which was also known as the Garden Grove Company.
129. Chimney Rock was considered the halfway point between Winter Quarters and Salt Lake City, but it was not. Chimney Rock was by Clayton's calculation 452 ½ miles from Winter Quarters and 578 ½ miles to Great Salt Lake City.
130. Punctuation is in original.
131. Spring Creek.
132. Brown's official journal recorded that they "camped on the head of Spring Creek." Clayton wrote that Spring Creek was "south of the road. You do not cross it, but travel half a mile alongside. Good water, and many trout in it." See Clayton, *Latter-day Saints' Emigrants' Guide*, 11. At that point Watt had traveled 476 miles from Winter Quarters, and he stopped writing.
133. According to Clayton, this should be the day that Watt should have been able to see Laramie Peak. Punctuation is in original.
134. There is an insertion mark between *we* and *designed*, but no insertion.
135. Insertion mark below inserted phrase is crossed out.

136. If he is accurate with his mileage, using William Clayton's *Latter-day Saints' Emigrants' Guide*, he was probably about fifty miles west of Chimney Rock and twenty-two miles from Fort Laramie, and this letter was written on August 14 or 15. He mailed the letter or had someone else do it at Fort Laramie.
137. Punctuation is in original.
138. There is a crossed out insertion mark after *untruth*, but no insertion.
139. Long *e* is given in shorthand.

4. The End of the Trail

1. Elias Smith and Emily Smith Hoyt were siblings traveling in the same ten (subgroup) as Preston Thomas. See Family Search, https://www.familysearch.org/tree/person/details/KWJ5-K9G.
2. "John Brown Emigrating Company Journal"; for Preston F. Thomas as author of journal, see Preston F. Thomas, Pioneer Database, https://history.churchofjesuschrist.org/overlandtravel/pioneers/7934/preston-f-thomas. See also J. R. G. Baker, "Jane Rio Griffiths Baker Diary," Pioneer Database; J. R. Baker, "Diary of Jean Rio Baker," Saints by Sea; Smith, "Elias Smith Journals"; Emily Smith Hoyt, "Reminiscences and Diaries."
3. Baker, "Jane Rio Griffiths Baker Diary," August 15, 1851, Pioneer Database.
4. The Fort Laramie Treaty of 1851 was signed on September 17 between the United States and the Plains Indian tribes. These tribes were assigned certain areas of land, their traditional claims, where they were to hunt and live; it did not put these tribes on reservations. The treaty also provided safe passage for settlers to Oregon, Utah, and California. It was actually signed thirty miles downriver from Fort Laramie at the mouth of Horse Creek, where there was better grass for the horses. The treaty was broken soon after by the federal government, the tribes, and settlers. See "Treaty of Fort Laramie," Colorado Encyclopedia, accessed July 27, 2021, https://coloradoencyclopedia.org/article/treaty-fort-laramie. Baker, "Jane Rio Griffiths Baker Diary," August 28, 1851, Pioneer Database.
5. Baker, "Jane Rio Griffiths Baker Diary," September 1, 1851, Pioneer Database.
6. Brown, July 24, 1851. See appendix 2 for the list of people in Watt's ten.
7. For a detailed discussion of this correspondence and the beginning of the *Journal of Discourses*, see Watt, "Beginnings of the *Journal of Discourses*."
8. Watt, *Mormon Passage*, 129–30.
9. Watt, *Mormon Passage*, 128–36.
10. Watt, *Mormon Passage*, 119.

11. Watt, *Mormon Passage*, 141–59.
12. Watt, *Mormon Passage*, 163.
13. Watt, *Mormon Passage*, 162, 166, 283.
14. Watt, *Mormon Passage*, 172.
15. Watt, *Mormon Passage*, 173–74.
16. Watt, *Mormon Passage*, 171.
17. Watt, *Mormon Passage*, 164.
18. Watt, *Mormon Passage*, 169.
19. Watt, *Mormon Passage*, 169–70. See also Reorganized Church of Jesus Christ of Latter Day Saints (RLDS) deceased files, early reorganization minutes. 1852–71, Book A, p. 627; Nebraska City, Nebraska, RLDS branch records and Starr Creek, Kansas, RLDS branch records, Community of Christ Archives, Independence, Missouri. Jane Brown first lived in Nebraska City, Nebraska, and then Starr Creek, Kansas. For a complete list of Watt's wives and children, see appendix 3.
20. Watt, *Mormon Passage*, 138, 188–96.
21. "Deseret State Fair," *Deseret News*, October 13, 1858, 8, 139.
22. Watt, *Mormon Passage*, 197–99.
23. Bowles, *Across the Continent*, 243.
24. Thomas Stenhouse, "The Irrespressible George—A Utah Man," *Semi-Weekly Telegraph*, October 16, 1865, 3.
25. George D. Watt, "Asparagus," *Semi-Weekly Telegraph*, March 19, 1866, 2. This article was also published in the *Deseret Evening News*, March 18, 1865, 5.
26. George D. Watt, "Shade Trees," *Deseret Evening News*, April 4, 1866, 2–3.
27. George D. Watt, "Dip[h]theria," *Semi-Weekly Telegraph*, October 24, 1867, 3.
28. George D. Watt, "A Talk," *Semi-Weekly Telegraph*, October 31, 1867, 3; November 14, 1867, 4; November 21, 1867, 1.
29. Watt, *Mormon Passage*, 218–19.
30. Watt, *Mormon Passage*, 220–23. Watt was amazed at the small number of members of the church left in Britain. He commented that in 1851 he spoke at a meeting in Liverpool held in one of the finest halls in the city to a congregation of nearly one thousand people. In March 1867 he again addressed the Liverpool Saints but in a small room measuring ten feet wide and twenty-five feet long to not more than twenty persons. Watt, *Mormon Passage*, 220.
31. Watt, *Mormon Passage*, 222–24.
32. Watt, *Mormon Passage*, 223–24.
33. Watt, *Mormon Passage*, 229.
34. Watt, *Mormon Passage*, 246.
35. Watt, *Mormon Passage*, 254.

36. Watt, *Mormon Passage*, 255–56.
37. Watt, *Mormon Passage*, 257–62.
38. Members of the Church of Jesus Christ of Latter-day Saints believe that persons who have died can be baptized vicariously; a living person is baptized for the deceased. Watt's wife Elizabeth received permission from Wilford Woodruff, the fourth president of the church, for Watt to be baptized vicariously. On February 3, 1892, his son Richard was rebaptized for him in the Logan, Utah, temple. Watt, *Mormon Passage*, 280–81.
39. Watt, *Mormon Passage*, 275–76.

5. *Sermons by Orson Pratt*

1. "James W. Cummings Company (1851)," Pioneer Database, https://history.churchofjesuschrist.org/overlandtravel/companies/97/james-w-cummings-company-1851.
2. See "James W. Cummings Company." Watt did not mention the Pratts' other children, nor any children on board, except to note births, serious illnesses, deaths, and burials. A family portrait painted by Frederick Hawkins Piercy in Liverpool, ca. 1850, includes the Pratt children: Orson Pratt Jr., Marinthia Altheria, Laron, and Celestia Louisa Pratt. England, *Life and Thought*, 158.
3. Three sermons by Orson Pratt, transcribed from George D. Watt's shorthand record by LaJean Purcell Carruth.
4. The fourth sermon appears to have been added later. The notebook only contains shorthand records of three sermons.
5. John Toone.
6. Anne Toone.
7. Punctuation is in original.
8. I.e., *except*.
9. *These* is written at the end of one line and again at the beginning of the next line.
10. *Doctrine and Covenants*, section 76.
11. Obvious intent: *it was*.
12. See Acts 2:27.
13. Written: *Peter*; obvious intent: *David*.
14. Punctuation is in original.
15. See 1 Corinthians 5:4–5.
16. See 2 Peter 3:8.
17. See Acts 3:19–20.
18. Written: *forgiveness*; apparent intent: *forgiven*.

19. Punctuation is in original.
20. Punctuation is in original.
21. Punctuation is in original.
22. Word may be crossed out.
23. I.e., a prayer.
24. Quotation marks are in original.
25. Quotation marks are in original.
26. Word may be crossed out.
27. See Exodus 32:1–8.
28. See Deuteronomy 9:14.
29. This could be a stray ink mark.
30. See Ezekiel 20:25.
31. See *Doctrine and Covenants* 103:16.
32. Apparent intent: *their*.
33. See *Doctrine and Covenants* 35:25.
34. See *Doctrine and Covenants* 38:33.
35. Orson Pratt may have become excited and spoken more quickly here, which would have made it more difficult to report his words; the shorthand in this passage is more difficult to read than in the rest of the sermon.
36. See Ether 2:8.
37. *And* is written at the end of one line and again at the beginning of the next line.
38. See Ether 2:9.
39. See Ether 8:22, 24.
40. See Luke 21:24.
41. See Isaiah 11:12.
42. Quotation marks are in original.
43. Quotation marks and period are in original.
44. Underlining is in original.
45. See Isaiah 49:22–23. Terminal quotation mark is in original.
46. See Daniel 2:34, 45.
47. See Isaiah 11:12.
48. See Psalms 110:3. Terminal quotation mark is in original.
49. Obvious intent: *with all their hearts*.
50. See Ezekiel 20:33–36. Punctuation is in original.
51. See Ezekiel 20:38.
52. See Ezekiel 20:38.
53. See *Doctrine and Covenants* 90:36.
54. Likely intent: *What would I feel about, [if I knew I was going to be] translated?*

55. Images 25–28 contain shorthand doodling or practice; there is no meaningful content. A small piece of blue paper pasted to the cover of the notebook (image 25) reads: ***4 Disscourses by Orson Pratt upon the Ocean. 1851.***
56. See Isaiah 55:8–9.
57. See Hebrews 12:6.
58. See *Doctrine and Covenants* 56:4, 103:12.
59. Probable intent: *habitations*.
60. George D. Watt apparently missed reporting several words in the process of turning the page.
61. See *Doctrine and Covenants* 104:15.
62. See Daniel 7:27.
63. The previous sentences could be punctuated in a number of ways, with different meaning. The only indication in shorthand is a space before *But*, which indicates this word is the beginning of a phrase.
64. See Alma 40:12.
65. See 1 Corinthians. 15:50.
66. See Ezekiel 37:3–10.
67. See Ezekiel 37:11.
68. See Ezekiel 37:12.
69. *Faith* is likely an aborted attempt to write *forth*.
70. See Philippians 3:21.
71. Watt wrote *for* at the end of one line and again at the beginning of the next line.
72. See Psalms 2:8.
73. Matthew 5:5.
74. See 2 Timothy 4:7–8.
75. See 2 Timothy 4:8.
76. See Revelation 1:6.

Appendix 2

1. For Pioneer Database, see "About the Pioneer Database," https://history.churchofjesuschrist.org/content/pioneer-database/about.
2. For Saints by Sea Database, see "Find Your Ancestor's Voyage," https://saintsbysea.lib.byu.edu/.

Appendix 3

1. See FamilySearch, https://www.familysearch.org/tree/person/details/KWNG-4KG.

Appendix 4

1. Church History Department Pitman Shorthand transcriptions, 2013–2020; Addresses and sermons, 1851–1874; Heber C. Kimball, 1852–1868; Heber C. Kimball, 1859 August 7; Church History Library, https://catalog.churchofjesuschrist.org/assets?id=64531491-4f46-4a19-8769-410a7745b4a8&crate=0&index=0.
2. Church History Department Pitman Shorthand transcriptions, 2013–2020; Addresses and sermons, 1851–1874; John Taylor, 1852–1875; John Taylor, 1872 May 26; Church History Library, https://catalog.churchofjesuschrist.org/assets?id=0af21da9-88ed-4a50-9956-e5ce45f90627&crate=0&index=0.

Appendix 5

1. "About the Pioneer Database," https://history.churchofjesuschrist.org/content/pioneer-database/about. The railroad reached Ogden, Utah, in 1869.

Bibliography

Archives and Manuscripts

Baker, Jane Rio Griffiths. "Jane Rio Griffiths Baker Diary, 1851–1852 March and 1969 September–1880 May, 9–55." Pioneer Database. https://history.churchofjesuschrist.org/overlandtravel/sources/99686100627483881700-eng/jane-rio-griffiths-baker-diary-1851-january-1852-march-and-1869-september-1880-may-9-55?firstName=George%20Darling&surname=.

Baker, Jean Rio. "Diary of Jean Rio Baker: Liverpool to New Orleans, 23 Jan 1851–20 Mar 1851." Saints by Sea, entry for February 26, 1851. https://saintsbysea.lib.byu.edu/mii/account/479?netherlands=on&europe=on&scandinavia=on&keywords=jean+rio+baker&mii=on&sweden=on.

Brown, John. Journal, 1851. As recorded by Preston Thomas, Church History Library. Church of Jesus Christ of Latter-day Saints, Salt Lake City.

Chatterly, John. [Autobiography]. In "Utah Pioneer Biographies." 44 vols. 7:72–75. Pioneer Database, Church of Jesus Christ of Latter-day Saints. https://history.churchofjesuschrist.org/overlandtravel/sources/4887/chatterly-john-autobiography-in-utah-pioneer.biographies.

"European Mission Emigration Records, 1849–1925." Church History Library. Church of Jesus Christ of Latter-day Saints, Salt Lake City. https://catalog.churchofjesuschrist.org/assets?id=38b87d5b-7d50-48b0-969f-3b213d784175&crate=0&index=0.

Hindley, Jane Charters Robinson. Jane C. Robinson Hindley Journals, 1855–1905. https://catalog.churchofjesuschrist.org/record?id=e30d7aa0-255a-46c1-a8d9-5212f0f15cb6&view=summary.

Hoyt, Emily Smith. "Reminiscences and Diaries, 1851–1893." Church History Library, Church of Jesus Christ of Latter-day Saints, Salt Lake City. https://catalog.churchofjesuschrist.org/record/74ea6026-07b2-43e1-bee0-32427f92c6c6/0?view=brows.

Smith, Elias. "Elias Smith Journals, 1836–1888, Journal, 1851 May–1854 October, 13–35 [images 14–36]." Pioneer Database, Church of Jesus Christ of Latter-day Saints. https://history.churchofjesuschrist.org/overlandtravel/sources

/4895/elias-smith-journals-1836-1888-journal-1851-may-1854-october-13-35-images-14-36.

Smith, Joseph. The Joseph Smith Papers. http://josephsmithpapers.org/.

Williams, Robert. "Robert Williams Autobiography, circa 1859." MS 8358. Microfilm of manuscript. https://catalog.churchofjesuschrist.org/record?id=7fae6364-bfe4-4f36-a43c-6004ec14db59&view=summary. Partial typescript available at Pioneer Database, https://history.churchofjesuschrist.org/overlandtravel/sources/63114480343893306440-eng/robert-williams-autobiography-circa-1859-118-25?firstName=Robert&surname=Williams.

Published Sources

Adams, Silas. *The History of the Town of Bowdoinham, 1762–1912*. Fairfield ME: Fairfield Publishing, 1912. https://books.google.com/books?id=viUzAQAAIAAJ&printsec=frontcover&source=gbs_ge_summary_r&cad=0#v=onepage&q&f=false.

Allen, James B., and Glen M. Leonard. *The Story of the Latter-day Saints*. 2nd ed. Salt Lake City: Deseret Book, 1976.

Allen, James B., Ronald K. Esplin, and David J. Whittaker. *Men with a Mission, 1837–1841: The Quorum of the Twelve Apostles in the British Isles*. Salt Lake City: Deseret Book, 1992.

Arrington, Leonard J. *Great Basin Kingdom: An Economic History of the Latter-day Saints, 1830–1890*. Cambridge MA: Harvard University Press, 1958.

Bitton, Davis. *George Q. Cannon: A Biography*. Salt Lake City: Deseret Book, 1999.

Bowles, Samuel. *Across the Continent: A Summer's Journey to the Rocky Mountains, the Mormons, and the Pacific States and Speaker Colfax*. Springfield MA: S. & Company, 1886.

Cannon, M. Hamlin. "Migration of English Mormons to America." *American Historical Review* 52, no. 3 (April 1947): 441.

Chadwick, Owen. *The Victorian Church*. Part 1. Ecclesiastical History of England. New York: Oxford University Press, 1966.

Chappell, Phil E. *A History of the Missouri River*. Topeka KS: State Printing Office, 1911.

Church History Department (2008–); Publications Division. "Church History Department Pitman Shorthand Transcriptions, 2013–2020." https://catalog.churchofjesuschrist.org/record?id=5df3b7da-d0a5-437b-8268-7dde8a87c76e&view=summary.

Clark, James R., ed. *Messages of the First Presidency of the Church of Jesus Christ of Latter-day Saints*. Vol. 2. Salt Lake City: Bookcraft, 1965.

Clayton, William. *The Latter-day Saints' Emigrants' Guide*. St. Louis MO: Republican Steam Power Press—Chambers & Knapp, 1848.

Cowan, Richard O. "Church Growth in England, 1841–1914." In *Truth Will Prevail: The Rise of the Church of Jesus Christ of Latter-day Saints in the British Isles, 1837–1987*, edited by Larry C. Porter, James R. Moss, and V. Ben Bloxham. Solihull, UK: Corporation of the President of the Church of Jesus Christ of Latter-day Saints, 1987.

Dana, Richard Henry, Jr. *The Seaman's Manual: A Treatise on Practical Seamanship*. London: Edward Moxon, 1863.

———. *Two Years before the Mast*. Orinda CA: Sea Wolf Press, 2020. First published 1899 by D. Appleton (New York).

Dirkmaat, Gerrit, and LaJean Purcell Carruth. "The Prophets Have Spoken, but What Did They Say? Examining the Differences between George D. Watt's Shorthand Notes and the Sermons Published in the Journal of Discourses." *BYU Studies* 54, no. 4 (2015): 25–118.

Doctrine and Covenants of the Church of Jesus Christ of Latter-day Saints. Salt Lake City: Church of Jesus Christ of Latter-day Saints, 2007.

Doxey, Cynthia. "The Church in Britain and the 1851 Religious Census." *Mormon Historical Studies* 4, no. 1 (Spring 2003): 106–38.

"Emigration." *Latter-day Saints' Millennial Star* 1, no. 10 (February 1841): 263.

England, Breck. *The Life and Thought of Orson Pratt*. Salt Lake City: University of Utah Press, 1985.

"Epistle of the Twelve." *Latter-day Saints' Millennial Star* 1, no. 12 (April 1841): 311.

Farmer, Thomas L., and Fred E. Woods. "Sanctuary on the Mississippi: St. Louis as a Way Station for Mormon Emigration." *Confluence* 9, no. 2 (Spring/Summer 2018): 42–55.

Gillespie, Michael. *Wild River, Wooden Boats*. Stoddard WI: Heritage Press, 2000.

Hafen, Leroy. "Handcarts to Zion, 1856–1860." *Utah Historical Quarterly* 24, no. 1 (January 1956).

Hartley, William G. "Atlantic Crossing on the Ship *Olympus*." *New Era*, July 1978, 11–13. https://www.churchofjesuschrist.org/study/new-era/1978/07/atlantic-crossing-on-the-ship-olympus?lang=eng.

———. *Faithful and Fearless: Major Howard Egan*. Salt Lake City: University of Utah Press, 2017.

Hartley, William G., and A. Gary Anderson. *Sacred Places: A Comprehensive Guide to Early LDS Historical Sites*. Vol. 5, *Iowa and Nebraska*. Salt Lake City: Deseret Book, 2006.

Hartley, William G., and Fred E. Woods. *Explosion of the Steamboat Saluda*. Salt Lake City: Millennial Press, 2002.

———. "Explosion of the Steamboat Saluda: Tragedy and Compassion at Lexington, Missouri, in 1852." *Missouri Historical Review* 99, no. 4 (July 2005): 281–305.

Hulmston, John K. "Mormon Immigration in the 1860s: The Story of the Church Trains." *Utah Historical Quarterly* 58 (Winter 1990): 32–48.

Jenson, Andrew. "Church Emigration." *Contributor* 12, no. 12 (October 1891): 441.

Kane, Adam I. *The Western River Steamboat*. College Station: Texas A&M University Press, 2004.

Kimball, Stanley B., ed. *The Latter-day Saints' Emigrants' Guide*, by William Clayton. Gerald MO: Patrice Press, 1983.

Liefring, Christina, and Paula Rose. "Steamboat Travel Was Dirty and Dangerous, Especially on the Missouri River." Produced by Kansas City Public Radio, July 14, 2015. http://www.kcur.org/post/steamboat-travel-was-dirty-and-dangerous-especially-missouri-river#stream/0.

Madsen, Susan Arrington, and Fred E. Woods. *I Sailed to Zion*. Salt Lake City: Deseret Book, 2000.

Mandal, Nisith Ranjan. *Ship Construction and Welding*. Springer Series on Naval Architecture, Marine Engineering, Shipbuilding and Shipping. Singapore: Springer Nature Singapore, 2017.

Moon, Francis. "Letter of Francis Moon." The *Latter-day Saints' Millennial Star* 1, no. 10 (February 1841): 254–55.

Mountjoy, Eileen. "History of Coke." Indiana University of Pennsylvania. https://www.iup.edu/archives/coal/mining-history/history-of-coke.

Mulder, William. *Homeward to Zion: The Mormon Migration from Scandinavia*. Minneapolis: University of Minnesota Press, 1957.

Murdoch, Alexander. "The Emigrant Experience." In *British Emigration, 1603–1914*. London: Palgrave Macmillan, 2004.

Orton, Chad M. "This Shall Be Our Covenant: Brigham Young and D&C 136." *Religious Educator* 19, no. 2 (2018): 119–51.

Pitman, Ben. *Manual of Phonography*. Cincinnati OH: Phonographic Institute, 1855.

Plewe, Brandon S., ed. *Mapping Mormonism: An Atlas of Latter-day Saint History*. Provo UT: BYU Press, 2012.

Raiders of the Lost Archives. "Confederate Prisoners and the Aleck Scott, February 1862." https://scrc1.wordpress.com/2012/03/06/confederate-prisoners-on-the-steamboat-aleck-scott-february-1862-3.

Roberts, B. H. *A Comprehensive History of the Church of Jesus Christ of Latter-day Saints*. 6 vols. Salt Lake City: Deseret News Press, 1930.

Smith, Joseph. *History of the Church of Jesus Christ of Latter-day Saints*. Edited by B. H. Roberts. 7 vols., 4th ed. Salt Lake City: Deseret News, 1965.

Sonne, Conway B. *Saints on the Seas: A Maritime History of Mormon Migration, 1839–1890*. Salt Lake City: University of Utah Press, 1983.

———. *Ships, Saints, and Mariners: A Maritime Encyclopedia of Mormon Migration, 1830–1890*. Salt Lake City: University of Utah Press, 1987.

Taylor, P. A. M. *Expectations Westward: The Mormons and the Emigration of Their British Converts in the Nineteenth Century*. Ithaca NY: Cornell University Press, 1966.

Taylor, Thomas, to Brigham Young Jr. 30 May 1866 in the New York Emigration Book, 22 March 1866–10 July 1866, 34 CHL quoted In "Two Sides of a River: Mormon Transmigration through Quincy, Illinois, and Hannibal, Missouri." *Mormon Historical Studies* 2, no. 1 (2001): 141.

"Treaty of Fort Laramie." Colorado Encyclopedia. https://coloradoencyclopedia.org/article/treaty-fort-laramie.

Unruh, John D., Jr. *The Plains Across: The Overland Emigrants and the Trans-Mississippi West, 1840–1860*. Chicago: University of Illinois Press, 1993.

Watt, Ronald G. "The Beginnings of the *Journal of Discourses*: A Confrontation between George D. Watt and Willard Richards." *Utah Historical Quarterly* 75 (Spring 2007): 134–48.

———. *The Mormon Passage of George D. Watt, First British Convert, Scribe for Zion*. Logan: Utah State University Press, 2009.

———. "Sailing 'The Old Ship Zion': The Life of George D. Watt." *BYU Studies* 18 (Fall 1977): 48–65.

Whitney, Orson F. *Life of Heber C. Kimball*. Salt Lake City: Bookcraft, 1967.

Woods, Fred E. *Gathering to Nauvoo*. American Fork UT: Covenant Communications, 2001.

———. "Gathering to Zion." In *Unto Every Nation: Gospel Light Reaches Every Land*, edited by Donald Q. Cannon and Richard O. Cowan, 43–58. Salt Lake City: Deseret Book, 2003.

———. "A Gifted Gentleman in Perpetual Motion: John Taylor as an Emigration Agent." In *John Taylor Champion of Liberty*, edited by Mary Jane Woodger. Brigham Young University Church History Symposium. Provo UT: Religious Studies Center, BYU, 2009.

———. "The Knights at Castle Garden: Latter-day Saint Immigration Agents at New York." In *Regional Studies in Church History*. Vol. 3: *New York and Pennsylvania*, edited by Alexander L. Baugh and Andrew H. Hedges, 103–24. Provo UT: BYU Religious Studies Center, 2002.

———. "Norfolk and the Mormon Folk: Latter-day Saint Immigration through the Old Dominion (1887–1890)." *Mormon Historical Studies* 1 no. 1 (Spring 2000): 73–92.

———. "Perpetual Emigrating Fund." *Encyclopedia of Latter-day Saint History*, edited by Arnold K. Garr, Donald Q. Cannon, and Richard O. Cowan, 910. Salt Lake City: Deseret Book, 2000.

———. "Sea-Going Saints." *Ensign* (September 2001): 54–60.

———. "The Tide of Mormon Migration Flowing through the Port of Liverpool, England." *British Journal of Mormon Studies* 1, no. 1 (Spring 2008): 64–91.

———. "Two Sides of a River: Mormon Transmigration through Quincy, Illinois, and Hannibal, Missouri." *Mormon Historical Studies* 2, no. 1 (2001): 119–47.

Woods, Fred E., and Thomas Farmer. *When the Saints Came Marching In: A History of the Latter-day Saints in St. Louis*. Salt Lake City: Millennial Press, 2009.

Young, Brigham. Letter of Brigham Young to Elder Franklin D. Richards. "Foreign Correspondence." *Latter-day Saints' Millennial Star* 16, no. 43 (28 October 1854): 684.

———. "Letter of Brigham Young to Franklin D. Richards." *Latter-day Saints' Millennial Star* 17, no. 51 (December 22, 1855): 813–14.

Zobell, Albert L., Jr. *Under the Midnight Sun: Centennial History of the Scandinavian Missions*. Salt Lake City: Deseret Book, 1950.

Index

Page numbers in italics indicate illustrations.

CPSIA information can be obtained
at www.ICGtesting.com
Printed in the USA
LVHW010037290322
714682LV00003B/131

9 781496 229878